Global Perspectives on FOSTER FAMILY CARE

edited by

Matthew Colton
and
Margaret Williams

RHP

Russell House Publishing

First published in 2006 by:
Russell House Publishing Ltd.
4 St. George's House
Uplyme Road
Lyme Regis
Dorset DT7 3LS

Tel: 01297–443948
Fax: 01297–442722
e-mail: help@russellhouse.co.uk

A catalogue record for this book is available from the British Library.

British Library Cataloguing-in-publication Data:

ISBN: 1-903855-88-8
978-1-903855-88-1

Typeset by Alden Group, UK

Printed by Alden Group, UK

Contents

About the Authors

Argentina

María Elvira Dezeo de Nicora specialises in Psychopedagogy and Criminology (Lovain University, Belgium). She was the Chair of Child and Adolescent Psychology at Universidad del Salvador (City of Buenos Aires). Together with her husband and daughters, she founded Fundación Emmanuel. Since 1988, she has shared her family with the first foster children at the Fundación. She is the current Vice President and Head of the Professional Team in that institution. The e-mail address of Fundación Emmanuel is emmanuel@emmanuel.org.ar. The website address is www.emmanuel.org.ar.

China

Robert Glover has 25 years experience working in social services in the UK. Initially working in the residential sector, he managed a therapeutic unit for difficult teenagers before becoming a fostering officer. As a Service Manager, he oversaw the full range of social services from under fives to secure units for adolescents. Robert is a qualified social worker with CSS and CQSW as well as CMS.

France

Michel Corbillon began his career as a professional social worker, including periods as a community worker and as a residential care worker. He then completed a PhD (sociology) on the topic of intellectual deficiency. In 1984, he founded a research group on child care ('Groupe de recherché sur la reproduction et l'innovation sociale'). He has participated in several research projects undertaken by the group, including a national study of child welfare services in France.

Dr Corbillon is now a Professor in Educational Sciences, University of Paris X-Nanterre. He manages the research laboratory Education familiale et intervention sociale aupres des familles. He is a member of the executive committee of the European Scientific Association on Residential and Foster Care for Children and Adolescents (EUSARF). He sits on the editorial board of *La revue internationale de l'education familiale* and of the *International Journal for Residential and Family Care*. He has published many articles and books on children in care and child welfare services.

India

Najma Goriawalla is a graduate in social work and has been working in the field for over 30 years. Her special interests are family and child welfare and community development. She has been associated with several organisations in her specialised fields in various capacities. She is the past president and presently a consultant with the Indian Association for the Promotion of Adoption and Child Welfare, Mumbai, a family and child welfare agency established in 1970. She has several publications to her credit in her specialised fields.

Kaumudi Telang is a qualified social worker who has worked in the field for 34 years. Her special interests are family and child welfare and work with senior citizens. She is the immediate past President of the Indian Association for the Promotion of Adoption and Child Welfare and is presently working as a Project Director. As well, she has been associated with many organisations working in her fields of interest. She has been invited as a resource person to several national and international fora.

Japan

Kozo Iwasaki graduated from the George Warren Brown School of Social Work, Washington University, in St. Louis. He has worked as a social worker in the field of child protection for more than 16 years. He has written one book in English *Child Welfare in Context: An International Perspective*, published by Aikawa Books in 2001 and has published many other articles on child welfare in Japanese books and journals. He was a professor at Iwate Prefectural University until his move to Hirosakigakuin University where he is now a professor in the School of Social Work. He is also a Vice President of the Japanese Association of Social Workers.

Poland

Zofia-Waleria Stelmaszuk PhD is a lecturer at Warsaw University Faculty of Pedagogics, Section of Child and Family. Her publications include books and articles in the areas of child welfare practice, residential and foster care, family reunification and family support. Dr Stelmaszuk is actively involved in child welfare organisations at the local, national and international levels. She is a member of the executive board of EUSARF (European Scientific Association for Residential and Foster Care for Children and Adolescents) and of the editorial board of the *International Journal of Child and Family Welfare*. Her research, teaching and writing activities have been devoted to the prevention of long-term institutional placements for children and to the development of community-based child and family services in Poland.

South Africa

Wilfried van Delft is a social worker and clinical psychologist. He is a professor in social work at the University of South Africa and teaches human behaviour and research. He is also practicing as a psychotherapist and consults for a variety of child and family welfare organisations with specific reference to foster care and adoption. He is a member of the South African Council for Social Service Professions which is the governing body of social work in South Africa. He is married to Trudie Gericke who is a social worker specialising in adoption.

Sweden

Ingrid Hojer BA, MA, PhD in Social Work is a senior lecturer and researcher at the Department of Social Work, University of Gothenburg. She has had a great deal of experience working with children and families as a social worker. Her research is mainly in the area of child welfare, in particular foster care. She has undertaken two main studies, one on the impact of foster care on the foster carers themselves, and one on the impact of foster care on the sons and daughters of foster carers. She is also involved in a project concerning the development of foster care in Croatia. She is a member of the Research Program: 'Parenting and Childhood in Modern Family Cultures'.

United Kingdom

Clive Sellick is a senior lecturer in Social Work at the University of East Anglia (UEA) Norwich, England. He is Director of the school's international programmes including its MA in International Child Welfare and has considerable links overseas, particularly in Eastern Europe where he has conducted several study tours to aid the development of social work practice in Romania and Moldova. He is a former social worker, team leader and magistrate. His research interest is fostering and in particular in developing the research mindedness of foster care practitioners, in the collation, synthesis and analysis of data and in evaluating fostering services across the public, private and independent sectors. He has recently completed a review of innovative fostering practice in the UK for the Social Care Institute for Excellence. He is the author and joint author of many articles and chapters and books.

United States

Yvonne A. Unrau PhD is Associate Professor at the School of Social Work, Western Michigan University. She earned her Masters of Social Work from the University of Calgary in 1990 and her PhD (social work) from the University of Utah in 1995. Her research interest is studying services and outcomes to vulnerable children and families, with a particular focus on those who have experienced foster care. She is co-author of three books: *Evaluation in the Human Services; Introduction to Social Work Research* and *Evaluation; and Quantitative and Qualitative Approaches*, 7th edition.

Kathryn Conley Wehrmann PhD is an assistant professor and graduate programme director at Illinois State University. After receiving her MSW in 1982, and prior to obtaining her PhD in social work, Dr Wehrmann worked for the State of Illinois Department of Children and Family Services as a caseworker and administrator. Many of Dr Wehrmann's research, teaching and service efforts focus on child welfare issues. She has also had the opportunity to expand her interest to researching child welfare reform in post-revolutionary Romania as a Senior Fulbright Scholar.

Judy Martin PhD is a professor in the Social Work Professional Program at the University of Wisconsin Green Bay. She is the author of *Foster Family Care* and the co-author of *Child Welfare Services*. She has examined gender issues in physically abusive families, adult outcomes for battered children, and the impact of unemployment on fathering roles. She is interested in studying the experiences of foster parents as they strive to establish meaningful relationships with the foster children placed in their care.

The Editors

Matthew Colton obtained his Doctorate at the University of Oxford in 1987. He joined the University of Wales Swansea in 1989 and was awarded a Personal Chair in 2000. He successfully served as head of Applied Social Studies at Swansea from 1998–2004. He also holds a Professorship at the Regional Centre for Child and Adolescent Mental Health, Norwegian University of Science and Technology, Trondheim. He was elected an Academician of the Academy for Social Sciences in 2002.

Professor Colton has published widely within the field of child and family welfare. He began his research career in Oxford with studies on foster family and institutional care practices and the educational progress of foster children, and his subsequent research has included an international comparative study on stigma and child welfare (funded by the European Commission), and a study of sexual abuse by men who work with children (Leverhulme Research Fellowship). His current research includes work on intra- and extra-familial child sexual abusers. He recently led a review of family foster care in Wales on behalf of the Welsh Assembly Government. He has served on the editorial boards of several international research journals and presented plenary papers at a large number of international conferences. He is an honorary member of the European Scientific Association for Foster and Residential Care and previously served for many years on the Association's Executive Committee.

Margaret Williams PhD is an Associate Professor in the Faculty of Social Work at the University of Calgary, Canada. She is Director of Graduate Student Affairs for the faculty and has built an extensive international network through placing students overseas as well as through her own writing and research. She teaches child welfare and is responsible for the Child and Family concentration within the graduate programme.

Dr Williams has published extensively in the field of child welfare. Her PhD thesis was based on the partnership of social workers with the biological parents of children in care under the United Kingdom Children Act 1989. Subsequent research has included a study of outcomes for sexual abuse treatment programmes across Canada and an international study on the stigma associated with receiving child welfare services. Current research is focused on outcome studies related to a new child welfare model being piloted in Alberta whereby families within the child welfare system may receive either child protection services or the less intrusive service of family enhancement.

Dr Williams is a member of the European Scientific Association for Foster and Residential Care and an Associate Editor for the *International Journal of Child & Family Welfare*. She has been for many years a member of the Standing Committee on Youth and Adolescents which provides a voice on youth-related research at the Canadian Institutes of Health Research table.

Preface

Almost 10 years ago, the editors of the present volume published a book called *The World of Foster Care: An International Sourcebook on Foster Family Care Systems* (Colton and Williams, 1997). As its title suggests, that book was intended as an international reference book, providing, in one volume, an easily accessible and fairly comprehensive description of the role and structure of foster care systems in 21 different countries of the world. Each chapter was written by a local expert and covered the following topics: jurisdiction, history and origins, administration and organisation, foster children and carers, financial support for carers, major problems and trends, role of national foster carer organisations and research.

Trends in Foster Care

Analysis of this information revealed a number of international trends in the purpose and practice of foster care. In relation to purpose, we discerned a two-part trend away from severing children's family and community attachments towards family support and normalisation. Second, with respect to practice, we identified a move towards diversification so that more children with a wider range of needs could be cared for. At one end of the continuum, placement with relatives was being encouraged; at the other end, professional carers were being recruited and trained to work with older children and young people who have multiple difficulties. Between these poles, foster carers were offering part-time day, after-school, respite and holiday care, and full-time care for younger, or less troubled, children.

These trends are still evident today, together with other trends which we have identified in the concluding chapter of this book. Within the large literature on foster care, there are very few books which focus on the comparison of foster systems in different countries. The enthusiastic reception of *The World of Foster Care* convinced us that a more up-to-date, complementary volume was necessary. However, we also felt that such a book should be more focused, concentrating on a smaller number of countries which provided a wide range in terms of geography, political and cultural traditions, and the status of foster care within the country's child welfare system. In Argentina and China, for example, foster care is still in its infancy whereas the well-established foster care system in Japan is in danger of disappearing.

Of particular interest in these diverse countries is the relationship between political, social welfare, and religious systems. There are relationships, for example, between a nation's cultural and religious traditions, its economic profile, the welfare model it adopts, its attitudes towards socially divisive forces such as race, poverty, age and gender, and the position of child abuse on its social agenda. There are other relationships between the approach to child-care provision (child protection vs. family support), the foster care system, the legislative framework, training for professionals, and the extent and effects of research.

The diversity of this book

This book attempts to explore these relationships through a selection of countries which, taken together, reflect global trends in foster family care. The 10 countries selected span the continents of Africa, Asia, Europe, and North and South America and include representatives of some of the major models of welfare systems: liberal, social-democratic, and post-communist. They also differ widely with respect to racial mix, economic conditions, the value placed on ancestral ties, and the role of religion in social care.
The 10 countries included in this volume are as follows:

- Argentina
- China
- France
- India
- Japan
- Poland
- South Africa
- Sweden
- United Kingdom
- United States

The Authors

The contributing authors from these countries all have considerable knowledge, experience and expertise in both the art and science of family foster care. In addition to their academic qualifications, many hold office in various organisations related to foster care in their countries. Perhaps more importantly, they have practical experience in the foster care field, acting as therapists or consultants or administrators in foster care agencies. All in all, they are particularly well placed to represent global perspectives on contemporary policy, practice and research issues relating to this vital child welfare resource.

The Countries

Among the countries selected, *Argentina* and *China* provide examples of countries with very different traditions and political systems, where foster care is just beginning. In Argentina, foster care is viewed as an expression of solidarity within communities, while in China, the motive to foster derives largely from the desire to have a second child in a country where population growth is being curbed through a one-child-only policy. *India*, while predominantly Hindu, includes members of most of the major world religions and has a strong tradition of assistance to others as a way of attaining salvation. It also has one of the largest child populations in the world, estimated at 400 million, and its long history of kinship care has played a vital role in meeting the needs of children.

In *Japan*, as noted, foster care appears to be dying, partly because Japanese people value blood-ties and do not wish to have unrelated children living in their homes, and partly due to the lack of a religious tradition, like Christianity, which is active in social care. *Poland*, which serves as a representative of eastern European post-communist states, has engaged in formal foster care since 1736 when staff from the Father Baudouin Home for Children first tried placing foundlings into the care of recommended paid foster mothers. The near-demise of foster care under the communist state and its rise again in the 1970s provide an interesting glimpse into the effects on foster care of differing political ideologies.

South Africa is struggling to deal with the HIV/AIDS crisis in a context of racial tension and endemic poverty and unemployment. Kinship care has come into prominence almost by default as grandparents and other relatives struggle to care for children whose own parents are deceased or incapacitated due to AIDS. The great need for foster placements has meant that licensing has been abandoned as impractical, support services for foster carers are almost non-existent, especially in rural areas, and foster care is no longer a specialised function but may be offered by any agency with social workers in its employ. New forms of foster care – for example, a foster carer moving into a home where the parents have died – are being contemplated in response to the crisis.

Sweden, on the Scandinavian Peninsula, is ethnically relatively homogeneous, and has a history of foster care stretching from the 18th century. Like *France*, it embraces a largely institutional (as opposed to residual) approach to social welfare and, also like France, it is moving towards increased professionalisation of foster carers at the same time as it is encouraging social workers to seek foster care placements within the child's own extended family and social network. The quality of foster care is an important issue in Sweden (one study showed that between 40 and 50 per cent of placements of teenagers ended in breakdown) and another issue is the difficulty of recruiting foster carers in a country where professional careers are highly prized by both men and women.

France, in common with all other countries, is also experiencing difficulty in recruiting foster parents. In France, the organised placement of children in foster family care extends back to the 12th century and the charitable tradition of the Catholic Church has played a major role in the development of care for abused and abandoned children. Today, the religious aspect which has been so significant in the field of child welfare in the past has almost completely disappeared and most foster care services are contracted to non-profit agencies through a 'private' sector which is publicly funded.

The *United Kingdom* and the *United States*, while very similar in many respects, tend to have different approaches to social welfare. In both countries, there is an ongoing tension between the institutional and individualistic (residual) approaches but in the United States, the residual approach has prevailed overall whereas, in the United Kingdom, the government has championed a 'third way' between state monopoly welfare and private market provision.

The structure of the chapters

In order to be able to make comparisons between these 10 very different countries, we provided our contributing authors with a chapter outline that asked them not only to describe their country's foster care system under the given headings but also to provide an analysis of the information. Authors were asked to include the following information about their countries:

- Jurisdiction (geography and demography, including migration).
- The dominant political system, in light of the models noted above.
- The dominant ideology of welfare, including competing ideas about the welfare system.
- History and origins of foster care within the welfare system, including the author's reflection on those factors (cultural, religious, economic or political) which have had a major influence on the current foster care model.
- Legal framework.
- Service provision in the area of foster care in terms of (1) administration and organisation, including resources and training for professionals; and (2) current practice.
- Major issues.
- Messages from research.
- Future trends.
- Sources of further reading in the form of an annotated bibliography.
- Summary of main points.

However, each author was asked not just to present information but also to include the following considerations:

- The rights of the child – for example, the degree to which the United Nations Convention is implemented.
- The role of the family. Feminist critiques have drawn attention to the role of the family as a distinguishing criterion in understanding welfare state formations in Europe (Balbo, 1983; Tejero and Torrabadella, 1999). They have emphasised the interrelationship of the family, the state and the market, thus 'gendering' welfare states (Sainsbury, 1994). According to the strategic perspective, a family may be understood not just as an institution nor just as a mechanism through which other social spheres operate, but as an agent of social change. For example, in a patriarchal and capitalist order, incentives from the state may encourage a male breadwinner and rely on unpaid female labour for the care of the young, the sick and the elderly. Changes in gender roles within the family in succeeding generations will affect the labour market and the welfare system, obviously including the foster care system.
- The impact of religion on foster care policy.
- The impact of economic factors on foster care policy.
- The impact of political relationships on foster care policy, locally, nationally and internationally. For example, what is the impact, if any, of the European Union on foster care in European countries, and what is the impact of the relationship between federal and state governments in the United States?
- The effects of globalisation on foster care services.
- The effects of cultural diversity on foster care services. Some critics of the welfare state hold that the welfare state involves the misapplication of generic concepts to diverse individuals and groups which, in turn, has produced *dis*welfare by forcing those individuals and groups into particular ways of life or, alternatively, by effectively excluding them from the benefits of state provision (Ashenden, 1999).

Following these guidelines has been a challenge for some authors since not all factors are relevant to the foster care systems in their countries. Indeed, some authors have decided that their material would be best presented in a different way and the editors have respected their decision in this regard. The chapter on China, for example, has no list of references because that author is describing the first foster care initiative to be implemented in China so publications on the Chinese experience are not yet available.

With respect to the language difficulties which are very much to the forefront in a book of this type, readers should note that some chapters have been extensively edited and may therefore contain errors due to the editor's lack of understanding of what was intended. In addition, the process of copying references to books written in languages other than English may have entailed some sacrifice of accents. We apologise to any author whose work has been distorted in this way.

The Purpose of This Book

It should be noted that this book is not primarily a textbook, although sections of it – particularly the introductory and concluding chapters and the chapter summaries – might be of interest to classes dealing with comparative social policy, international issues, and child welfare. The sources of further reading provided by the authors will be invaluable to students in social welfare programmes world-wide, particularly those who are in international concentrations. Further, the trend in university teaching is towards providing comparative materials so that students might appreciate the similarities and differences between their own social systems and those of other countries. It will probably not be long before it is common practice to run a course – on child welfare, for example – in which the students are resident in different countries and obtain credit for the same course through different universities. Such courses will require textbooks, or web-based materials, very different from those texts which are presently being produced. This book, although not intended primarily as a textbook at the present time, may well be a forerunner of what textbooks might become.

This book is aimed at students at the graduate and undergraduate levels, teachers, scholars, policymakers, and providers in the fields of child-care, social work, administration and public policy. We hope that all our readers will enjoy the insight the book affords into the philosophies, policies and practices of foster care systems in the selected countries.

1 Argentina

Maria Dezeo de Nicora

Jurisdiction

The Republic of Argentina occupies an area of 3.8 million square kilometres in the southern part of South America, between the Andes to the west and the Atlantic Ocean to the east. It is bordered by Chile (South and West), Bolivia and Paraguay (North) and Brazil and Uruguay (Northeast). Argentina comprises 23 provinces and the autonomous city of Buenos Aires, the capital of the country. The population density varies widely, ranging from 86.2 inhabitants per square kilometre in urban areas to two inhabitants per square kilometre in the southern province of Tierra del Fuego. Eighty per cent of the total population of 37.7 million people live in the province of Buenos Aires.

Argentina is a multi-ethnic and pluri-cultural nation whose people are descended both from South-American Natives and from an important flow of European immigrants at the beginning of the 20th century (mainly Spaniards and Italians). For Argentinian society to be perceived as really pluri-cultural and equitable, it is important to remember the heritage of the native peoples. Spanish is the official language and there is freedom of religion, Catholicism being dominant.

According to the constitution, passed in 1853 and reformed in 1994, Argentina is a federal republic with a representative government which has executive, legislative and judicial powers. The executive component consists of a president and a vice-president who are elected by secret ballot, hold power for four years and can be re-elected for one consecutive period only. Voting is mandatory for citizens of both sexes, 18 years of age and older. The legislature comprises two chambers, Senators and Deputies. The judiciary comprises the Supreme Court and minor courts of law.

Research undertaken by the Department of Economics, University of La Plata in May 2002, *Demographic Characteristics and Progress in Argentina*, highlights some of the changes that have taken place due to the depression that the Argentinian economy is currently experiencing (Departamento de Economía de la Universidad Nacional de La Plata, 2002). In 1992, 81 per cent of children lived in two-parent families. In 2002, that figure was 72 per cent, showing an increase in one-parent homes, mostly headed by women. In 1980, six per cent of the people in Greater Buenos Aires[1] lived below the poverty line. In 2001, that percentage was as high as 35 per cent. Conditions in the rest of the country reflect the same level of change, though often over a shorter period of time. Large families have suffered particularly. In 2000, 50 per cent of families with six or more members in the Greater Buenos Aires area were living below the poverty line. Nevertheless, there is no evidence that changes in family income have in any way altered fertility decisions.

The increase in poverty over the last two decades has not affected all demographic groups equally: for example, in 2000, 47.1 per cent of children below the age of 12 lived in families with an income lower than the official poverty line but the percentage of adults above 65 years of age living in poverty was significantly lower (13.9%).

The increase in social vulnerability over the last two decades in Argentina is evident not only through the numbers living in poverty, but through social and employment indicators. Vulnerability has grown in different economic contexts, even during the period of economic expansion in the 1990s. The increase has been particularly apparent in one-parent homes headed by women with little education

[1] Greater Buenos Aires: An area that surrounds the Autonomous City of Buenos Aires where there is the highest population density.

and in homes with many family members, where the head of the family is relatively uneducated.

Educational attainment is an important indicator of vulnerability. In 2001, 9.9 per cent of youths from poor families dropped out of school while the percentage was 7.6 for youths from families of higher economic status. In poor homes, the birth of a new son or daughter increases the probability of other young family members dropping out.

Both educational attainment and access to social security vary with family configuration. Youths from one-parent homes fare worst, with a 15 per cent rate of school drop out and a 53 per cent lower probability of having access to social security. Young people from two-parent homes have a drop out rate of five per cent and a 17 per cent lower probability of access to social security: and youths from extended family homes, where relatives and their families live together, have a drop-out rate of 15 per cent and a lower probability of access to social security of 10 per cent.

The Argentinian State has policies whose purpose is to ensure equality in education and social security access. In theory, all citizens have access to public and free education and medical assistance in hospitals and health care centres. However, in practice, even if we ignore the differences in quality between private and public services, the public services are insufficient to guarantee equal access.

In 2003, UNICEF issued a report based on data provided by *Instituto Nacional de Estadísticas y Censos* (National Institute of Statistics and Surveys) and by the Ministries of Employment, Health and Economy (General Information, 27th Nov. 2003). The report states that:

- 7 out of 10 children are poor. That is, 4.9 million children (71.1%) are poor and 40.5% are indigent (their basic needs are not met).
- Between 2001 and 2003, 1.15 million children have become poor. Every day, 1,570 children become poor.
- 16 out of 1,000 children die before they reach the age of one year.
- In 2001, 43 out of every 100,000 women died in childbirth.
- 46% of children below the age of two are at risk of malnutrition.
- 50% of children below the age of two, and 20% of school age children, suffer from anaemia.
- A high proportion of children below the age of five do not have access to education. In 2001, the rate was 1 in 4.
- Approximately 1 million children under the age of 15 are working.
- Between 1997 and 2002, there was an increase in the number of children below 15 years of age working in urban areas: from 250,000 to 840,000.

As is shown in a document produced by *Área de Estudios Sociales de Estadísticas Argentinas* (Social Studies Area on Argentinian Statistics) under *Marco de Diálogo Nacional* (National Dialogue Framework) poverty is a contextual phenomenon and it is manifested in different dimensions: income (employment and salary); human development (basic needs); risk and vulnerability (volatility and precariousness of employment and income and low social security); and voice and power (limited participation in the political process).

Experience with social programmes shows that they are useful in supporting the populations eligible to receive their benefits but they are not useful at all in reducing poverty and inequality. Income concentration tends to reinforce the concentration of political power and, thus, to perpetuate and increase poverty and inequality. This highlights the relevance of the political dimension of poverty since the voice and power of people below the poverty line tend to be reduced even in democratic political systems. At present, in Argentina, there is a proliferation of different social programmes addressing different problems at different levels of government. These overlap and thus create barriers to efficient coverage and implementation. Political manipulation is reflected in a lack of transparency in allocating funding, and there is a conflictive state/society relationship in the implementation of all section programmes (General Section (4th January, 2004). Clientelismo del Presdiente: *La Nacion* 10).

In Argentina, almost 20 per cent of homes are dependent on social programming. The largest state programme to fight poverty has an annual budget of $3,500,000. It provides a monthly payment of $150 (about USD 50) to approximately 1.8 million unemployed breadwinners, in exchange for, ideally, four hours of mandatory work on the part of the beneficiaries. The programme does not provide universal coverage for all the unemployed (there are 5 million unemployed – almost half the working population) and it does not provide sufficient funds to lift beneficiaries over the indigence threshold (report by *Centro de Estudios Legales y Sociales* (*CELS*) Social and Legal Studies Centre, May 2003). Officials from the national government acknowledge that there are flaws in distribution and even the President, Dr Néstor Kirchner, has made reference to 'political consumers'. In addition, the programme does not promote income redistribution but only targeted assistance. Nowadays, the policy is to direct the unemployed towards productive work as a means of exit from this purely 'assistance' model. However, the CELS report claims that this policy is unsound since there are no stable jobs to absorb the retrained unemployed unless they replace other workers. For workers presently employed, the threat of being replaced only deepens the precariousness of their position.

The Origins of Foster Care

The preceding paragraphs provide a context for the establishment of foster care in Argentina. It has long been a concern to *Fundación Emmanuel* that foster care in Argentina is a forgotten avenue, neglected by both governmental and non-governmental organisations. A large number of children from poor families whose parents are unable to care for them, children with special needs, and children considered 'unadoptable' because of their age are housed in institutions. It was because of these concerns that *Fundación Emmanuel* was born in 1985. This was the first institution to establish foster care in Argentina.

Fundación Emmanuel defines foster care as providing a space in a family, for as long as needed, to children and adolescents who, for whatever reason, cannot live with their own families, recognising their stories and identities, and allowing for re-attachment with their origins, always from a framework of respect, support and trust.

In 1985, a working team was established to give legal and statutory shape to *Fundación Emmanuel* and to develop a theoretical framework to guide the placement of children in foster families. The goals of the *Fundación* were as follows:

- To foster children at social risk, so that they can exercise their right to live with a family, providing them with a context that respects their identity.
- To encourage families to share their homes with children who are not their own and to recruit, train and support such families.
- To strengthen and support birth families so that they can continue to have bonds with their children and can work together with foster families.
- To facilitate the development of supporting networks within communities by bringing together the relevant actors.
- To provide advice and training to professionals and organisations interested in the place of foster care within the child-care system.

In 1988, the first foster family at *Fundación Emmanuel* welcomed a group of seven siblings, two of them highly handicapped, who had not previously had the opportunity to enjoy a stable family life. This experience was used as a jumping-off point to call for other volunteers and to demonstrate what could be achieved through providing support to new foster families.

In the years since 1988, a number of programmes have arisen in Argentina under the foster care umbrella. Some do not seem to be 'foster care' in the sense that *Fundación Emmanuel* defines the term, and the differences do not lie merely in terminology but reflect different ethical and philosophical frameworks regarding the care of children at risk and their relationships with their birth families. It is as well, therefore, to look at the various terms in current use, in an attempt to clarify the conceptual differences.

Family placement: In many countries which have a long tradition in foster care, the term 'foster care' is synonymous with the term 'family placement' in that 'family placement' is what happens when a child enters 'foster care'. In Argentina, 'family placement' is a protective measure, employed in cases where a child is either separated from their family or is excluded from it because of the difficulty the birth family is experiencing in performing parental duties.

The emphasis is on safeguarding the child's well-being and, in practice, this is often accomplished by minimising any interaction with the birth family. By contrast, foster care provides a response to a family in need and recognises the right of the family to ask for assistance when experiencing difficulty. This 'rights' approach means that the birth family continues to play a vital role in the child's life, appreciates the assistance offered by the foster family, and is recognised by the foster family as essential to the child's well-being.

Substitute family: Substituting means replacing, changing, taking one thing instead of another. A foster family is not intended to be a substitute family in the sense that the foster parents are the child's new parents and the birth parents are no longer in the picture. Instead, both the foster and birth families act in a complementary manner, each making its contribution to meeting the needs of the child.

Wardship: Since, in Argentina, a national legal framework for foster care does not exist, foster care may be mistaken for wardship. Wardship means caring for a minor, providing them with material and spiritual assistance, without being their legal representative. Wardship provides limited room for the birth family and, in general, the family welcoming the child is not supported in the complex process of reintegrating the child with the birth family.

Transitory family: This is a family that provides a placement to a child on a short-term basis. Sometimes, it is recommended to such families that they try not to establish an attachment to the child since attachment may create difficulties when the child must move on.

Although the expected duration of family placement can be categorised by the Juvenile Court of Law as short, middle, or long-term, the 'rights' approach inherent in foster care means that time (or transience) in foster care is measured in terms of the need of the child and family receiving the foster care service. The placement will therefore last as long as it needs to last depending on each foster care situation and the resolution of the causes that gave rise to foster care.

Service Provision

When we were asked to write a chapter for this book, we invited all the Provincial Secretaries or Offices for Children, Adolescents and Families to participate in the chapter by sending information. We only received information from the provinces of Río Negro, Chubut and San Juan, whom we would like to thank for their prompt co-operation. We will describe the legislation and programmes used by these provinces but we must not forget that there are other districts that have implemented foster care, although it is not mentioned in the law.

Before describing them briefly, we would like to share with you the stipulations made by the Committee on the Rights of the Child (United Nations, October, 2002) in response to a report presented by Argentina regarding Article 44 of the Convention on the Rights of the Child.

The committee said, in effect, that it was glad to see some advance, such as legislation regarding minors in provinces such as Mendoza, Chubut and the Autonomous City of Buenos Aires. It acknowledged that Argentina was facing many difficulties in implementing the convention due to the socio-economic-political crisis, and that increased poverty was hindering the complete fulfilment and exercise of the rights acknowledged in the convention. However, the committee was worried about the current national legislation regarding minors (Law 10.903 – Patronage Act) based on the doctrine of the 'irregular situation' where minors are subject to judicial protection. The committee highly recommended revision of that legislation.

Regarding family and alternative care (Art. 5, 18 [para. 1–2]; 19–21; 25, 27 [para. 4], and 39 of the Convention) the committee was highly concerned about the number of minors, mainly children from poor families, who were deprived of a family setting and placed in public assistance homes or institutions, far away from their own homes, more often than not. It recommended, in the light of Article 20, the taking of effective measures so that minors were placed in institutions only as a last resort, and access to homes and other alternatives for the care of children in a family setting was promoted and increased.

As already noted, Argentina lacks a national law that responds to the Convention on the Rights of the Child, although some provinces have enforced and updated their provincial laws to comply with it. Even if the term 'foster care' is not used in every province, the spirit of foster care is still present in the legislation and programmes in that emphasis is placed on respect for the child's own story and the story of their birth family.

Since 2002, the province of Rio Negro has had a provincial programme called 'Family Strengthening', decree N° 325/03, which falls within the framework provided by Law N° 3097/97, 'Integral protection to and promotion of the rights of the child and adolescent'. This programme is for families at risk who require support from the state. Its aim is to try to resolve family attachment issues so that risk to the child is reduced. In some cases, temporary protection is provided for the child through a programme called 'Solidarity Family'. Here, the child is placed with another family, for no longer than a year, until assistance provided to the birth family has ameliorated the situation sufficiently to allow the child to return home. Another programme, called 'Solidarity Home', serves children and adolescents who have had difficulty developing attachments to their birth family. Because of their 'at-risk' situation at home, they are placed under legal care for as long as is needed, sometimes returning to live with their birth families and sometimes not.

Both these programmes are implemented through the participation of families in the child's community who are willing to provide temporary support to children and adolescents in need. Each jurisdiction has a list of interested families and has the assistance of a professional team, comprising social workers and psychologists, for programme assessment. Selected families are financially supported, according to their needs.

In December 1997, the province of Chubut passed provincial Law N° 4317 'Integral Protection of Children, Adolescents and Families'. Article 25 states that every child and adolescent has the right to be raised and educated in a family, preferably in their own families in their own communities and, only exceptionally, in other families. Article 59 stipulates the role of an alternative (or foster) family as complementary to the role of the birth family in cases where children or adolescents are at risk.

To some extent, this law acts as a framework for new legislation. What is particularly interesting about it is that, when it talks about protection, it considers protection not just in the sense of physical protection but in a more holistic sense as protection of rights. It also supports intervention with the birth family to help it deal with the difficulties that gave rise to the child's need for protection, and to facilitate, whenever possible, the return of the child or adolescent to the birth family.

In addition, the province of Chubut has made agreements with several districts to enforce 'rights protection services', and has made progress in the launching of a Family Strengthening programme to provide birth families or extended families with subsidies, in order to promote permanence and the socialisation of children and adolescents within the family.

The Autonomous City of Buenos Aires, in its law 114 (3/12/98), in Chapter 2 'Special Measures for the Protection of Rights', states in Article 36 that these measures are for the special protection of children who are threatened, or vulnerable or whose rights are not being observed: the measures are time-limited and are applicable for as long as the causes still exist. Article 42 talks about alternative ways to house children when there is no family or no permission to live with a family, so that children can live with people they know, either members of their extended family or friends in the community. Article 43 supports and strengthens family attachment, thus **separating poverty from the court of law**; and Article 44 considers **institutionalisation as exceptional and subsidiary**, since protective measures should never involve denial of freedom.

The province of San Juan reports that the new law N° 7338 concerns protection for children and adolescents. In Book 2, Chapter 2°, Articles 57–63 inclusive, the law makes reference to the placement of children with alternative families. It has not been implemented yet but a non-governmental organisation (NGO) has been charged with the implementation.

Fundación Emmanuel is promoting a national law on foster care as pertaining to family rights. Such a law is expected to avoid the danger of placing foster care under the judiciary or of creating a new system of placing children with alternate families that reproduces the old, known flaws of the already existing systems. Experience has shown that, once rights begin to be promoted, families are able to exercise their rights. When *Fundación Emmanuel* began its mission, the only requests for foster care it received were from the juvenile courts of law. Then, it began to work jointly with professional teams from institutes, schools, health care centres, and community groups; and today, it is parents themselves who come to *Fundación Emmanuel* requesting the help of a foster family to ensure the well-being of their children until they can overcome the difficult circumstances that have led them to make the request. Readers will recall that, in Argentina, a high percentage of children are fostered due to the economic crisis, which has not only increased poverty at a structural level but has also given rise to families who are newly poor and are experiencing crisis as a result of their new economic condition.

When the birth family, as the child's natural developmental setting, is minimised and disregarded, it is because of the belief that intervention is necessary because the child has been abandoned (with all the possible meanings of the word 'abandonment') or because the responsible adults concerned with the child are not performing their parental roles appropriately. In fact, the issue is not about an abandoned child but about a family which is experiencing a crisis and, in many cases, does not have an opportunity to exercise its rights. Thus, disregarding the family means disregarding the right that the family has to ask for help.

In 1985, a working team was established, whose mandate was to study a possible declaration by the UN about the rights and responsibilities of the family. In order to fulfil its mandate, the team gathered 58 documents from the UN related to 26 social topics. Its intention was to produce a coherent and exhaustive document, laying out family functions, responsibilities and rights. The draft of this document was issued to the Board of the Committee of the Family in Vienna on December 16, 1992. The final document, issued in 1993, says that:

1. Programmes and activities concerning social well-being shall be formulated so that they strengthen and revitalise the functions of families.
2. Every policy, on both national and international levels, in both developed and developing countries, shall consider its impact upon the family (Cots, 1994).

This is why foster care is a family right that the family can claim when experiencing a crisis. Such an acknowledgement challenges the idea that the child must be considered a 'subject for protection' and must be cared for by the state, with the family losing its right to be involved in decision-making pertaining to the child's life. In other words, the document challenges the idea that parental rights and duties should be transferred to the state when the state is caring for the child because the parents have demonstrated their inability to exercise their rights and fulfil their duties. It accepts that all families may experience crisis on occasion and that families in crisis retain the right to seek outside support which may allow them to resolve their conflicts. This philosophy, already stated in recommendations and declarations, needs to be enshrined in social policies with the participation of government and non-governmental organisations.

We must remember that Argentina has always favoured equal rights for 'those who live in our nation', according to the constitution. That view strengthened the social fabric. The neighbour was part of the extended family and showed concern for other neighbours living in the community. An example is the 'nursing mother', a mother who had given birth to her own baby and shared her milk with another mother who could not nurse her baby. The nursing mother gave away part of herself that went beyond the food and focused on the needs of the other mother and baby in her community. Many adults still remember their 'nursing mothers' and proudly introduce their 'nursing brothers'. These memories serve to enrich foster care and demonstrate a way in which rivalry gives place to sharing, and prejudice to the acceptance of difference.

Those working with *Fundación Emmanuel* have experienced foster care as a natural response from one family to another one. Yet, although many foster families have succeeded on their own, others have come to the *Fundación* to ask for advice and support from professionals, since 'goodwill' does not replace the training and support that every foster family needs. The *Fundación*'s intent is to preserve the neighbourly spirit which nourishes foster care but which has been blurred by the successive socio-economic-cultural crises that Argentina has been experiencing. These crises have led many to protect themselves rather than reaching out to others, increasing social isolation. But on the other hand, there have also arisen numerous proposals from communities, expressing their solidarity and resulting in concrete plans to modify existing systems through active participation by the beneficiaries of the modified systems.

Given that foster care in Argentina was initiated by an NGO (*Fundación Emmanuel*) as a solidarity response to families in need, the underlying philosophy was not based on the idea of an agency as a service provider but on the idea of families within a community helping other families in need. This is the reason why foster care is spreading more easily in the non-profit sector, supported by foundations and civil associations.

The concept of solidarity within a community does not denote political customers or paternalistic ideas about protection or residualistic notions of charitable assistance to the unfortunate. Instead, solidarity confirms the right of families in need to receive assistance. The exercise of that right results in a foster care system where preparation, training and support are provided to both birth and foster families as a matter of course.

Foundations or associations providing foster care are responsible to the pertinent national body and are also guided and supported by professional teams, which oversee the foster care programme's theoretical framework and methodological approach. Every Argentinean institution working with children and adolescents needs an explicit mandate at national and provincial levels from the *Inspección General de Justicia* (General Supervision from the Judiciary) which must be presented with an annual budget and report on activities. Every institution must also be enrolled in the *Centro Nacional de Organizaciones de la Comunidad (CENOC), del Consejo Nacional de Coordinación de Políticas Sociales de la Presidencia de la Nación* (National Centre of Community Organisations, from the Board of Social Policies Coordination, from the National State) or in the pertinent provincial or municipal offices, and they are supervised by provincial Boards, Secretaries or Undersecretaries for Childhood and Adolescence.

Despite the fact that many of the NGOs emerged from religious movements, mainly Catholic or Protestant, very few organisations which work with children in Argentina provide foster care. Community groups with more secular concerns are becoming more aware of their resources and responsibilities with respect to families in need and are establishing natural supporting networks in the provinces and great urban areas.

Major Issues

Those responsible for national, provincial and municipal public policies have been inviting *Fundación Emmanuel* to implement foster care ever since its inception. However, a succession of different administrations, inattention to prevention programmes and the lack of promotion of foster care, among other things, have resulted in foster care programmes being implemented piecemeal, with no long-term realisation.

A good example is the agreement signed between *Fundación Emmanuel* and the National Board for Childhood, Adolescence and Family (*Consejo Nacional de Niñez, Adolescencia y Familia*). Disposition No 245/00, titled *Necesitamos Abrazos* (We Need Hugs) called for *Fundación Emmanuel* to assess, select and train foster families to welcome children with special needs: that is, groups of siblings, older children, and adolescents with or without health problems, and with or without attachment with their birth families. The agreement lasted only six months.

In 2001, the National Board promoted the presentation of preparatory material for the 13th International Biennial Conference IFCO Argentina 2003, called 'Spreading the Wings of Foster Care'. Disposition No 196/01 stated that it was of the utmost importance to support and strengthen the exchange of knowledge on the topic, regarding both theory and practice. The National Board deals with the promotion of the rights of children and adolescents at social risk so that they can exercise their rights to live with a family and to have their identity respected, according to the terms of the national plan to implement the Convention on the Rights of the Child. In May 2003, the President of the National Board signed an agreement with *Fundación Emmanuel*. Article 1 of the agreement states that 'the Board and the *Fundación* are to execute jointly, simultaneously and in coordination, all actions leading to the implementation of the foster care process in or between families, so that children and their families can exercise their right to foster care.'

Article 2 reads: 'To coordinate the actions tending to spread, encourage, and strengthen the right to foster care of children and their families.' This agreement represented another initiative on the part of the National Board to consolidate public policies which fit with the perspective of rights stated in the Convention on the Rights of the Child, and which went beyond the traditional practice. Unfortunately, the new administration of 2003 does not recognise the agreement described above, and does not respond to requests that the process, already begun, should be continued.

Apart from the information available from the National Board of Childhood, Adolescence and the Family, and from the Undersecretary for Minors of the Province of Buenos Aires, it is not known how many children are in out-of-home care under the auspices of traditional programmes: for example, 'amas externas' (transitory family placement for children between birth and 5 years of age) 'little homes', housing eight to 10 children each and developed by the state for the protection of children whose parents cannot care for them for various reasons; and transitory homes, housing children referred by order from a juvenile court of law. It is also unknown how many children live away from their families on the streets or with neighbours or relatives. Data from the National Board show that, currently, 657 children are placed in 'little homes' and 95 'amas externas' care for 464 minors. It is worth while mentioning that, although these programmes are deemed to be 'transitory' (short or middle-term) 60 per cent of children and adolescents under the protection of the state do not leave their placements until they become adult (Palomar, 2003).

Information from the Undersecretary for Minors of the Province of Buenos Aires shows that between 10,000 and 12,000 children and adolescents are institutionalised because they need assistance or protection. One-third of these are assisted by the state and two-thirds by non-governmental organisations; 688 children and adolescents live in 86 'little homes', housing eight to 10 children and adolescents each.

In the province of Buenos Aires, 70 per cent of adults in prison come from these institutions. Not only does that figure show the ineffectiveness of institutional placements for children, but also, and above all, the lack of humanity in such placements.

For *Fundación Emmanuel*, the fact that a child is in conflict with the law does not mean that the child cannot be welcomed into a foster family, though there is no legislation around this and courts still do not request foster placement. *Fundación Emmanuel* believes that criteria for acceptance of a foster child should not be based on previous acts committed by the child but on the child's bio-psycho-social characteristics. What is important is whether the child will allow him or herself to live with a family, and that such a motivation is more than a verbally expressed desire.

We would also like to emphasise that if foster care is not perceived as a means of strengthening families, it is running the risk of continuing to implement programmes that increase family vulnerability. For this reason, the approach must involve all three of the major actors in the foster care environment: the child, the birth family and the foster family. The participation of these actors in all phases of the foster care process, from assessment to training to support, must be recognised not only by professional teams, but also by all the other services and systems (for example, schools and health care organisations) that interact with the birth and foster families.

The lack of a national legal framework hinders the transformation of the perception of the child from an object needing protection to a subject having rights. Without this change in perspective, there is a danger that traditional ways of 'protecting the child' will be carried on under new names. Thus, it is essential to bring into force a national law that respects the essence, spirit and identity of foster care.

It is a matter of concern that, although other types of programmes serving families provide financial support to their families (scholarships or subsidies, ranging from USD 66 to USD 200, according to the province and the child's needs) it would seem that many officers responsible for public policies believe that, because foster care represents solidarity within a community, therefore it does not need to be paid for. One of *Fundación Emmanuel*'s main challenges is to make officials aware of foster care as a process that needs budgets and resources. These resources could be drawn from programmes which place children in institutions — programmes which have been shown to be uneconomical, inefficient, and inhumane.

Fundación Emmanuel is making continuing attempts to promote foster care through public awareness campaigns, drives to recruit foster families, attempts to interest the media, and training for professionals and volunteers from government and non-governmental organisations. These efforts are succeeding in slowly establishing foster care within Argentinean communities and in decisive areas of government and NGOs.

A milestone in foster care in Argentina and in Latin America was the 13th International Biennial Conference IFCO Argentina 2003 - 'Spreading the Wings of Foster Care' — organised by *Fundación Emmanuel* in the city of La Plata, capital of the province of Buenos Aires. This conference allowed not only for academic exchange, but also, and mainly, for enrichment through experience. It was a moment *Fundación Emmanuel* certainly shared with many readers of this chapter.

Conclusion

We are convinced that our achievements in implementing foster care in Argentina and spreading it in Latin America have not been in vain. Many provinces have updated their legislation; many governmental and non-governmental organisations have adhered to this new view of the child and their family in need; public policy makers have become aware that old policies only supported and encouraged systems of marginalisation and that speeches accepting the Convention were often no more than empty words. All these have helped to achieve the aim of our *Fundación*: that institutionalisation should become a ghost from the past and the right to live with a family should be exercised by every child and adolescent around the world.

References

Consejo Nacional de Niñez, Adolescencia y Familia (2003) *Políticas y Estrategias de Derechos en el Área de Niñez, Adolescencia y Familia. Crónicas de los Encuentros Federales Regionales.* Buenos Aires, Argentina.

Consejo Nacional de Niñez, Adolescencia y Familia (2003) *Informe de Gestión 2002/2003.* Buenos Aires, Argentina.

Convención Internacional sobre los Derechos del Niño, National Law N°. 23.849, enforced on 27/9/90.

Cots, J. (1994). *Familia: Derechos y Responsabilidades.* Colección Al Servico del Nino, BICE, 145.

Departamento de Economía de la Universidad Nacional de La Plata (2002) *Características demográficas y pobreza en la Argentina.* http://bisi.siempro.gov.ar/bisi/eds/cuadros/cuadro.jps?cuadro = B8.

General Infomation (27th November, 2003). Interview with UNICEF Regional Director, Nils Arne Katsberg, in Buenos Aires: La Nacion. 17.

General Information (4th January, 2004). Clarin 28 and 29.

Ley del Niño y el Adolescente de la Provincia de Mendoza – Ley 6354 (1997). Mendoza, Argentina.

Palomar, J. (2003) *Hogares en tránsito. Un largo camino a casa.* Revista La Nación. 58–63.

Social Studies Area of Charity Argentina 2002. *Elements to design a social policy in Argentina.* www.caritas.org.ar.

United Nations (2002) Consideration of the reports issued by States Parties, according to art. 44 of the Convention. *Conclusions by the Commission on the Rights of the Child: Argentina.*

2 China

Robert Glover

Jurisdiction

With an area of 3,705,408 square miles (9,956,961 square kilometres) China is twice the size of Western Europe. It has 31 provinces, including five 'autonomous regions' and four city municipalities. China is a highly diverse country and its terrain ranges from plains, deltas and hills in the east to mountains, high plateaux and deserts in the west. To the south its climate is tropical, while to the north it is sub-arctic. Less than one-sixth of China is suitable for agriculture and the most fertile areas lie in the eastern third of the country, which is economically the most developed region.

The Chinese imperial system came to an end in 1911, when the Qing (Manchu) dynasty was overthrown and China was proclaimed a republic, partly through the efforts of revolutionaries such as Sun Yat-sen. The country then entered a period of warlordism until in 1927 the Nationalist Party or 'Kuomintang' (KMT), under its leader Chiang Kai-shek, established a central government in Nanjing. The Chinese Communist Party (CCP) was founded in 1921 but broke with the KMT and was forced to flee into the interior in the Long March in 1934/35. Both KMT and CCP forces opposed Japan during World War Two but a civil war broke out from 1945–1949. CCP forces under Mao Zedong routed their KMT opponents and in 1949 Mao announced the establishment of the People's Republic of China. KMT elements fled to the island of Taiwan.

The period between 1949 and Mao's death in 1976 was characterised by an ambitious political and economic restructuring programme which involved the collectivisation of industry, the establishment of communes and the redistribution of land. The Cultural Revolution from 1966–1976 brought enormous upheaval in the political system and Mao had to rely on the armed forces to maintain order and exercise control.

In December 1978 the CCP, inspired by Deng Xiaoping, launched a wide-ranging programme of economic and social reform which sought to modernise the economy, develop China's external relations (the 'open door policy'), especially with the West, and implement a gradual and limited liberalisation of Chinese society.

Political opposition to the more liberal reforms forced periods of retrenchment and in June 1989, following the brutal suppression of pro-democracy demonstrators in Beijing, political control swung firmly into the hands of conservative elements within the CCP. The Chinese government labelled the demonstrations a 'counter-revolutionary rebellion' and clamped down on dissent. Prominent dissidents fled the country or went into hiding. Many activists were arrested. Jiang Zemin, former Mayor and later Party Secretary of Shanghai replaced Party General Secretary Zhao Ziyang. Jiang was appointed to the additional post of State President in March 1993. Since then, the Party leadership has continued the economic reform programme, while also seeking to improve China's standing in the international community. Jiang retired as President in March 2003 and was replaced by Vice-President Hu Jintao.

China's current process of 'modernisation' is of a speed, scale and scope probably unprecedented in human history. 1998 was the 20th anniversary year of China's 'reform and opening up' policies, which have achieved fairly steady economic growth over the 20 year period. The growth is occurring especially within an emerging, highly dynamic, market-driven sector, more in coastal than in inland provinces and regions.

Opening to global market forces may increase disparities, and pressure on the poorest in China, in the short-term; however, the hope is for everyone to benefit economically. The impact of recent outbreaks of Severe Acute Respiratory Syndrome (SARS) has yet to be measured. Every year, major natural disasters such as heavy rains, floods, snowstorms, drought and earthquakes cause heavy economic losses including hundreds of human casualties throughout China. Children are often the most vulnerable victims of such natural disasters. Many families lose their means of production and are left unable to support the cost of children's education, health care or other basic services.

Overall estimates by government indicate that infant and under-five mortality have declined. The maternal mortality rate has decreased from 89 per 100,000 live births in 1990 to about 53 per 100,000 live births in 2000. Although the decline is impressive, the rate of decline has been falling over the decade. There is also wide variation within the country: even between provinces there can be three-fold differences. Major causes for infant deaths are Acute Respiratory Infections, problems of the newborn, neonatal tetanus, diarrhoeal diseases and injuries. Causes of child mortality (one to four years) are pneumonia, diarrhoeal diseases and injuries.

HIV/AIDS was first reported in China in 1985. In September 2002 the Chinese government estimated that about a million people were infected with the HIV virus in China. The United Nations believes that this is still an underestimate and warns that as many as 1.5 million Chinese have the virus, with an estimated increase to 20 million by the end of the decade. Although cases have been detected in all provinces, HIV transmission is primarily focused among intravenous drug users in certain provinces (e.g., Yunnan and Xinjiang). In 1998 the Chinese government set out policy objectives and strategies to deal with HIV/AIDS and introduced measures such as HIV screening for all blood for clinical use and information campaigns.

Dominant Political System

The State Council of the People's Republic of China, namely the Central People's Government, is the highest executive organ of state power, as well as the highest organ of state administration. The State Council is composed of a premier, vice-premiers, state councillors, ministers in charge of ministries and commissions, the auditor-general and the secretary-general. The premier of the State Council is nominated by the president, reviewed by the NPC (National People's Congress), and appointed and removed by the president. Other members of the State Council are nominated by the premier, reviewed by the NPC or its Standing Committee, and appointed and removed by the president. In the State Council, a single term of each office is five years, and incumbents cannot be reappointed after two successive terms.

The State Council follows the system of premier responsibility in work while various ministries and commissions under the State Council follow the system of ministerial responsibility. In dealing with foreign affairs, state councillors can conduct important activities on behalf of the premier after being entrusted by the premier of the State Council. The auditor-general is the head of the State Auditing Administration, in charge of auditing and supervising state finances. The secretary-general, under the premier, is responsible for the day-to-day work of the State Council and is in charge of the general office of the State Council.

The State Council is responsible for carrying out the principles and policies of the Communist Party of China as well as the regulations and laws adopted by the NPC, and dealing with such affairs as China's internal politics, diplomacy, national defence, finance, economy, culture and education.

Under the current constitution, the State Council exercises the power of administrative legislation, the power to submit proposals, the power of administrative leadership, the power of economic management, the power of diplomatic administration, the power of social administration, and other powers granted by the NPC and its Standing Committee.

At the 16th Communist Party Congress in November 2002 Jiang Zemin stepped down from his position as Party General Secretary to make way for a new 'fourth' generation of leaders. Prior to this, he had pressed ahead with a major political campaign, the 'Three Representatives', which addresses key concerns surrounding the Party's continuing role and relevance at a time of major domestic and international change.

Hu Jintao succeeded Jiang as Party General Secretary. The new state leadership positions were announced at the National People's Congress (NPC), which met from 5–18 March 2003. Hu Jintao was named President and Wen

Jiabao became Premier. Wu Bangguo replaced Li Peng as NPC Chairman. The new leadership have made it clear that they will continue the current policy main priorities of economic growth, internal stability and opening up to the world.

History and Origins of Foster Family Care for Children

In 1949 there were an estimated 500 million people in China. China's population in 1999 was about 1.2 billion — the most populated nation in the world.

Faced with a seemingly out-of-control population explosion, China implemented strict family planning controls in the 1970s with the aim of limiting the population to 1.2 billion by the year 2000. Those controls — especially the 'one-child-only' rule – have been largely successful. China's birth rate has dropped, and officials estimate that without the family planning campaign, the Chinese population would now be more than 1.5 billion. However, the controls also had other consequences; for example, an increase in the number of children, especially girls, being abandoned and put into orphanages. In 1996 orphanages in China were in crisis with overcrowding, lack of resources and no staff training. This crisis was certainly a factor in the establishment, in September 1988, of the Joint Shanghai Foster Care and Training Program, the first formal foster care project with management and training standards to be set up in China. This project will be further discussed later in the chapter.

Analysts say the biggest threat to China's efforts at population control is the growing number of transients — a 'floating population' now estimated at more than 100 million, of mostly rural labourers and their families who travel to China's cities in search of work. Such transients tend to ignore the government's family planning policies. China's life expectancy average also has doubled since 1949, to 70 years. Longer living Chinese, with fewer births, could cause China to soon become the fastest aging nation in history.

For the past 20 years, 'encouraging' Chinese couples to limit the size of their families to one child has been employed as a means of controlling that country's soaring population growth. Restrictions on adoption by Chinese couples with existing children are now being eased. Provisions for this first appeared in the amended Adoption Law that went into effect April 1, 1999.

These changes are expected to affect the face of international adoption since the number of children in Chinese orphanages could drop dramatically over the next three to five years. It should be noted that children adopted from China are estimated to represent somewhere between one-quarter to one-third of the worldwide total of out-of-country placements.

Adoptions of Chinese children within China soared from 201 in 1989 to 5,053 in 2002, and the one-child policy certainly has to be considered a major factor in this enormous jump. Family planning will continue to be strongly encouraged by the Chinese government, and many alternative forms of contraception will be made available. Abortion also remains a legal alternative.

China's social welfare institutions for children play a role in the country's efforts to care for children. The welfare institutions accept orphans who have lost their parents during natural disasters or accidents, and also those abandoned by their parents because they are disabled mentally or physically, or because they have contracted a serious illness.

Each welfare home for children has drawn up guidelines concerning aspects of both internal management and the children's lives – upbringing, nursing, medical care, rehabilitation, scientific research, community rehabilitation, training, and support services.

Apart from welfare institutions set up by the Ministry of Civil Affairs and managed by the local Civil Affairs Bureaux, to take care of orphans and abandoned children, China encourages citizens to adopt these children so that they can enjoy a normal family life.

The Joint Shanghai Foster Care and Training Program

The Joint Shanghai Foster Care and Training Program was established in September 1998 as a three year programme (subsequently extended by one year) to establish foster care in Shanghai through the adaptation of foster care practices used in the UK to the Chinese situation. It was a partnership between Care for Children (CFC), a UK registered charity, and the Shanghai Social

Services, a part of the Shanghai Civil Affairs Bureau. CFC was partly funded for the first three years of the project by the UK government Department for International Development.

The purpose of the Shanghai Foster Care and Training Program was to develop, within the Shanghai Children's Welfare Institute, de-institutionalised alternatives for caring for abandoned or orphaned children under their jurisdiction, in particular, long-term foster care in a family environment. This involved the development of policies and practices appropriate in the Chinese context and the production of training materials for use in the training facility. Once the programme was successfully established, the experience gained could be used to set up a training facility in Shanghai to train staff from Shanghai and elsewhere in China in foster care. It was hoped that such a training facility would influence social policy and practice throughout China.

Two effects of the programme only indirectly related to the placement of foster children have to do with the social work profession and the alleviation of poverty. Social work is not yet a recognised profession in China but Care for Children is introducing methods of training and empowering individuals to undertake standard social work roles in their communities, which will do much to establish the profession. With respect to poverty alleviation, the following extract from a report by Care for Children's President, Lord Laming, is of interest:

> *During the succeeding months the social workers observed the progress of each child. But also they noted a growing concern by the families that, whilst they could comply with the required standards in the home, they were worried about the state of the drains in the village. They feared that if the foster child was sick, it might be thought they were to blame. The authorities offered to make good the drains if the community gave an assurance that they would be used properly. At another meeting the foster parents expressed concerns that the foster children were getting greater opportunities than their own children. Again the authorities offered to enlarge the school if the parents would ensure that their own children attended regularly even during harvest or at times of other demands.*

And so the story continued of how the quality of life in the villages was being steadily improved.

This observation by Lord Laming reveals that the relatively simple notion of ensuring a good standard of foster care can transform the welfare of a whole community.

There is a big difference between the type of foster care in the West (short-term) and the practice that is being encouraged in China. Most children in the West come into care through some form of abuse in the past, and may have contact with their natural families. Children in China, many of whom are disabled, come into care through abandonment because of their disability or gender, so their traumas are very different. They have no contact with their natural families so we look for permanent families through long-term foster care.

We use long-term foster care (permanence) for placing children with disabilities. This is because the foster parents need added support and training to be able to care for the child. We encourage attachment and bonding between the child and its substitute parents but continue to monitor and support the families.

In China there is a great motivation to foster long-term, as many couples have had their only child and want to raise another, often a girl if they have had a son. Adoption is an obvious solution here. However, we felt that to allow so many people to adopt without the initial support of foster care could lead to adoptive parents working in isolation and a higher breakdown and abuse rate. After a period of three to five years of foster care, many families do adopt the child placed with them.

When we work with local authorities, usually an orphanage, we select and train a group of the institution's staff to become family placement workers. We have adopted the UK National Standards for Foster Care along with the codes of practice and assessment procedures recommended by the British Association for Adoption and Foster Care. (BAAF, 1999) These have been translated and culturally amended to make a comparable Chinese version that works very well. Family placement workers recruit and assess foster parents, match foster parents with children (who are selected by the management of the Children's Welfare Centre) and support placements.

The programme has now been in operation for four years. Its achievements over that time can best be described under the following three headings: Shanghai foster care project; Training programme; and Relationship development.

Shanghai foster care project

A team of 12 staff dedicated to the foster care service, operating under the auspices of the Shanghai Children's Welfare Institute, was established. This team included doctors, nurses and teachers who were trained to assess the needs of both children and parents in the pre-placement stage of fostering. The team also developed skills in training families to care for children with disabilities and were able to monitor the progress of the children and support the families effectively in the community. Supporting the team were staff from the Shanghai Children's Welfare Institution, the Shanghai Social Services, the Shanghai Charity Foundation and the East China Normal University. The All China Women's Federation provided volunteer support for the foster families in the community. Robert Glover, the CFC consultant to the programme, was based with the team at the Shanghai Children's Welfare Institution in Pu Yu Shi Lu.

Recruitment of foster carers surpassed original expectations. More than 700 families applied. By the end of the project, 400 children had been placed, surpassing the original target of 300 children, and foster carer self-help groups had been initiated in five localities. The children ranged in age from birth to 12 years and many had mild physical or learning disabilities. When the project ended in 2002, an average of 10 children continued to be placed every month.

The first group of children, placed in early 1998, have been in their foster homes for five years at the time of writing. At 7 per cent, the placement breakdown ratio is lower than that experienced in the UK but it is recognised that the programme still has a limited history. Significant positive changes have been observed in many children following their move to foster families. In particular, several children who had in the past been felt to have serious learning difficulties have made significant progress.

In May 2000, an independent evaluation was completed by Professors Thoburn and Beckett from the University of East Anglia and Professors Shen and Zeng from the East China Normal University. Further details can be found in their evaluation report, which is available upon request.

The local authority remained the legal parent of each child placed and the foster family expected to raise the child to independence. Payment to foster families was fully funded by the Shanghai Civil Affairs Bureau and the Shanghai Charity Foundation. Each family received a monthly payment (on average RMB 300 equivalent to USD 35) to cover the child's medical, educational and living costs. The philosophy underlying the payment was that people should not be able to make money from fostering but neither should they lose financially. In fact, some families initially refused the money and were only persuaded to take it by being told that it was for the child and not for them. As well as the regular support visits from their family placement worker, there were monthly foster parent support groups which had an incredible 100 per cent turnout. CFC put on a free meal at a local restaurant and all the parents came to discuss and help and support one another. This was deemed to be one of CFC's best investments.

Training programme

CFC funded the consultant, the translation and cultural tailoring of materials, the development of practice procedures, the training of foster parents and staff, service delivery, and the promotion of policy and practice development at a national level.

Various training methods were developed including:

- In service training.
- Seminar and specialist topic training.
- One-year postgraduate child-care course at the East China Normal University.
- Study and work visit placements to the UK.
- Masters degree in International Child Welfare in the UK.

These provided the necessary training for the day-to-day needs of the child-care service and the theoretical underpinning for ongoing development and problem resolution. Overall, the project is undoubtedly an impressive achievement on a number of grounds:

- The establishment of a highly effective partnership between Shanghai Social Services and CFC.
- The number of placements achieved in a short time, the number of foster parents recruited, and the interest generated.

- The stability of placements for children who are generally considered 'hard to place' and 'hard to parent'.
- The diversity of placements.
- The creative interplay of British and Chinese experience which will inform both British and Chinese projects in the future.
- The benefits to many of the children, who have progressed rapidly since moving from institutional care to foster care.
- The establishment and training of a team of 12 child-care workers able to sustain the project independently when CFC's involvement ended.
- The establishment of a set of training programmes in Shanghai and the UK able to support the continued training of staff and development of the programme in Shanghai.
- The development of Shanghai standards and guidelines in foster care.
- The achievement of full funding commitments from all intended sources and operation within the original budget.

Relationship development: Child-care conference

In July 2000, China's first National Child-care Conference was organised by Care for Children and Shanghai Social Services. Representatives involved in child-care were invited from Civil Affairs Bureaux and non-government organisations across China. Representatives from 135 Civil Affairs Bureau and 65 other child-care organisations attended. The conference provided information on the Shanghai Program as well as providing an opportunity for other child-care organisations to share their experiences and issues. A second successful National Child-care Conference was held in June 2002.

Following from the conference:

- Cities across China expressed interest in replicating the Shanghai Program.
- CFC received concrete invitations from some cities for assistance in establishing their programmes.
- CFC participated in a working party under the Ministry of Civil Affairs to draft National Standards for child-care.
- CFC was invited to contribute to a programme focusing on the needs of children with disabilities across China.
- CFC commenced co-operation with Kunming Children's Welfare Institute, Chengdu Children's Welfare Institute and Ningxi Children's Welfare Institute.
- The success of CFC working in partnership with the Shanghai government has led to an invitation from the Ministry of Civil Affairs in Beijing to work together with the China Social Work Association (an organ of the central government) on a national programme in 15 of the poorest provinces. On the 29th May 2003 CFC signed a five-year contract to replicate the successful Shanghai project in 15 provinces (85% of geographical China). This could change the face of social welfare in China.

Areas still Needing Development in Shanghai Social Services

While the foster care service was established in the first four years of the programme, further work is still needed to strengthen and develop it. In particular:

- The foster parent self-help groups are new and need support to function effectively.
- The foster care team needs to consolidate their training with practical experience and further on the job training.
- The effectiveness of the training programmes need to be assessed.
- Practice guidelines and standards need to be agreed.
- Foster care policy and legislation need to be drafted.
- An autonomous family placement department needs to be developed.
- A staff development system needs to be put in place to ensure continued enhancement of skills.
- More work needs to be done around the placement of 'hard to place' children,

usually older children and children with more serious disabilities.

- A research and evaluation section within the family placement department needs to be developed.
- Community family centres need to be established to support foster families in their communities.
- 'Preparation for independence' training needs to be developed for children and young people leaving care.

Lessons Emerging

While many adaptations had to be made it was apparent that, as in the UK, foster care could provide a more effective and lower cost approach to meeting the needs of children in care. The primary differences between the Shanghai Program and current practice in the UK related to:

- Statutory checks of foster families.
- Motivation of prospective foster families.
- Community support for foster families.
- Background reasons for children coming into care.
- China's limited social care history.
- China's limited understanding of child protection issues.
- A greater focus on practice in China with limited policy development.
- The lack of legislation or national guidelines on foster care in China.

It will take time to determine how much these are a reflection of the early stage of the programme and how much they reflect the cultural and environmental differences between China and the U.K.

Conclusion

The objectives of the Shanghai Foster Care and Training Program were achieved in the four years. The basic foster care programme was well established and operating effectively, with 400 children placed by the end of 2002. Short-term training courses were established with staff making use of the training in their day-to-day work. A full year diploma programme was set up in Shanghai.

It was encouraging and extremely rewarding to see the Shanghai project become more and more independent during the first four years. The staff worked well in grasping and owning the concepts, allowing the international consultant to step back during the fourth year.

The danger from the initial success is that Shanghai sees itself as expert in foster care and may decide to go it alone. Much of the development, research and evaluation are related to the life span of the child. Many placements do not get tested until the child reaches adolescence; therefore no family placement is truly mature until it has been in existence for at least 20 years.

The need placed before Care for Children is unchanged: to establish family based care, so that orphaned and abandoned children can grow and develop in the love and care of a family environment. The size of this need however, has been propelled onto a national scale, which is where our challenge now lies.

3 France

Michel Corbillon

Jurisdiction

Situated on the Atlantic Coast of Europe, France has a surface area of about 549,000 square kilometres and a population of about 61,000,000 (INSEE, 2003). With respect to population, contrasting changes are occurring at both ends of the age distribution curve: the proportion of people under 20 years old (currently 25.1 per cent of the population) is diminishing, while the proportion of those over 60 (currently 20.6 per cent of the population) is increasing. The present demographic situation is comparable to that in other European countries: a slight decrease in the mortality rate and a tendency for couples to be slightly older when they have children than in the past. However, despite increased age at childbirth, the fertility rate is high at 1.9. According to data published by INSEE, the unemployment rate was 9.8 per cent in the first trimester of 2004 (INSEE website). There was a decrease in this rate at the end of the 1990s but it has been rising regularly during the last months of 2003 and in 2004.

In 1983, a number of areas – especially child protection, which had been the exclusive responsibility of the state - were transferred to local government departments under a move towards decentralisation. These departments (départements) reflect divisions which stem from the French Revolution. Metropolitan France includes 95 departments, the nature and population of which vary widely. In relation to children, the central government retains only legislative and statutory power and the authority to assume control, mainly with respect to legislative matters. The local General Council (Conseil Général) is now in charge of the organisation of child welfare services and facilities, staff management, financing, and the fixing of the fee scale for services. Between 1984 and 1986, laws and decrees defined this transfer of responsibility. Several principles, still in effect today, were asserted or reaffirmed:

- Priority is given to keeping the child in their natural family, with help provided by social services.
- Importance is placed on maintaining the full responsibility of families who find it temporarily necessary to entrust their children to other agencies, especially through the provision of better information concerning their rights and duties, and by closer involvement of the families in decisions taken concerning their children.
- There is an obligation to reassess the situation of each child at least once a year.

The placement system for children is included in the broader field of social services. The placement of children and teenagers is entrusted to several institutions in France: the Child Care Office (Aide Sociale à l'Enfance), the judiciary protection of minors (Protection Judiciaire de la Jeunesse), maladjusted children's services, and infant and juvenile psychiatric services.

Two ministries in particular are in charge of the monitoring of services: the Ministry of Social Affairs and the Justice Ministry. However, the authority of the former was reduced by the decentralisation process, in favour of local government. The Education Ministry, which is directly involved in education and remedial classes for children suffering various forms of delayed development (needing special classes and staff with specific qualifications) is barely represented at all in the placement administration.

The various responsible authorities (local government or state) entrust the children to services managed directly by them, or to institutions managed by private associations. In the vast majority of cases, these are associations associated with the 1901 Act: non-profit making institutions, whose funding is exclusively public.

Dominant Political System

Since the 1980s, some changes have occurred in the French political system. In particular, there has been a shift in traditional voting patterns and a weakening of the long-standing ideological differences between the major political parties. The last 20 years have seen transfers of power between right wing parties (conservative) and the socialist party (social-democrat). The last transfer of power occurred in 2001 when the right wing parties replaced the socialists.

History and Origins of Foster Family Care for Children and Youth

In France, the history of placement in family foster care falls within the broader scope of the history of child welfare, which is often concerned with the protection of society from 'dangerous' children and young people. Individuals and families have always intervened in order to rescue abandoned children or to take advantage of their situation: 'We can agree that placement into family foster care has been practiced since high antiquity, if we mean by that phrase that a child is brought up by a family other than its own natural family' (Soulé and Bouchard, 1983: 13). In France, it seems that even if similar systems existed prior to that period (especially in the form of charitable residential homes for abandoned children), organised placement in family foster care appeared in the 12 century. The Order of the Holy Spirit of Montpellier is generally credited with having played a crucial role in the development of institutions for abandoned children. The younger children were first entrusted to the care of nannies (nourrices), and then admitted to the local institution, which could house up to 600 children. This same religious order went on to found similar establishments in France and throughout Europe with the help of the Catholic Church.

In the Middle Ages, both abandoned children and the children of well-off families were placed in the care of nannies. Appalling transportation conditions, combined with the harsh living conditions of the nannies themselves, caused the death of many infants. Many go-betweens – 'transporters', 'leaders', 'recommandaresses' – set up an organisation around family foster care, to the extent that some historians have spoken of a 'child fostering industry'.

Towards the end of the Middle Ages, the circumstances of foundlings seems to have deteriorated as wars and famines hindered the work of charitable bodies. Exposure under church porches, child-trafficking and death, were commonplace. Indeed, at La Couche – a shelter for abandoned children established in Paris in 1570 – children were sold for 10 pennies a head to beggars, traveling acrobats, or magicians. The death rate was very high: 100 per cent in some shelters. It was against this background that Saint Vincent de Paul succeeded in forging the beginnings of 'modern' child fostering methods. With the help of charitable brotherhoods, he sought to promote changes in people's perceptions concerning abandoned children and most particularly illegitimate children. In 1638, he created the Oeuvre des Enfants Trouvés, a charitable organisation for foundlings, which was later transferred to the authority of the Assistance Publique (state-run relief) of the Seine district in Paris. Tangible and technical changes in methods were developed: experiments were undertaken on feeding babies with cow's milk, attention was paid to the health of the children, and concern was expressed about their later social and professional integration into society. A system was developed whereby foster families were paid for caring for abandoned children up to six years of age. This system was associated with a closer monitoring of nannies or foster mothers who had to be recommended by a parish priest.

The proportion of abandoned children rose dramatically during the 18th century due to three factors: a large increase in the number of illegitimate births; an improvement in living conditions among placed children (which led to an increase in placements); and the institution of the 'turn', a revolving, cylindrical platform in the wall of a shelter for children, on which the unwanted baby was placed, to be taken in by the organisation on the other side of the wall.

The French Revolution secularised and brought about the reorganisation of the relief system. Before the Revolution, the relief system had been organised by the Church but afterwards it became part of the duties of the state. Although secular relief measures were not standardised, the work of the revolutionaries in this field was of major importance, and was to shape attitudes, practices, and laws to come.

The 19th century was marked by an increase in financial support for child welfare, technological innovations and also, to a certain extent, by a rationalisation of the administrative framework. The Napoleonic decree of January 1811 was an important stage in this development of child welfare, since it defined the eligibility criteria for admission to public institutions, the obligations due to placed children, and the amount of money to be set aside for their care. It also established a system for monitoring placement conditions, appointing 'special commissioners', who were replaced, in 1870, by 'inspectors for assisted children'. More and more, placement within a family setting was being considered beneficial for children.

In the 20th century, a national welfare policy developed regarding placement. After a period marked by the first educational experiments, by the principles of preventive action, and by the separation of abandoned or mentally deficient children from other types of 'marginals' or people in care, the development of increasingly sophisticated educational and preventive measures was intensified. The decree of 29 November 1953 (as well as subsequent decrees between 1954 and 1956) modified the French structure of social relief measures. The term Aide Sociale à l'Enfance (ASE - Youth Welfare Service) was coined, as a substitute for Assistance Publique (Social Relief).

Various legislative reforms marked the evolution of social policies regarding the protection of children, but as far as foster family placement is concerned, the most significant change was introduced by the law of 17 May 1977, which granted official status to the nannies or foster parents, who consequently became 'mother assistants' (assistante maternelle). The circular of 20 December 1979 detailed eligibility conditions for optional training. A law dated 12 July 1992, together with guidelines for its implementation, increased the professional status of mother assistants (foster parents). At the time of writing, December 2003, it is anticipated that Parliament will see a new Bill, intended to improve the foster parents' status regarding allowances, paid vacations, training, and so forth.

Therapeutic placements in foster families have a short history, even though mentally challenged children have been cared for in families over quite a long period. A decree of 1952 legalised placement in foster family care for physically or mentally handicapped persons. Various experiments, particularly in Paris, were undertaken towards the end of the 1960s, with the result that foster family care came to be considered part of the therapeutic process. However, it was the law of 10 July 1989 and the order of 1 October 1990 which provided a legal basis for therapeutic family fostering. Foster family care had now become a tool which could be used by local psychiatric services (Brunier, 1993, pp 47–48).

Service Provision

In France, foster family care is designed for infants, teenagers and adults, including the elderly, and families (for instance taking into care a mother and child). Foster placements for adults are particularly concerned with the care of the mentally ill. For example, for over a century, two villages in the Centre region of France, Dun-sur-Auron and Ainay-le-Château, have carried on a tradition of caring for the mentally ill in a family environment. The different types of foster family care developed in response to living conditions inside residential institutions, which were often viewed as dehumanising. Foster family placement appears a more appropriate solution: it is considered as warmer and more 'normal', especially where young children are concerned. Nevertheless, this very perception creates a tension between the advantages of a 'natural' family-type environment and the recent demand for professionalisation.

Of particular importance is the Act of 12 July 1992 concerning foster parents which alters the Code of the Family and of Social Welfare and the Code of Health and Labour. That law and the guidelines for its implementation have led to changes in the organisation of family foster care and imply a genuine professionalisation of foster parents. A clear distinction is made between certification and recruiting, a contract must be signed prior to employment, and monthly wages for foster parents and training obligations on the part of the employer are set out. The law recognises foster parents as non-incumbent staff members (i.e. lacking the rights of the French civil servant).

Three main categories of foster family care can be distinguished: the category defined by the Aide Sociale à l'Enfance, specialised placements and therapeutic placements. These three categories apply in three different situations and are undertaken within three major areas: social, medico-social and health related. These three areas are not completely distinct, and the populations involved are quite similar, but they are nevertheless financed and regulated along different lines (Oui, 1993, p. 23).

Foster family care involves a process which includes the certification, recruiting, training and monitoring of the foster parents. Any paid person who fosters a child at home is required to have been certified as a foster parent by the president of the General Council of the department where the foster parent resides. The district services for maternal and infant protection are responsible for the certification procedure. Certification is intended to verify that 'fostering conditions guarantee the health, the security and the development of the children who are cared for' (Act of 12 July 1992, Art. 1). This certification procedure is the same throughout France, regardless of the type of fostering provided. Certification criteria are clearly stipulated by law, but they allow a margin for interpretation by local authorities. The certification indicates whether permanent fostering is permitted, and details the number and the ages of the children allowed to be cared for by the foster parent, as well as the times at which the children will be looked after, if necessary. Unless otherwise authorised (for example, when siblings are fostered in the same family), no more than three children may be taken into one family at a time. Certification is given for five years, with the possibility of renewal. It may be cancelled, modified or suspended if certain conditions are not met. In such cases, the president of the General Council must first confer with a joint consultative commission, including members of the district authority and foster parents.

Some tasks are the responsibility of the district authorities for child care, regardless of the type of foster family care; others concern the employer who can be a legal representative by public law (mainly the General Council, but also hospitals) or connected with private associations (services for maladjusted or handicapped children or adolescents). According to the law, recruiting is now distinct from certification since hiring an employee is involved. The conditions which apply in the case of dismissal are also detailed by the law.

Monitoring and support for the foster parents are nearly always associated with the monitoring of the placed children. These vary widely between one local government and another and according to different types of placement. A few departments have created a special interdisciplinary team to complete this task, while other departments entrust this task to the Youth Welfare Services or to the interdisciplinary social service.

In other types of placement – specialised and therapeutic – the follow-up and monitoring of foster families, birth parents and children are crucial issues in the debate. Myriam David (1997), an expert on the subject of foster family care and the author of an important book on the topic, remarks that since 1965 – when the first symposium of the services dealing with such forms of placement took place – the majority of specialised placements have led to practical improvements which inspired those in charge of the Youth Welfare Services. This has a bearing on the conditions of admission, the regular follow-up of each case, the use of interdisciplinary teams, the reinforcement of the work accomplished with the foster families, collaboration with the birth parents, and the possibility of treating the child.

Finally, some heads of residential care units choose to integrate their establishments within the institutional framework of foster family care, so that the carers are certified as foster families.

It might be noted that the religious aspect which has been so significant in the field of child welfare in the past has, with few exceptions, almost completely disappeared today. It is important to point out that the French situation is characterised by ample recourse to the 'private' sector — which, in fact, is publicly funded, though most of the work is contracted to non-profit agencies.

Children and Young People Placed in Foster Family Care

Foster family care, as we have seen above, concerns various types of children and young people. Today, foster care is not restricted, as it was before, to a given age, deficiency or handicap category. It is mainly used for those children whose parents are temporarily or permanently unable to bring them up due to social or psycho-social problems. The Youth Welfare Service is in charge of such situations. Nevertheless, there are still a few types of children who are not approved for placement within the system: for example, children with severe handicaps or severe behavioural problems.

Different sources show some differences in the assessment of the number of children and young people placed in foster family care, partly because a number of censuses commissioned by the state were produced on the basis of unreliable data provided by local governments. Of the 134,800 children and young people cared for by the Youth Welfare Service, about 55 per cent are fostered in families (DREES, 2003: 10). A small increase in the family placement rate has been seen lately but, over the last 20 years, increases have been relatively minor. It should be noted that the rates are quite different from one department to another, with no clear explanations for this phenomenon, except perhaps the 'classical' interpretation which is linked to history, and especially to the existence of a long tradition of foster or residential care depending on the department.

With respect to therapeutic foster family care, a study published 10 years ago has shown that 540 children are involved in this type of placement (Cebula and Horel, 1993). The number of children cared for in the context of specialised foster family care is more difficult to evaluate since these are independent services. There is, and in some cases there has existed over a long period, a limited amount of foster family care specially designed for other populations: drug addicts, for instance.

Foster Family Care Providers

The status of foster parents varies according to the type of employer. They can be non-incumbent staff from the local authorities (this applies to the majority of foster parents) or they can belong to the state-run hospital system (therapeutic placements). If the employer is a private service, the foster parents are employees under private law, and are governed by current collective agreements. In 1977, legislation granted professional status to foster parents. In 1992, this law was revised to take into account social evolution and increasing professionalisation. For example, the revisions called for more training, more recognition of the professional status of foster parents, and better provision regarding pay and conditions of work.

Lately, the number of foster families has slightly increased; there are an estimated 46,000 foster parents today (Assistantes et assistants maternels, 2002) compared with 40,000 at the beginning of the 1990s. However, looking at the 1979 figure of 70,000, it is apparent that fewer professionals are involved in permanent fostering today than was formerly the case. The decrease has been caused by the falling numbers of children being placed in care, especially in the Youth Welfare Service.

Professional training has become compulsory and must amount to at least 120 hours during the first three years of practice. The forthcoming 2004 law should increase the number of hours required of full-time foster parents. A decree of 27 November 1992 outlined the major areas to be covered in training: child development, the special factors relating to the separation of children from their families, the profession of foster parent, and the institutional and legal framework. The foster parent is paid during her training period. (Since 99% of foster parents are female, the feminine pronoun is not inappropriate here). Funding for her wages and for the training is covered by the employer, who must also provide for the care of the foster children during her absence.

In addition to an employment contract specific to the function of a foster parent, a separate contract is drawn up between the foster parent and her employer with respect to each child or young person cared for on a permanent basis. This contract details the role of the foster family and of the service responsible for the placement, conditions of admission and departure of the child from care, the timeframe, and the procedure for contacting the service in case of emergency.

Legislation takes into account the need to monitor the performance of the foster parents, as well as the importance of considering them as full partners rather than merely as employees, so local government is in charge of the professional monitoring of the foster parents. Moreover, the foster parent must be consulted about any decision relating to the foster child taken by the representative of the service which employs her.

Foster parents also take part in the regular assessment of the foster child's situation.

Local associations and private foster parents can belong to one of two national federations which together had 18,000 members in 2003 (Sellenet, 2003, p. 128). The Union Fédérative des Associations de Familles d'Accueil et Assistantes Maternelles publishes a quaterly periodical *L'arc* and runs an information centre which caters for foster families (through a hotline and the periodical). The other federation is the Amicale Nationale des Familles d'Accueil et Assistantes Maternelles sans Frontières. These two federations are concerned with both registered carers (foster family care) and day care services. Their roles are identical: their purpose is to inform their members, play a role in their training, represent them in collective procedures and promote the position of foster parents. These federations were involved in the debate of previous laws and are still involved today. Apart from the federations' journals, some publications are directed to foster parents such as *L'accueil familial en revue* (Ed. IPI, 50 rue Samson, 75013 Paris, France) and a new monthly magazine, *Assistantes Maternelles*, of which the first issue was published on October 1st, 2003. A specific trade union has been in existence for a number of years, called Syndicat national professionnel des assistants et assistants maternels, and the national trade unions have a foster family unit in their federations, which includes the staff of local authorities. The following contact information may be helpful:

- Union Fédérative des Associations de Familles d'Accueil et Assistantes Maternelles, 13 place de Rungis, 75013 Paris, France; Telephone (+33) 01 45 81 08 96; www.uf-am.org.
- Amicale Nationale des Familles d'Accueil et Assistantes Maternelles sans Frontières, 239, rue des quatre roues, 86000 Poitiers, France; Telephone (+33) 05 49.88.23.06.

Financial Support for Foster Carers

Funding differs according to the situation of the birth family and the reasons for the child's placement. The departments are in charge of placements for social reasons, while the national health service (Sécurité Sociale) looks after placements for medico-social reasons. Foster family placement has often been favoured because it is less costly than residential placement. However, in addition to the wages of the foster parents, an accurate evaluation of the cost of foster family care ought to take into account those expenditures related to the certification, professional training and monitoring of foster parents. Such an assessment is difficult since these costs are not differentiated from the other costs of the services concerned.

The foster parent's wages are guaranteed during the fostering period: therefore, temporary absences of the child have no financial consequences for the carer. If fostering is periodic (for a period less than or equal to 15 consecutive days), a day is paid inclusively at a rate equal to three times the minimum legal hourly wage (about 17.5 euros, that is about USD 21, using the exchange rate in December 2003). If fostering is continuous, the monthly rate is equal to 84.5 times the minimum legal hourly wage per month, which amounts to about half a month's pay at minimum wage per fostered child (about 485 euros or USD 580). In addition to this, money is paid for the child's keep. Payment ceases when the child leaves care, but compensation is paid for three months if the employer is unable to place another child in the care of the foster parent.

Major Issues in Foster Family Care

Some difficulties seem to be inherent in foster family care and are acute today, although recent legislation has introduced a few significant measures which make it easier to address certain problems. For instance, the 1992 Act specifies that all those persons living at the home of a foster parent certified to take care of children on a permanent basis, constitute a foster family, but the role of the foster parent's husband is not always easy and her own children may find it difficult to assume the role of foster siblings. On the other hand, if everything works well, there is a risk that the foster family may attempt to claim the foster child as its own. Nowadays, it seems that such problems less often lead to outright conflicts between the administration and foster parents who refuse to allow foster children to be withdrawn from care than was formerly the case. A few years ago, the media reported such incidents regularly. Nevertheless, it is obvious that tensions exist over whether children should draw their feelings of identity from the birth or foster home, and these tensions are manifested in the difficulties encountered in contacts with the birth family and the attachment felt by the foster family to a child who lives permanently in their home.

With respect to the birth family, it is difficult to avoid the parents feeling that they are considered to be 'bad parents' since another family has shown a better ability to care for the child. As in any situation where placement is concerned, there always remains a risk that the birth parents will relinquish their parental role.

A major issue is the recruitment of foster families. Finding foster families has proved to be difficult in large cities, especially in the Parisian area, where housing conditions often lead to a lack of space.

There is no doubt that the relationship between foster families and social institutions or services is one of the most important issues at stake with regard to the foster parents' new status. Social workers eventually become senior staff and are required to become supervisors and assume monitoring responsibilities, a role which they find hard to fulfil because of lack of training. It will probably require a few more years for relationships to change before foster parents, the social services and social workers can collaborate fully.

Future Trends in Foster Family Care

Some of the major trends have been mentioned previously and work is still in progress:

- The professionalisation of foster parents and the improvement of their status. The forthcoming law regarding this question was mentioned earlier in the chapter.
- The development of team work including the other institutional partners involved in the placement.
- A growing concern for the role of the birth parents in placement matters.

Some trends have to do with the evolution of perceptions concerning placement. For example, more attention is being paid to the individual needs of each child by placing children with relatives whenever possible, placing them in close proximity to the birth family where possible, and making birth parents aware of their continuing responsibility. Specialists think it important to work more precisely and comprehensively on preparing the placement. A recently re-edited book concludes that 'we must avoid precipitating familial separation as much as possible. Admissions and separations must be planned'. (David, 2003: 98).

Finally, there is a trend which is not new but is perhaps particularly strong in France: the increasing role played by psychologists, mainly psychoanalysts, in collecting evaluation data from service staff, foster parents, children, and birth parents. As is the case with other social activities, evaluation has become mandatory in foster care services (law of 2 January 2002 'renovation of social and medico-social actions'). The creation of an Evaluation Council (Conseil supérieur de l'évaluation) should allow follow-up studies pertaining to the different types of foster care to be undertaken. In the future, it would be helpful if evaluations conducted by specific services could be generalised outside the local context.

Foster Care Research

Research regarding placement in general in France is quite scarce, particularly research based on 'academic' scientific criteria (Corbillon, 1993). This lack is even more pronounced concerning foster family placement. Many of the works which have a practical orientation focus on foster family care, covering such topics as the recruitment of foster parents, their training and status, the relationships between foster families and birth families, and so on. In these studies, the organisational aspects of foster family care and the professional issues are seldom addressed. In most cases, they are studies conducted by specific services, and their conclusions relate only to the local context. Often, social workers going back to graduate studies contribute to knowledge in this area. The dissertation national directory indicates that five dissertations are in progress on the placement question in Education Sciences, Psychology and Sociology respectively. Moreover, a dissertation in Education Sciences defended lately in Paris X (Chapon, 2003) proposes to dissociate placements from classic family models, considering the foster family as a centre of pluri-parentality by focusing on familial links that appear during the placement process. This approach suggests that the foster family acts as a substitute for the birth family to a greater or lesser degree. Depending on the type of placement and the kind of relationships that are forged within the foster family, the attitude of the foster parent towards her role falls somewhere on a continuum between being certain that she should behave towards the child as a substitute mother and being uncertain as to what her role should be. Other models are based on the sharing of the maternal role between the foster and birth families, or the predominance of one of the families.

It should be kept in mind that, over the past 30 years, numerous authors, influenced by psychoanalytic trends, have emphasised the trauma experienced by children separated from their parents. These authors have generally been far more critical of residential care. In particular, an important book by David, re-edited in 1997, draws on the long experience of the author in that field. On the basis of her observations, David accounts for the difficulties encountered by the various actors involved in foster family care. Her conclusion, highlighted on the back cover of her book, is that it is necessary to 'combine with social and educational measures, a permanent and specific therapeutic follow-up', centred on the child.

Much work has been done by GRAPE, a research association which has been focusing for several years on questions related to children's separations from their family and their placements in foster care families (Bass et Lernout, 2000; Bass et Pellé, 2002). In addition, the following three recent studies should be noted:

- Ruhaud's 1997 study analyses parental authority in foster families. It shows that parental authority can be established by the foster carer through a 'generative' attitude in Erikson's terminology: that is, a capacity to forsee a good future for the child when planning the child's care and education.
- An important study by Gheorgiu (2002) explores long-term outcomes with respect to young people served by the Youth Welfare Service at Seine Saint Denis (north of Paris). It shows better results for study participants who lived in foster families compared to those who lived in residential care. It is worth noting, however, that the children studied did not always experience both settings or compare both experiences.
- Sellenet's (2003) *Assistantes maternelles qui êtes-vous*? presents the foster parents' environment and helps us understand how they experience 'the pleasures and difficulties of their job', and their relationships with the institutions employing them and with the child's parents in 'their meticulous work with the children'.

Conclusion

France has made considerable progress towards the professionalisation of foster parents and the improvement of their status. One aspect of this move towards professionalisation is the need to develop teamwork between foster families, social workers and the organisations involved in the placement – an area in which there is still some way to go though progress has been made.

Another aspect of professonalisation is evaluation which became mandatory in foster care services as of January 2002. The creation of an Evaluation Council should facilitate follow-up studies pertaining to different types of foster care.

While foster care services emphasise professionalisation, there is also a growing concern for the role of the birth parents in placement matters. More attention is being paid to the individual needs of each child by placing children with relatives where appropriate, placing them in close proximity to the birth family if possible, and making birth parents aware of their continuing responsibility. While there might appear to be some inherent conflict between the twin emphases of professional carers on the one hand and kin carers on the other, both types of care are necessary to ensure that children are provided with the services most appropriate to their needs and situation.

References

Assistantes et assistants maternels (2002) Rapport au Ministre délégué à la famille et à l'enfance.

Bass, D., Lernout, Y. (Eds.) (2000). *Le placement familial en Europe; une question de justice ?* Paris: GRAPE.

Bass, D. and Pellé, A. (Eds.) (2002) *Le placement familial en Europe, une vielle histoire à réinventer.* Ramonville Saint-Agne: Erès.

Brunier, J. (1993) En France. In Wetsch-Benqué, M. et div. (Eds.) *Les interactions en accueil familial.* Ramonville Saint-Agne: Erès.

Cébula, J.C. and Horel, C. (1993) *L'Accueil familial organisé à l'hôpital.* Rapport de recherche. Paris: IFREP.

Cébula, J.C. and Horel, C. (1994) *Le placement familial de l'aide sociale à l'enfance.* Paris: La Documentation française.

Chapon, N. (2003) *Relations affectives et parentalité en situation de placement familial.* Thèse de Sciences de l'éducation. Université de Nanterre.

Corbillon, M. (1993) France. In Colton, M. and Hellinckx, W. (Eds.) *Child care in the E.C.* Arena: Aldershot.

David, M. (1997) (2nd edn) *Le placement familial, de la pratique à la théorie.* Paris: E.S.F.

David, M. (2003) *Enfants, parents, famille d'accueil. Un dispositif de soins: l'accueil familial permanent.* 2nd edn. Ramonville Saint-Agne: Erès.

DREES, Ministère des Affaires sociales, du travail et de la solidarité (2003) Les bénéficiaires de l'aide sociale départementale en 2002. *Etudes et résultats.* N° 255.

Gheorghiu, M. et al. (2002) *Rapport final de la recherche longitudinale sur le devenir des personnes sorties de l'ASE de Seine-Saint-Denis entre 1980 et 2000.* Document dactylographié.

INSEE (2003) *La France en bref.* Paris: Editions de l'INSEE.

INSEE website. Institut national de la statistique et des etudes economiques.

Oui, A. (1993) Le placement familial, un concept en évolution. *Le placement familial, un lieu commun ?* Ramonville Saint-Agne: Erès.

Ruhaud, B. (1997) *Accueil familial et autorité parentale.* Paris: L'Harmattan.

Sellenet, C. (2003) *Assistantes maternelles qui êtes-vous ?* Savigny-sur-Orge: Pro Pages Editions.

Soulé, M. et al. (1983) *Le placement familial.* Paris: ESF.

4 India

Najma Goriawalla and Kaumudi Telang

Jurisdiction

India achieved independence from British rule in 1947. The India of today is a federation of 28 states and seven territories. It is a secular and democratic republic with a constitution enshrining a parliamentary form of government. There are many political parties representing ideologies which range from capitalism to communism.

India's population of around 1.08 billion includes members of most of the major world religions. Hindus, followers of Hinduism, the dominant religion, comprise 80.41 per cent of the population. Muslims, the second largest religious group, represent 11.67 per cent. Christians (representing diverse Christian religious denominations) comprise 2.32 per cent, followed by Sikhs, Buddhists, Jains and others (Census of India, 2001). The states of India, some of them comparable to countries in Europe, Africa and Asia in size and population vary greatly with regard to language, culture, and human and economic development. Nevertheless, a fine but strong thread of unity links the diversity.

Welfare System and Organisation of Social Services

Social welfare policy has evolved against the backdrop of India's ancient culture and civilisation. The religious philosophy governing the lives of the people emphasises the need for charity and assistance to others in attaining salvation. Hence there has always been a built-in mechanism for providing service and social security through the joint family system, kinship and other social institutions.

The struggle for independence involved intensification of efforts in the areas of social welfare, social action and social reform. After independence, social welfare policy followed the dual approach of enacting social legislation and implementing welfare programmes (Government of India, 1981). The Constitution of India, adopted in 1950, includes the goal of a Welfare State and provides the inspiration for social welfare activities as an organised part of national development. Article 38 of the Constitution enjoins that the 'State shall strive to promote the welfare of the people by securing and protecting as effectively as it may, a social order in which justice – social, economic and political - shall inform all the institutions of the national life' (Government of India, 1955).

In order to concretise and give shape to the provisions in the Constitution, a programme of economic and social development was launched in 1951, through a series of Five Year Plans. This has resulted in the initiation of several planned social welfare activities for socially and physically handicapped women and children from the underprivileged sections of the community.

Child Development and Policy Framework

India has one of the largest child populations in the world, estimated at 400 million (Voluntary Health Association of India, 2002: viii). The two main legal and policy instruments that pertain to the child in India are the Indian Constitution adopted in 1950 and the United Nations Convention on the Rights of the Child (CRC) ratified by India in December 1992. Taken together with the National Policy for Children (1974) and the National Plan of Action (1992) they seek to provide adequate service to children to ensure their full physical, mental and social development. To attain these objectives several measures are listed, including strategies for children in general as well as for 'marginalised children'. The term 'marginalised children' 'generally refers to children under patriarchal, feudal and other forms of societal control subject to desertion, destitution, geographical isolation, and stigmatisation, legal infirmities of parentage and citizen status'

(Sujaya, 2002: viii). A National Children's Board has been constituted to provide focus and to ensure continuous planning and coordination of all essential child welfare services. A separate Bill termed The National Commission for Children Bill 2001, has recently been framed by the Government of India. The envisaged functions of the Commission are examining laws pertaining to children, overseeing their proper implementation, conducting research, and intervening in courts on behalf of children, amongst others.

Government Structures

The Ministry of Human Resource Development (MHRD) was specially set up in 1985, with the aim of integrating efforts for the development of human potential in the areas of education, women and child development, arts and culture, youth affairs and sports. The Department of Women and Child Development (DWCD) was set up in the same year as part of the MHRD, to focus on the holistic development of women and children and the realisation of their rights. It serves as a pivotal agency for children's development. It is directly responsible for the care of pre-school children whereas other Ministries (for example, Labour, Health and Family Welfare, Education, Social Justice and Empowerment) look after matters relevant to children in addition to their regular responsibilities.

Central Social Welfare Board (CSWB)

In order to emphasise the importance of the development of welfare services and the growth of the voluntary sector in India, the Central Social Welfare Board (CSWB), an autonomous body, was created by statute in 1953 and was registered as a Charitable Company in 1969. The CSWB formulates various schemes and programmes for women and children. Funding for the schemes is provided by the Department of Women and Child Development. Temporary foster care for the children of families in crisis is one such scheme sponsored by the CSWB.

History and Origins of Foster Family Care

India has a strong foster care tradition. The joint family structure, bound with close family ties, has traditionally played a vital role in meeting the needs of children so that neither the death of their parents, nor unhappy family circumstances would lead to their destitution and desertion. Another unique form of informal foster care prevalent in the past was the 'Gurukul' system, where students lived in the homes of their teachers and enjoyed all the benefits of family life during their training period. Hindu tradition and law (Dharmashastra) allowed the teacher and his wife to assume the role of their ward's parents at socio-religious ceremonies if the student was left destitute. These support systems eroded over time due to industrialisation and urbanisation. Futhermore the deterioration of family and social values led to the neglect, delinquency, abandonment and destitution of children. Institutions were set up privately and later on by the state with legal support. Enactment of the Children Acts (1948, 1960), modelled on British laws, provided residential care and rehabilitative services for these children.

The Indian Conference of Social Work, an affiliate of the then International Conference of Social Work (renamed International Council of Social Welfare) first took up the subject of organising foster care services as an alternative to institutionalisation in the 1940s, borrowing from the western concept of foster care. However it took two decades for the service to emerge. The first reference to the provision of family care as an alternative to committing a child to an institution appears in the Children Act 1948 (Bombay). This Act under part V, section 45, provided for committing children to the care of a fit person approved by the court for such period as the court deemed fit. This provision, though available, was used to a very limited extent.

Under the Children Act 1960, experiments were conducted in three states whereby some children were permitted to be cared for in selected homes instead of in institutions. The homes were selected based on a report by the probation officer about the finances, health, educational status and motivation of interested families. An additional safeguard was introduced in the form of a bond, with or without surety, posted by the fit person to the court, towards the care of the child. Generally the families offered to care for the child free of charge, out of humanitarian motives. In some places a maintenance allowance of Rs. 50/- (50 rupees or just over 1 USD at current exchange rates) per child per month, was granted by the Juvenile Court, designated to adjudicate and dispose of these matters. Most of the children were orphans, placed on a permanent basis. This practice continued under the Juvenile Justice Act 1986 which repealed the earlier Children Acts that were in force in different states in India. In some progressive states such as Maharashtra, the High Court of Bombay introduced the practice of legalising the permanent foster care placements through adoption or legal guardianship to safeguard the interests of the child.

Development of Formal Foster Care Services

Pilot foster care projects

A formal foster care scheme was introduced for the first time during the Third Five Year Plan (1961–65) by the Central Social Welfare Board (CSWB). The philosophy underlying the scheme was stated as follows: 'whenever, due to desertion, long illness, imprisonment, death etc. of a parent or parents a child has been removed from his home, it is advisable to place him in an environment which is as near home as possible' (Subramanian, 1973: 60). Three pilot projects were initiated on an experimental basis by NGOs working for women and children, in Madras in 1964 followed by two agencies in Mumbai in 1965 and 1969 respectively. While implementing these projects, special care was taken to match the child's background with that of the foster family and to maintain the child's ties with the birth parent. A monthly allowance of Rs.50/- in addition to initial non-recurring expenses of Rs.30/- were provided to the foster family. The birth parent was encouraged to contribute some amount for the child's care out of a sense of responsibility. The grant was subsequently raised to Rs.75/- per month per child. By 1972, 84 children were covered under the scheme (Subramanium, 1973). The service was provided to children referred directly by or through the juvenile court.

Though the three agencies continued to run the project, the scheme did not gain favour for several reasons. Socio-cultural factors (religion, ethnicity, eating habits, living conditions etc.) and economic barriers acted as deterrents to accepting a child from an unrelated family. The problem of housing in overcrowded cities got in the way of making room for an unknown child. Moreover the meagre allowances that were paid for the child's maintenance, let alone for the services of the foster parents, was a problem in motivating families to take up the responsibility. The birth parents, too, preferred to place the children in institutions, as they were apprehensive about having their children live with an unknown family. The absence of any legal provisions to safeguard the interests of the child, foster parents, birth parents or the welfare agency was another hindrance in the implementation of the project.

Foster care scheme of the ministry of social welfare

The Ministry of Social Welfare in the central government launched a 'Scheme for Children in Need of Care and Protection' in 1974, which included, among others, a foster care scheme. The objective was to provide a near home atmosphere in a foster family to children who became destitute at a very early age. The scheme envisaged placement of a child on the basis of understanding the child's needs, assessing the foster family, and proper matching, supervision and follow up. NGOs working for children and families were entrusted to operate the scheme under the guidance of professionally trained social workers. A foster care allowance of Rs.75/- was sanctioned. The scheme was confined mainly to children below the age of six years on the grounds that children adjust easily at a tender age, whereas older children were likely to be exploited, having their services used for assistance in the home. A grant in aid was provided for a unit of 50 children, covering both recurring and non-recurring expenditure up to 90 per cent, with the implementing agency bearing the remaining 10 per cent.

The response to the scheme, however, was very poor, as the grant in aid for implementation and the foster care allowance were both found to be inadequate. The scheme was revised in 1978. The foster care allowance was increased to Rs. 250/- per child on the condition that, out of the sanctioned unit of 50 children, the NGOs should bear the expenses for 10 children, as well as 20 per cent of the total expenditure. The scheme failed as NGOs found it difficult to raise the required funds. Moreover, the grant was given by way of reimbursement and payment was inordinately delayed. In 'A Review of Children in Difficult Situations in India,' around 40 agencies providing foster care services were identified during the period 1982–83 (Rane, Naidu and Kapadia, 1986).

Within the same period an expert group was constituted by the Ministry of Welfare in co-operation with UNICEF to review and revise existing central government schemes for children in need of care and protection and to formulate draft non-institutional schemes for the Ministry's consideration. Observing that the existing foster care scheme had not made headway, the scheme was revised in terms of its objectives, scope and funding. A supplementary proposal for 'foster day care' was also made. Regretfully, the government has not acted on this initiative.

Foster care initiatives in some states

While the central government formulates schemes for children, applicable to the whole country, state governments also plan independent schemes depending on the needs of the region, since child welfare falls within the current list of government responsibilities. Initiatives in foster care have been undertaken by some states — in some instances, influenced by the foresight and vision of the individuals in charge.

In the state of **Gujarat**, the Social Defence Department initiated implementation of the Ministry of Social Welfare Scheme of Foster Care. The scheme was implemented by the District Probation and After Care Association through the Juvenile Court. Foster families were paid an allowance of Rs.75/- per child per month, later raised to Rs.250/- per month per child, with an additional contribution of Rs.100/- per child from the state government. The scheme however has not made much headway.

In 1963, the **New Delhi Administration** initiated foster care services under the provisions of the Children Act 1960 that empower the Child Welfare Board to commit a neglected child in the care of parent, guardian or other fit person (Section 16 (1)). The scheme entitled 'Foster Care Home Service' was enforced by the Directorate of Social Welfare. Abandoned children from Observation Homes and Children's Homes were identified for foster placement. An 'Investigation Report' on the socio-economic and health status of the prospective foster parents, their motives, and so forth, was made before placement. By 1977, 356 children up to the age of 15 years (172 males and 184 females) had been placed (Lalitha, Singh and Yaday, 1977). Foster families were paid Rs.100/- per month per child. A study to evaluate the scheme (Lalitha et al., 1977) revealed that parents were motivated to foster with the intention of adopting. Both the implementing authority and the foster parents perceived the programme as pre-adoption foster care. The Administration has framed draft New Foster Care Placement Rules based on the provisions of the new Juvenile Justice (Care and Protection) Act, 2000. The adoption of these Rules is awaited.

In the state of Maharashtra, the initiation of the Bal Sangopan Yojana (Foster Care Scheme) in February 1995 was precipitated by a surprise visit from the then Director of the Women and Child Welfare Directorate to a well-established institution. Greatly moved by the pathetic condition of the children in the institution, she convened an experts' meeting of representatives from UNICEF, academicians, and family and child welfare organisations providing non-residential services for children, to consider ways and means of preventing the institutionalisation of children through family support. The deinsitutionalisation of children already institutionalised was also a consideration since there has been a shift in focus from institutionalisation to a family-based approach. In general, deinstitutionalisation is seen as an option when: (1) the birth family sought institutionalisation for the child because of poverty and there is now a possibility of restoring the child to the birth or extended family by providing family support; and (2) the child is orphaned and eligible for adoption. Orphaned children often languish in institutions, particularly those run under state auspices, because staff have neither the motivation nor the resources to explore the adoption alternative.

The state government and UNICEF jointly initiated the Foster Care Scheme, with UNICEF providing administrative support to five NGOs for three years. The rationale for the scheme includes the statement, 'recognising the child's right to a family, this scheme focuses on the prevention of family disintegration and ensuring that the child is brought up in its own or a substitute family environment instead of in an institution' (Non-Institutional Scheme of Bal Sangopan Yojana: 1).

The scheme is being implemented only through NGOs or through district offices when there is no competent NGO in the area. NGOs with at least three years of experience in the field of family and child welfare and employing professionally qualified social workers are eligible. The scheme is being implemented by 11 organisations. Five are offering non-institutional services, whereas the rest are running residential homes. An amount of Rs.250/- per month per child is provided for maintenance, to the family. An additional amount of Rs.50/- per month per child is provided to the NGO towards administrative costs. At present there are more than 600 children covered under the scheme. An additional 100 children are also covered by the district offices.

The scheme applies to children under the age of 18 years residing in and outside institutions, and is applicable to: children who are orphaned, destitute and ineligible for adoption; children of single parents, broken families, or unwed mothers; children whose parents are severely ill, dead, divorced or have marital discord; children who are abused or neglected; and child labourers.

Eligible foster parents include the child's relatives, neighbours or close acquaintances, whether married or single. If these are not available then unrelated foster parents can be selected. In the case of single parents, the child's biological parent has also been declared eligible. In this respect the scheme deviates from the formal concept of foster care, advocating strengthening the child's birth family and thereby preventing family disintegration as the first alternative.

In a unique arrangement, in the city of Mumbai, an NGO, authorised by the state government, is represented at the sittings of the Child Welfare Committee (appointed to adjudicate under the juvenile justice system) once a week, when new applications for institutionalisation of children are received. This representation facilitates immediate intervention in exploring the foster care option. If, after due investigation, such an arrangement is found feasible, the case is closed at the committee level and placed under the Bal Sangopan Yojana. The agency is thereafter responsible to periodically report the progress of the case to the state government.

The response to this scheme has been so encouraging that the demand outweighs the sanctioned provision of funds. Agencies have raised their own funds to help a few more children. This has motivated the state government to consider extending the scope of the scheme to cover more areas in the region, as well as to increase the coverage for children.

In the **State of Karnataka** the foster care scheme was implemented in 1996–97 mainly for children committed by the court under the Juvenile Justice Act 1986. Three NGOs were authorised to implement the scheme, with a coordinating agency given responsibility to monitor the programme. One of the NGOs also experimented with group homes on somewhat similar lines to the SOS Children's Villages. SOS Children's Villages comprise a number of group homes. In each group home, a house mother, who is compensated for her services, provides care to 10–15 children of varying ages. For the foster care scheme in Karnataka. The sanctioned maintenance allowance was fixed at Rs. 500/- per month per child. The scheme was later withdrawn, however, because of bureaucratic delays in giving release orders as well as transfer orders from institutions to foster families scattered over the state. A Draft Foster Care Scheme has been prepared for submission to the state government.

Foster care during natural calamities

That the foster care scheme could be implemented even in times of natural calamities was proven when the Bal Sangopan Yojana covered two of the worst affected districts in the state of Maharashtra during the earthquake that occurred on 30th September 1993. Family disintegration and consequent institutionalisation were prevented through foster care support to extended family members such as grandparents and direct assistance to single parents. Conceptualised and funded by UNICEF, the programme was implemented by an NGO. Counselling and other support services were also provided to help families over the crisis. This initiative was found to be extremely cost effective compared with institutionalisation, particularly since devastation of this magnitude placed enormous demands on the government (Ghate, 1997).

Borrowing from this experience in Maharashtra, the Gujarat government extended its already existing foster care scheme for victims of the earthquake that had occurred on 26th January 2001, to 22 affected areas. The maintenance allowance was raised to Rs. 500/- per month per child. Following this, the number of children fostered, which had remained static at six, three years prior to the earthquake, went up to 89 in 2002–2003.

Another example is that of Orissa. In the year 2000, Orissa was hit by a cyclone which brought large-scale devastation in its wake. The Ersamma block in Jagatsingpur District, where 8,000 people were swept away in the deluge, was the worst affected area. The state government together with Action Aid, an NGO, jointly initiated 'Mamta Grihas' ('House of Love') to provide care and protection to children who had lost their parents and women who had lost their husbands. The hope was that the widowed women would look after the orphaned children, providing not only care for the children but healing for themselves.

At the beginning, 15 'mamta grihas' were set up, and gradually the number rose to 25 homes, in which about 623 children received care. Ten to 15 children lived in each home and the government provided Rs. 500/- per child to the women running the home. A local group of volunteers (sneha-samitis) monitored the children's progress to ensure that the children were benefiting from the placement. Within a year after the cyclone, the majority of the children had been restored to their relatives. Five or six of the women, however, kept children who had no relatives without any further financial support from the government.

Foster family care as an alternative to institutional care for children awaiting adoption

The Central Adoption Resource Agency (CARA), an autonomous body established by the Ministry of Social Welfare of the government of India framed 'Revised Guidelines to Regulate Matters Relating to Adoption of Indian Children' in 1995. The guidelines provided for recognition (licensing) of agencies engaged in adoption placement within and outside the country. Only agencies having institutional facilities were considered eligible. Two agencies, committed to promoting family care for children, had departed from the normal practice of setting up an institution, by initiating a pre-adoption foster care programme for children. They were denied recognition. It was only after protracted lobbying (for two years) invoking the spirit of the Convention on the Rights of the Child, to which India was a signatory, that pre-adoption foster family care arrangements were accepted, and specific guidelines for 'Foster Family Care as an Alternative to Institutional Care for Children Awaiting Adoption' (1998) were formulated (Government of India, 1998).

At the outset, the guidelines clarify that they do not refer to children placed in foster care with prospective adoptive families. The criteria for an agency to qualify for this service, as well as eligibility criteria for foster families, have been laid down. Only children below the age of six years (except in the case of siblings, one of whom is younger than six) can be fostered. A foster care agreement between the agency and the foster parent has to be made with legal responsibility for the child remaining with the agency. The number of families per agency is restricted to 20. The roles and responsibilities of the agency, and rules regarding monitoring and supervision have also been laid down. The agency is expected to meet the expenses for foster care, and is permitted to recover the amount (up to a limit of Rs. 70/- per child per day, stipulated by CARA) from the adoptive parents.

Foster care and the Juvenile Justice (Care and Protection) Act 2000 (JJA)

The umbrella Act for children who are neglected or delinquent is the Juvenile Justice (Care and

Protection) Act 2000. This Act has sought to consolidate and amend the law relating to juveniles in conflict with law and children in need of care and protection, to harmonise with the standards prescribed in the Convention on the Rights of the Child the United Nations Standard Minimum Rules for the Administration of Juvenile Justice 1985 (the Beijing rules), the United Nations Rules for the Protection of Juveniles Deprived of their Liberty (1990) and all other relevant international instruments. Existing ambiguity in the age of 'child' is clarified, defining a child as a person who has not reached the age of 18 years. The salient objectives of the Act are to provide a uniform legal framework of justice, adopting a child-friendly approach, to ensure a speedy and sensitive system of rehabilitation and social reintegration for the child, and to develop greater coordination between the formal system and NGOs working for children.

The Act has introduced a separate chapter on the rehabilitation and social reintegration of children through adoption, foster care, and sponsorship. The Act provides for temporary foster care for children awaiting adoption, and for short-term and long-term foster care placement in another family as befits the child's circumstances. In the latter case, birth parents are permitted to maintain ongoing contacts with the child with the possibility of being eventually reunited with them. The Model Rules, framed for the implementation of the Act throughout the country, have not provided any guidelines for the implementation of the foster care and sponsorship alternatives. Most of the states have yet to frame their own rules. Even Child Welfare Committees designated to adjudicate in these matters have not been constituted in most states.

Quality institutional care and alternatives for children (QUIC and CA)

A noteworthy initiative launched nationally in 2002 is the QUIC and CA campaign. It is a network of residential care institutions and child welfare agencies, aimed at 'ensuring quality care in residential institutions for children and facilitating family and community-based alternatives for social reintegration and deinstitutionalisation' (Shashtri, 2002: 1). The process includes direct intervention programmes, information sharing, capacity building, direct participation of children amongst others, and reviewing and influencing policies and programmes pertaining to children. The experience and expertise of the partners should prove valuable in facilitating the objectives of the initiative.

Children in Foster Care

The initiatives taken by different authorities at different points of time, though scattered and piecemeal, illustrate the intent of policy makers and service providers to secure the child's right to grow up in a family environment. Foster family care intervention programmes are aimed at both deinstitutionalisation and the prevention of institutionalisation. However, considering the magnitude of the problem of children in need of care and protection, the existing services are inadequate, both in terms of quality and number, and the beneficiaries are few. The estimated number of destitute, orphan children in India in 1991 was 12.32 million as compared with an estimated total of 30 million orphans. There were 304 million children in 1991. Thus, destitute orphan children comprise 4.1 per cent of the child population. It was also estimated that there were about 150,000 children in more than 1,000 institutions in the country (Pinto, 1994). In 1997–1998 there were only 613 children's state run homes, including juvenile, observation, special, and other homes (NIPCCD, 1998: 391). The total residential capacity was around 36,000 (Chandy, 2002). Though no nationwide statistics have been compiled on the number of children receiving foster care, it is obvious that this number is a miniscule drop in a vast ocean.

Most of the schemes have laid down criteria for children to be considered for foster placement. These include orphans, abandoned or destitute children or those belonging to dysfunctional families. There is no reference to children who are disabled or delinquent. Only in the Children Acts were provisions made to commit a delinquent child to a fit person. Hence, so far, foster family care has been limited to the placement of 'normal' children, unless the children are closely related to the foster family, or there is an informal arrangement between two families, formalised later. Because foster care is a new concept, it is difficult to recruit families, even for normal children. Moreover, lack of conviction on the part of stakeholders has precluded attempts to consider children with special needs.

Service Providers

Barring a few instances where government departments are involved, implementation of foster care programmes is left to NGOs. It has been the general pattern in the social welfare sector that schemes are sponsored by the government and grant in aid is provided to NGOs for implementation. NGOs are selected on the basis of criteria laid down in the scheme. Only NGOs registered or recognised under various statutes are eligible to operate foster care services. There is no separate license required (as is the case with adoption services, including pre-adoption foster care) for providing these services. Usually family and child welfare agencies offering a broad range of institutional and non-institutional services, with proven experience, employing professionally trained staff are eligible. Practice standards have been evolved mainly through individual efforts. There is, however, no uniformity in implementation. Moreover, poor co-ordination between the NGOs as well as with government authorities often results in duplication of efforts.

Foster care placements have no legal support. NGOs have to enter into a foster care agreement directly with the foster families. Conditions for agreement are not prescribed. In the case of Bal Sangopan Yojana, the agreement has to be made between the two sets of parents in a prescribed format. Monitoring and supervision of agency performance is most inadequate. Poor orientation of the scheme itself and the absence of clear monitoring guidelines, as well as the general perception about inspection processes, have confined inspections to merely checking of accounts and record maintenance.

Financial Support

From the various schemes described earlier, it is evident that the range of payments made to foster care providers, as well as administrative resources are well below the required levels. Payments are made to the foster parents as a maintenance allowance for the care of the child. Some agencies raise additional funds towards meeting the educational, medical and nutritional needs of the child. Stemming from the belief that family based care is more cost effective and child friendly, a lower maintenance allowance is allocated for foster care than for children in institutional care. For example, in the state of Maharashtra, the allowance for foster care under Bal Sangopan Yojana is Rs. 250/- per child per month plus Rs. 50/- towards administration. This amount, found to be inadequate at the outset, has not yet been revised. By contrast, the grant for institutional care has been raised to Rs. 750/- per child per month (Rs. 500/- for maintenance and Rs. 250/- for overheads). While it is true that cost effectiveness should not be measured in monetary terms alone, but in its contribution to the child's personal development, levels of funding must be sufficient to make the programme viable and effective.

Research

The Ministry of Human Resource Development, Government of India, plays a major role in sponsoring research in the social service sector. The majority of studies on children has been sponsored by the Ministry. Most of the studies, however, are descriptive, with little focus on analysis and interpretation of the collected data (Rane et al., 1986). Research studies are also conducted by Schools of Social Work and Departments of Psychology and Sociology in universities. The National Institute of Public Co-operation and Child Development (NIPCCD) has conducted a number of studies in child welfare. Some voluntary agencies are also engaged in research. International agencies, like UNICEF, ILO and WHO have also sponsored research studies.

Two studies undertaken so far, have dealt with the subject of foster care. 'A Study of Foster Care Service in New Delhi' sponsored by NIPCCD was undertaken by Lalitha, Singh and Yaday in 1976 (Lalitha et al., 1977). In 1986 a study on children in difficult situations was sponsored by UNICEF and undertaken by Rane, Naidu and Kapadia of the Unit for Child and Youth Research in the Tata Institute of Social Sciences, Mumbai. The report on this study *Children in Difficult Situations in India: A Review* (Rane et al.,1986) devotes one chapter (Chapter 6) to Non-institutional Services of Foster Care and Adoption. Both studies have been mentioned in the present chapter. There are no books devoted specifically to this topic but several articles have been written and presented at various fora. The articles are related to the promotion of a non-institutional approach to prevention, protection, welfare and the rehabilitation of children in difficult circumstances.

Major Issues

Though India has a strong foster care tradition, foster care as an organised child welfare service is a fairly recent phenomenon. A shift in focus, from a 'needs' to a 'rights' approach, and from an institutional to a family-oriented, community-based approach, has seen a plurality of initiatives in foster care under the auspices of NGOs and the various levels of government. Although this reflects a growing recognition of the foster care alternative, foster care programming has not made appreciable progress for several reasons:

- Stakeholders, particularly within the government, remain sceptical about foster care and doubt its efficacy when it comes to the placement of unrelated children.
- The hesitation in implementation also stems from the management perspective. Whereas it is relatively easy to supervise and monitor child-care in an institution, recruiting and supervising geographically scattered foster homes appears overwhelming. An unwillingness to take up new initiatives and bureaucratic delays also slow the process.
- The implementation of the programmes has suffered due to a lack of coherence in both the conceptual and operational aspects of the schemes. As a result the schemes have been differently interpreted and the approach to a large extent has been ad hoc, piecemeal and haphazard.
- Inadequate financial allocations for child-care and administrative costs have seriously hampered the service, further compounded by delays in the release of grants. To encourage more families to consider fostering a child, additional components with respect to service fees and costs of care needs to be introduced. Needless to say caution will have to be exercised to see that economic incentive is not the sole motivating factor.
- The wide socio-cultural diversity in Indian society is a major constraint, making it difficult to match the child's background with that of the foster family. Caring for unrelated children is still unconventional in the Indian social system. Hence few families volunteer for this service.
- Although only selected NGOs have been entrusted with the responsibility of operating the foster care programme, the quality of service and level of professionalism differ between them. No serious attempts have been made to address the training needs of such agencies. Neither have attempts been made to provide orientation to the related authorities. Lack of relevant knowledge and skills has also discouraged interested agencies from implementing the programme.
- The foster care programme has not been given concrete publicity. Community awareness about the programme is very low. At present personal contact is practically the only source through which interested families are recruited.
- Poor coordination between the stakeholders has also affected the development of the programme. This is because of lack of clarity about their roles and responsibilities.

Conclusion

From the situation prevailing today, it is evident that a lot of work lies ahead in promoting both the concept and practice of foster care in the country. The earlier initiatives under the Children Acts were treated by the implementing authorities, as well as by the respondents (foster parents) as an adoption-in-waiting programme. Subsequent schemes involved intervention programmes aimed at the prevention of institutionalisation and the promotion of family-oriented alternatives. The Juvenile Justice (Care and Protection) Act, 2000 has provided the policy framework for the promotion of non-institutional services. This will give an impetus to the development of a foster care programme. Already in some places, existing foster care schemes, which had not made much progress, are being remodelled within the JJA framework. The QUIC and CA movement is working to clearly define the approaches and strategies for implementation. Needless to say, the services will need to be professionally administered. Moreover sufficient, assured and timely funds must be made available for the programme to be viable and effective.

The Indian experience of giving priority to the placement of the children with their own birth families, relatives or kin under the Bal Sangopan Yojana has met with some degree of success. Given the cultural diversity, this practice should be encouraged, as placement within a familiar milieu facilitates adjustment. The placement of unrelated children, children with disabilities and children with other special needs appears difficult at this juncture since the concept is new, and specialised services and community resources are limited. The thrust towards greater reliance on family and community-based supports, holds promise. Only time will tell how the foster care programme will move forward.

Individual Acknowledgements

The authors would like to acknowledge the following individuals for their help in compiling this chapter.

Ms. Akerkar Supriya, Regional Manager, Action Aid, Bhubaneshwar, Orissa.

Ms. Ghate Bharati, Executive Director, Shishuadhar for the Child, Pune.

Mr. Patel Nathubhai, Hon Secretary, Voluntary Coordinating Agency, Gujarat State.

Ms. Apparao Hansa President, Indian Association for Promotion of Adoption and Child Welfare, Mumbai.

Dr. Ms. Kashyap Lina Head, Family and Child Welfare Dept., Tata Institute of Social Sciences, Mumbai.

Ms. Nichani Leena Advocate, High Court of Bombay.

Dr. Ms. Mehta Nilima Chairperson, Child Welfare Committee (JJA 2000), Mumbai.

Ms. Nayak Nina President, Karnataka Council for Child Welfare, Karnataka.

Ms. Matani Pushpa, Former Deputy Director, Child-Care, NIPPCD, New Delhi.

Ms. Modak Usha, Former Director, Family Service Centre, Mumbai.

References

Bharati, G. (2001) Bal Sangopan Yojana for the Quake Affected Children in Latur and Osmanabad. *Sharing*. Newsletter of the Indian Association for the Promotion of Adoption, Apr-Jun, V: 4.

Chandy, N. (2002) *Nobody's Children: Seen But Not Heard.* Voluntary Health Association of India: New Delhi.

Children Act 1948 (Bombay).

Children Act 1960.

Ghate (1997) Article in *Sharing*.

Government of India (1955) *Social Welfare in India.* Ministry of Information and Broadcasting.

Government of India (1981). *Social Welfare in India.* Ministry of Social Welfare.

Indian Institute of Population Studies (2001) *Census of India.* Indian Institute of Population Studies.

Juvenile Justice Act 1986.

Lalitha, Singh and Yaday (1977) *Foster Care Service in Delhi: A Study.* New Delhi: National Institute of Public Cooperation and Child Development.

National Institute of Public Cooperation and Child Development (1998) *Statistics of Children in India: Handbook 1998.* New Delhi: NIPCCD.

Pinto (1994) *Neglected and Delinquent Children: Approaches for Prevention, Protection, Welfare and Rehabilitation.* Paper presented at Sensitisation Program on Problems of Neglected and Delinquent Cjhidlren for Judicial Officers/Police Officers. National Institute of Public Co-operation and Child Development, New Delhi, Oct.

Rane, Naidu and Kapadia (1986) *Children in Difficult Situations in India: A Review.* UNICEF.

Shashtri, B. (2002) *QUIC and CA Annual Report, January-December 2002.*

Subramanium (1973) *Need and Scope for Foster Family Care in India.* National Seminar on Foster Care and Adoption of Children in India. Central Institute of Research and Training in Public Co-operation, January, New Delhi.

Sujaya, C.P. (2002) *The Marginalised Child: Seen but not Heard.* New Delhi: Voluntary Health Association of India.

Voluntary Health Association of India (2002) *Seen but not Heard: Sizing up the Problem.*

5 Japan

Kozo Iwasaki

Jurisdiction

Japan is divided into 47 prefectures as administrative divisions and is further split into towns or villages. Each of the 47 local jurisdictions has a governor and a unicameral assembly, both elected by popular vote every four years. All are required by national law to maintain departments of general affairs, finance, welfare, health, and labour. The governor is responsible for all activities supported through local taxation or the national government. Japan has a unitary rather than a federal system of government, in which local jurisdictions largely depend on national government both administratively and financially. However, trends over the last decade show that local governments are becoming more independent from the national government in their administration of policies and programmes.

Situated in Eastern Asia, Japan is an island chain between the North Pacific Ocean and the Sea of Japan, and is located at the east of the Korean Peninsula. It covers an area of 377,835 square kilometres, which is slightly smaller than California, and has a population of 127, 610,000 (Statistics Bureau, July, 2004).

The demographic pyramid resembles that of most other industrial countries. Sixty seven per cent of the population is aged between 15 and 64, 14.4 per cent is under 15 years of age, and 18.6 per cent is 65 and over. The trend shows an aging society with fewer children. It is projected that, in 2025, 13.1 per cent will be under 15 years, 59.5 per cent will be between 15 and 64, and 27.4 per cent will be 65 and over. In 2003, the average life expectancy at birth was 80.93 years, 77.63 years for men and 84.41 years for women. Japan is culturally very homogeneous. The population comprises 99 per cent Japanese and one per cent of others. Of this one per cent, 40 per cent are Korean, 19 per cent are Chinese, 14 per cent are Brazilian, 7 per cent are Filipino and 20 per cent have other ethnic origins.

The economy experienced a major slowdown starting in the 1990s, following three decades of unprecedented growth. In 2002, the GDP per capita (purchasing power parity) was USD 28,000.

Dominant Political System

The Japanese assembly is called Diet, and has two houses. They are the House of Representatives and the House of Councillors. Members of both houses are elected by universal adult suffrage. As of the last general election, the membership of the House of Representatives was reduced from 500 to 480 (Public Offices Election Law, revised February 2000). The four-year term is unchanged. The House of Councillors' membership is 252, with half of its members elected every third year for a six-year term.

Recent political trends show the emergence of a two-party system in Japanese politics: the Liberal Democratic Party (LDP) and the Democratic Party of Japan (DP). The Liberal Democratic Party (LDP) has been the dominant political party among many political parties in Japanese politics since World War II, except during 1994 to 1996 when the head of the Socialist Party of Japan (SPJ) occupied the position of Prime Minister and the national government consisted of multiple political parties. In the general election of 2003, there were more votes for the Democratic Party of Japan (DPJ) than for the Liberal Democratic Party (LDP), but the LDP continued to govern because of Japan's complicated electoral system. Although the DPJ has achieved equivalence with the LDP under the proportional representation system, the LDP is undoubtedly stronger in single-seat constituencies. There is, however, little difference between the policies of the two parties. The LDP may be more conservative than the DPJ. The Communist Party has regularly been supported by 3–5 per cent of the population through the years, while the Social Democratic Party has recently declined in popularity.

The increase of civil society in Japan may be the reason why the one dominant ruling political party, in power for a long time, has been losing ground. As Professor Susan J. Pharr (2003: 2) of Harvard University has pointed out:

> *The uneven distribution of resources and targeted states policies may still favour established interest associations, but newer citizen-initiated movements enjoy a dynamism and mass appeal that the former lack. Coinciding with a decline in popular confidence in government found until recently in virtually all the advanced industrial democracies, the general public-and some leaders-in Japan have concluded that the state lacks the flexibility and resources to cope with increasingly complex socioeconomic issues, and more and more citizens have responded with their own initiatives.*

Dominant Welfare System

The concept of social security appears in Article 25 of the Constitution of Japan. Article 25 stipulates as follows: 'All people shall have the right to maintain the minimum standards of wholesome and cultured living. In all spheres of life, the State shall use its endeavours for the promotion and extension of social welfare and security, and of public health.' The provision thus ensures people's rights to a quality standard of living and provides the legal basis for social security systems. 'Social security systems' is a general expression that includes the following: social insurance, including medical and pension insurance programmes; public assistance programmes to ensure a minimum standard of living; social welfare programmes for children, mothers with children, people with disabilities, and the elderly; medical care; and programmes for public and environmental health.

Japan had limited resources to deal with welfare issues in the aftermath of World War II. Welfare therefore began as a government initiative based on the administrative placement system (sochi-seido), which is a system whereby the government determines people's needs and provides welfare services accordingly. By the early 1960s, the major social welfare laws had been established, beginning with the Daily Life Security Law in 1946, followed by the Child Welfare Law in 1947, the Law for the Welfare of Physically Handicapped Persons in 1949, the Social Welfare Services Law in 1951, the National Pension Law in 1959, the Law for Mentally Retarded Persons in 1960, and the Law for the Welfare of the Aged in 1963. In the last decade, these laws have been revised significantly to meet the changing needs of the population in an aging society and to satisfy demands for services which are user-friendly and community-based. Welfare programmes for children and families include day-care centres, child abuse prevention programmes, social child-rearing (foster care or residential care), counselling services, support for programmes addressing child rearing and the healthy growth of children, support for single-parent families, and welfare programmes for women. Each local government provides various programmes for parents looking for help in child-rearing: for example, after-school care, and support centres where parents can get advice. In order to ensure that children do not have to wait to enter day-care centres, the Ministry is promoting the acceptance of younger children (birth to two years) into day-care centres. It is also promoting help with child-care in the home and respite for parents, as well as the relaxation of rules concerning day nurseries. Another measure being implemented aims to extend the ages covered by the child-allowance support system and to lessen the financial burden experienced by families engaged in caring for their children.

Provision of welfare for the elderly includes the long-term care insurance system, support programmes for self-reliant life in the community, and support for an active social life. Welfare for persons with disabilities includes provision of a place to live, counselling services, support programmes for community living, employment support, promotion of social and cultural activities, and additional welfare policies for persons with mental disabilities. Income support programmes include public assistance, services for the homeless, and disaster relief. All of the population is covered by one of several medical insurances.

History and Origins of Foster Family Care

An old handwritten document tells the story of Wake-no-Hiromushi, a lady of the court in the late 8th century who looked after many children orphaned by clan disputes. As Atsumi (1997) and Miyoshi (1963) note, it was common for the Royal

Family and aristocrats to entrust their children to acquaintances to be brought up. Later, this custom spread to the common people. In the 11th century, an aristocrat entrusted his daughter to a family in northern Kyoto which was the capital of Japan. Ever since then, people in the community have accepted foster children. The survey of 1922–3 showed that 98 children had been entrusted to families in a village where 482 families comprised the total village population (Kyoto-fu Shakaika, 1924). In the late 19th century and the early 20th century, it was not unusual for children to be fostered by farmers when their mothers died, had difficulty breast-feeding because of sickness or insufficient milk, or bore illegitimate children. These foster care arrangements were made through individual contracts (Takiguchi, 2003). During the same period, Ishii founded Okayama Orphanage, based on the methods of Barnado's Homes in England. Children, who could not live with their families because of famine or for some other reason, were brought up in homes housing eight to 10 children. The physically weak were fostered on farms where food was more likely to be plentiful (Shibata, 1964).

It was after World War II that the public foster care system was introduced in Japan (Takiguchi, 2003). The phrase 'foster parent', as it is used today, was first coined in the Child Welfare Law of 1947.

Service Provision in Foster Care

Each governor of a prefecture and mayor of a designated city is responsible for the local authority which provides foster care services within its geographical area. In providing services for deprived children, such local authorities must establish at least one Child Guidance Centre (CGC) in their prefectures and designated cities according to the Child Welfare Law. The law requires that the CGC perform primarily the following services with respect to the welfare of children:

- To give advice about all kinds of problems pertaining to children in response to requests by the children's families and others.
- To conduct investigations, and medical, psychological, pedagogical, sociological and psychiatric assessments concerning children and their families.
- To give guidance based on the investigations and assessments.
- To take temporary protective care of children when necessary.
- To provide counselling services for foster parents.
- To support foster parents by providing respite care.

The law also gives the CGC the authority to place children with foster parents, or with vocational guidance parents, or in children's or infants' homes. The CGC arranges adoption for children placed in institutions as well (Tozawa, Iwasaki and Motomura, 2003).

In Japan, there is a basic Child Welfare Law, enacted in 1947, and several laws relating to child welfare such as the Law on the Prevention of Child Abuse, enacted in 2000, the Law for the Welfare of Mother with Child and Widow, enacted in 1964, the Law for Punishing Acts related to Child Prostitution and Child Pornography, and for Protecting Children, enacted in 1999, and so forth.

Article 34 of the Child Welfare Law forbids forcing a child to beg or using a child for begging, forcing a child under 15 to engage in acrobatics (for example, in a circus), putting a child in a freak show, and other such things. It is also forbidden to violate the confidentiality of a client in a Child Guidance Centre, to use the title of 'certified child-care worker' without holding the qualification, and so forth. Laws concerning child prostitution and child pornography punish those who act as intermediaries in child prostitution and those who solicit other persons to commit child prostitution.

Foster Parent Recruitment Process

Foster care services are administered by the Child Guidance Centre (CGC) in every prefecture and designated city. Each prefecture and designated city must also have a Child Welfare Council which fills an advisory role with respect to child welfare matters. The CGC recruits prospective foster parents, screens them by conducting a home assessment, and sends the documented results of the assessment to the child welfare council for approval. On the recommendation of the council, the governor issues a document: Approval for Foster Parent. After being approved, the foster parents are registered as foster parent candidates for a period of five years. When initially registered, they must complete a training session to hone their child-rearing knowledge and skills, and then they await a call from the CGC to tell them that they have been matched with a child. Foster parents must be reviewed every five years in order to maintain their status and to be eligible for the foster parent support services which the CGC also provides.

Foster Family Care Providers

Foster parents must meet the following conditions:

- Be healthy in spirit, mind and body.
- Be knowledgeable about child-rearing, willing to raise a child and able to show affection towards a child.
- Be financially comfortable.
- Have no history of child abuse or difficulty in child-rearing.
- Have no record of violating laws pertaining to child welfare.

With the increase in numbers of abused or neglected children to be placed in out-of-home care, the Japanese Ministry of Health, Labour and Welfare (MHLW) revised the foster family care system and introduced a new system in 2002 (Ministerial Ordinance No.115 by the Minister of Health, Labour and Welfare). According to the Ordinance issued in 2002, foster parents should fall into one of the following four categories:

- **General foster parents** (Yoiku-satooya). These are foster parents, approved by the governor of a prefecture, who look after a child having no guardian or a child deemed to be inadequately cared for by their guardian.
- **Kinship care parents** (shinzoku-satooya). In order to be approved as kinship care parents, prospective foster parents must be related to the child within the third degree of kinship, such as grandparents, aunts or uncles. It must be the case that the child cannot expect to be looked after by their parents or care givers, because they are dead, under detention (e.g., in prison) or their whereabouts is unknown. The condition of being financially comfortable does not apply to kinship care foster parents as it does to other foster parents.
- **Short-term foster parents** (tanki-satooya). These are approved and qualified foster parents who care for a child for less than one year.
- **Specialised foster parents** (senmon-satooya). These parents care for children who have suffered traumatising experiences, such as child abuse and neglect, within the last two years. Specialised foster parents must have completed the training required for specialised foster parents and must satisfy one of the following conditions in addition to the conditions required for general foster parents: (a) they must have been registered and have had experience caring for foster children for more than three years; (b) they must have had equivalent experience with child welfare services for more than three years and this experience must be recognised as equivalent by the child welfare council and the governor. Equivalent experience might include work at a day-care centre, infant's home, children's home or other child-welfare facility, either as a child-care worker or a social worker. The training for specialised foster parents includes theories and principles of social welfare, child welfare and many other subjects, and includes a practical.

Since this new system of foster care, with the category of specialised foster parent, was only initiated on October 1st, 2002, there are no data yet available on how well it is working.

Children and Young People Placed in Foster Family Care

According to Article 25 of the Child Welfare Law (1947), 'Any person who discovers a child having no guardian or a child deemed to be inadequately cared for by his guardian shall notify a welfare office or Child Guidance Centre of this fact'. Article 27 says: 'The Governor of the prefecture shall take any of the following measures in regard to a child reported ... (3) place such children under the care of foster parents, hereinafter to mean such persons who have been deemed competent by the governor of the prefecture, and who wish to bring up a child whose supervision by its guardian is deemed inadequate ... '

Although foster care had been 'expected to play an important role in the promotion of child welfare services' (Atsumi, 1997: 177), after the emergence of the Child Welfare Law, the numbers of both registered foster parents and children placed in foster care did not increase but rather declined after showing a peak in 1957 (Table 1). As Table 2 shows, only 6.4 per cent of children who are placed out of their own homes are living in foster families in 2001. The remainder have been placed in residential institutions such as a children's home.

Table 2 shows the slight decline in the number of children in out-of-home care between 1975 and 2001, and a larger decline in the percentage of those in foster care.

Table 3 shows the age distribution of foster children in 2001. As might be expected, more

Table 1: Declining trend in foster care (Numbers refer to the end of each year)

Number of children placed in foster care	Number of registered foster parents	Number of foster parents with one or more children placed	Year	Remarks
9,478	18,498	8,537	1957	Highest number of children placed
8,337	19,275	7,332	1962	Highest number of foster parents
3,851	10,230	3,225	1975	
3,322	8,659	2,627	1985	
2,377	8,059	1,940	1995	

Source: Ministry of Health, Labour and Welfare (MHLW): Annual Report on Social Welfare Services

Table 2: Numbers of children in residential care and foster care respectively (as of October 1st in each year)

Foster care	Infant's Home	Children's Home	Total	Year
3,851(10.3%)	3,292(8.8%)	30,084(80.8%)	37,227(100%)	1975
3,322(9.0%)	2,710(7.4%)	30,787(83.6%)	36,819(100%)	1985
2,377(7.7%)	2,566(8.4%)	25,741(83.9%)	30,684(100%)	1995
2,211(6.4%)	2,912(8.4%)	29,610(85.2%)	34,733(100%)	2001

Source: MHLW: Annual Report on Social Welfare Services

Table 3: Age distribution of foster children in 2001

0 years old	1–6 years old	7–12 years old	13–15 years old	16 years old	Total
68(3.1%)	837(37.9%)	675(30.5%)	325(14.7%)	306(13.8%)	2211

Source: MHLW: Annual Report on Social Welfare Services

Table 4: Reasons for placement by percentage (as of March 1, 2002 except foster care March 31, 2002)

Reasons for Placement	Infant's Home	Children's Home	Foster Family
Parent's psychiatric condition	13.0	7.5	5.3
Born of unwed mother	12.2	–	–
Parent's employment status	11.2	14.2	6.9
Parent's hospitalisation	9.4	9.2	6.0
Whereabouts of parents unknown	9.9	14.9	17.9
Parents refuse to care for child	6.3	4.0	23.8
Parents divorce	5.3	8.5	4.6
Neglect by parents	3.3	8.6	5.7
Children with problems	0.5	5.4	0.8
Child abuse by parents	4.0	5.7	2.4
Abandoned children	3.0	0.9	7.3
Various other reasons	21.9	21.1	19.3

Source: Shoji, 2003, p. 292

children under the age of 6 are fostered than any other age group.

Table 4 shows one reason for placement is being born of an unwed mother. Unless there are abuse or neglect issues, placement of these children only occurs with the mother's consent. It is often the case that the child is the result of rape or is born to a high-school student who does not wish to raise the child. Such children are put up for adoption and are placed meanwhile in an infants' home.

Financial Support for Foster Carers

The Ministry of Health, Labour and Welfare sets annual national standards for payments to foster parents to cover the foster parent's labour and the costs of rearing the child. These payments are the shared responsibility of the national and prefectural governments. As of 2003, the foster parent's allowance is determined by the category into which the foster parent falls. The monthly allowance for a specialized foster parent is USD 851 and that of other foster parents is USD 283. An initial one-time payment of USD 306 is provided when the child is placed. Payments to cover the cost of living for the child depend on the age of the child. For a child five years old or younger, the monthly payment is USD 454 per child, and for a child aged 6 to 18 years it is USD 451 (US dollars are calculated using an exchange rate of 106 yen to the dollar). Although there are no school fees in primary and junior high school, payments of USD 20 for primary and USD 40 for junior high are paid monthly to cover the costs of stationery and incidentals. Monthly payments of USD 210 or USD 310 are provided respectively when children attend a public senior high school or a private senior high school. For school trips, there are annual payments of USD 198 for a sixth year pupil, USD 524 for a junior high school student, and USD 1,020 for a senior high school student. The Japanese school system includes primary schools, where students remain for the first six years of their school careers, and junior and senior high schools, where students remain for three years each. It is traditional that, in the last year of each of these periods, students are given the opportunity to travel and gain some experience of other places. It is these school trips that are paid for by the government on behalf of children in child welfare institutions, including foster children.

Costs incurred at school entry are also paid: USD 373 for primary school, USD 435 for junior high school and USD 524 for senior high school. Medical expenses and the cost of school lunches and vocational training are reimbursed in full. The standard payments to foster carers are criticized as being quite low because it is estimated that it costs USD 32,170 per year to maintain a primary-school aged child in a residential facility (Zenkoku-Satooyakai, 2003).

Major Issues in Foster Family Care

Although many researchers (Matsumoto, 1991; Miyoshi, 1963; Amino, et al., 1998; Kaneko, 1994; Shoji, 2003) and governments recognise the importance of foster family care, the number of foster families and children placed in their care has been declining and the system itself is in danger of disappearing (Shoji, 2000). The national government's efforts to reverse this trend are reflected in the new Ordinance of 2002.

There are many reasons for the failure of foster care to prosper in Japanese society:

- First, Japanese people value blood ties and do not wish to have non-related children living with them in their homes.
- Second, there are no religious traditions, like Christianity in Europe, which inspire interest in social care.
- Third, people lack confidence in their ability to parent children and tend to resort to books on the subject, many of which provide conflicting information.
- Fourth, there are inadequacies in the foster care system, such as the lack of training of some social workers employed by the Child Guidance Centres to work with foster families.
- Fifth, it is felt that birth parents who do not wish their children to be brought up by other families have a strong right to object.
- Sixth, there are insufficient foster families to accommodate the number of children who need to be fostered. Many foster parents really wish to adopt but there are few children available for adoption and the distinction between adoptive foster parents and non-adoptive foster parents is not clear.
- Seventh, the support system for foster parents is generally inadequate, although respite care for foster parents is now available.
- Finally, there is a lack of public awareness about foster care (Tozawa, Iwasaki and Motomura, 2003; Shoji, 2003).

Future Trends in Foster Family Care

As mentioned, the major trend is the decline and threatened disappearance of the foster family system. In order to promote the system, the following steps must be taken:

- The Child Welfare Law must be changed to make a clear distinction between adoptive foster parents and non-adoptive foster parents.
- Active publicity must be undertaken to make people more aware and to change their attitudes towards foster family care.
- The amount of money paid to foster carers must be increased, both in terms of salaries and child maintenance.
- Support services to foster carers must be improved.
- Child Guidance Centres must be staffed by competent, trained social workers.

Foster Care Research

There are three major institutes and associations studying foster care in Japan. One is the Japan Institute of Child and Family Studies, affiliated with the Boshi-aiikukai Foundation. This Institute publishes a journal, *Current Information on Child & Family Welfare*. Another, the Society for the Study of Adoption and Foster Care meets four times a year and publishes the journal, *Atarashi Kazoku: Yoshito Satooya no Kenkyu (The New Family: Study of Adoption and Foster Care)*, twice a year. There is also the Foster Parent Association of Japan which produces the *Newsletter for Foster Parents*. This association set up a study group to discuss 'how to promote foster care' and published a report (Zenkoku-Satooyakai, 2003).

Conclusion

In Japan, professionals in the field of child welfare acknowledge foster care as the best alternative kind of care for children who cannot be cared for in their own homes, in accordance with Article 20 of the Convention on the Rights of the Child. Nevertheless, the percentage of children in out-of-home care being fostered is still declining in spite of recent changes by the national government designed to promote foster family systems. The reasons for this decrease have been addressed in the chapter. While it is possible to address systemic reasons, cultural reasons (for example, opposition by birth parents to having their child placed in another family's home, and reluctance on the part of foster parents to accept a non-related child) are far more difficult to overcome.

References

Amino, T. et al. (1998) Research on Foster Family System: Foster Family System and its Operation. *JCFRI Bulletin*. 35, 181–208.

Atsumi, S. (1997) Japan. In Colton, M. and Williams, M. (Eds.) *The World of Foster Care: International Sourcebook on Foster Family Care Systems*. Gower House: Arena.

Ministry of Health, Labour and Welfare (MHLW) *Annual Report on Social Welfare Services*. Tokyo: MHLW also available from http://www.mhlw.go.jp/english/wp/wp-hw/index.html

Kaneko, T. (1994) *Hosupitarizumu no kenkyu (Study on hospitalism)*. Tokyo: Kawashimashoten.

Kyoto-fu Shakaika (Social Department of Kyoto Prefectural Government) (1924) *Rakuhokumeibutsu satogonohanashi (Northern Kyoto famous for fostering looked after children)*. Kyoto: Nakanishi Printing Company.

Matsumoto, T. (1991) *Jidofukushi no jisshoteki kenkyu (Emperical research on child welfare)*. Tokyo: Kenpakusha.

Miyoshi, A. (1963) *Satooyaseido no kenkyu (Study on foster family system)*. Tokyo: Nihon Jidofukushikyokai.

Pharr, S.J. (2003) Japan's Civil Society Today. *TsŪshin*. 9(2):2–3. Edwin O. Reischauer Institute of Japanese Studies, Harvard University.

Shibata, Y. (1964) *Ishii Juji no shougaito shisou (Life and idea of Ishii Juji)*. Tokyo: Shunju-sha.

Shoji, J. (2000) Korekarano satooyakyoiku (Training foster parents for the future). *Current Information on Child & Family Welfare*. 16:42–45.

Shoji, J. (2003) *Foster care: Satooya seido to satooya yoiku (Foster care: Foster care system and training of foster parents)*. Tokyo: Akashishoten.

Statistics Bureau, Ministry of Public Management, Home Affairs, Posts and Telecommunications. (2004) Population estimates: Monthly report July 2004 http://www.stat.go.jp/english/data/jinsui/tsuki/index.htm

Takiguchi, K. (2003) Satooyano hennsento satooyaseidono kaikaku (Changes of foster parents and reform of foster family system). *Mother and Child Wellbeing around the World*. 54: 2–5.

Tozawa, A., Iwasaki, K. and Motomura, M. (2003) Caring for Deprived Children in Japan. *Japanese Journal of Social Services*. 3: 93–105.

Zenkoku-Satooyakai (Foster Parent Association of Japan) (2003) *Satoota itakusokushin no arikata: Satooya itakusokushin no arikata kenkyukai hokoku (The report of Satoota itakusokushin no arikata kenkyukai on how to promote foster care placement)*. Tokyo: Zenkoku-Satooyakai.

6 Poland

Zofia Waleria Stelmaszuk

Jurisdiction: Political and Social Context

Poland is a republic in Central Europe bordered by Germany, the Kaliningrad oblast of Russia, Lithuania, Belarus, the Ukraine, the Czech Republic and Slovakia. Its northern border runs along the Baltic Sea coast. Poland covers an area of 312,685 square kilometres (Glowny Urzad Statystyczny, 2003a: 17) and its capital is Warsaw. There are 38,190,608 inhabitants, 61.8 per cent living in cities, and 38.2 per cent in rural areas (Glowny Urzad Statystyczny, 2004: 4,13). Nearly all of the population is ethnically Polish. Roman Catholicism is the dominant religion (90.1 per cent of the population) and there are also religious minorities: Russian Orthodox (1.34 per cent), Protestant (0.42 per cent) and other faiths (Glowny Urzad Statystyczny, 2003b: 14). The age of majority is 18, and there are currently 8,349,808 individuals aged under 18; in the last ten years the number of children has decreased by about two million (Glowny Urzad Statystyczny, 2004a: 4).

Poland is a former Soviet-bloc country, which is in the process of rebuilding a democratic society. Massive political opposition in the 1980s gave rise to the first non-communist government in 1989 and a transition to a free-market economy. In 1990, an open and free presidential election was held for the first time in Polish history, and 1991 saw the first free parliamentary election since the Second World War. In 1997 Poles enacted the new constitution guaranteeing social rights to all citizens.

The constitution guarantees special protection to children and families (Articles 71, 72). The Family Code (*Kodeks Rodzinny i Opiekunczy)* is the basic legal document regulating family relations and child protection. In 1987 an ombudsman was appointed and in 2000 a Children's Ombudsman. In 2004 Poland became a member of the European Union.

Poland is traditionally a rural country but it was industrialised after the Second World War and is currently facing many problems with the national economy. The political and economic transformation of the 1990s has caused hardship and upheavals in the lives of many Polish citizens. Although, during the last three years, there has been a substantial increase (14%) in the real average income of households, 25 per cent of the households examined in *Social Diagnosis 2003* lived below the poverty threshold. The highest percentages of households living in poverty were those households dependent on unearned sources of income (61%), or farming income (56%), and households with many children (53%) (Czapinski and Panek, 2004: 15). The unemployment rate at the end of December 2003 was 18 per cent of the economically active population, just as it was at the end of 2002 (Glowny Urzad Statystyczny 2004b: 16). Almost 13 per cent of households examined in *Social Diagnosis 2003* received assistance in some form (Czapinski and Panek, 2004: 16).

In the first quarter of 2004, the average gross monthly wage in the national economy was 2,332.17 zlotys (USD 615.88 as of June 2004). In the public sector it was 2,697.18 Zlotys (USD 712.27) while in the private sector it was 2,087.67 Zlotys (USD 551.31) (Glowny Urzad Statystyczny 2004b: 16).

Welfare System

State social welfare is aimed at enabling individuals and families to overcome difficult conditions which they are not able to do using their own resources. Social welfare is organised by the state in cooperation with social organisations, religious and charity associations, foundations and individuals. The Social Welfare Act (*Ustawa o pomocy spolecznej)* passed in 1990 was intended to provide government aid to the most vulnerable. The new Social Welfare Act of 2004 delegates many of the responsibilities to local communities.

Since the reform of Poland's administrative system, effective January 1999, a three-tiered system of government is in force as described below:

1. **Municipal government *(gmina)*.** This is the basic level of public administration introduced as early as 1990. The daily needs of the local community are met at this level. Social services for local inhabitants are provided by Social Welfare Centres *(Osrodek Pomocy Spolecznej)*. These centres are mandated to distribute financial aid to the needy as well as to offer social work services. There are 2,478 *gminas* in Poland.
2. **District government *(powiat)*.** This is the middle level of public administration designed to maintain many of the institutions of everyday public life. The agency responsible for the development, maintenance and monitoring of social services at a district level is the District Centre for Aid to Families *(Powiatowe Centrum Pomocy Rodzinie)*. These centres are mandated to fulfil a range of tasks such as: maintaining residential and foster family care; supplementing the basic services provided by *gminas* with more specialised services; supporting the social re-integration of ex-convicts and young people leaving care; and providing care for the homeless through the development of sheltered accommodation, etc. There are 314 *powiats*: 66 of the largest urban *gminas* have been endowed with *powiat* status.
3. **Regional government *(voivodship)*.** This level of public administration is endowed with an independent legal identity, its own budget, and extensive powers in the area of economic policy. The major tasks of the regional governments in the area of public services include, among others, overseeing health care and social welfare (e.g., counteracting unemployment through the development of regional strategies). There are 16 *voivodships* serving populations which range from 1 to 5 million people, with an average of approximately 2.4 million.

The state government exercises its statutory obligations of control over the social welfare system through the Ministry of Social Policy. Since the year 2000, the organisation of child welfare services has been the responsibility of the Ministry of Social Policy. Under the communist regime, child welfare was part of the national education system.

History and Origins of Foster Care

The first formal foster care programme was organised by the Father Baudouin Home for Children, a foundling hospital that opened in Warsaw in 1736. This institution was the first to try placing children in the care of 'known or recommended' paid foster mothers (Kolankiewicz, 1993: 161–2).

In the nineteenth century, when Poland was partitioned between Russia, Prussia and Austria, foster care was a widely applied form of child care in the Prussian sector, while, in the Russian sector, abandoned children were placed with paid wet nurses and nannies. Just before the First World War, Kazimierz Jezewski, a distinguished Polish educator, organised 'orphan nests', in which foster families caring for several children worked together on a 'model farm' provided by the state (Czajkowski, 1957; Kepski, 1991).

After Poland gained its independence in 1918, many foster care programmes were established, the best-known being the Lodz programme, founded in 1926 by the municipal authorities. In this programme, the qualifications required of foster families were set out, as were rules for systematic professional supervision (Puternicka, 1930). Foster children were guaranteed free schooling, medical care, medicine and hospitalisation, and even summer camps, with costs being covered by the city, and foster parents received remuneration (Majewska, 1948: 157–62). In 1931 the Committee of Foster Families was founded in Warsaw, and this helped to expand the idea of foster care on a country-wide basis. Starting in 1934, the then Ministry of Social Welfare mounted a Campaign for Foster Families to help promote the idea of fostering throughout the country (Babicki and Woytowicz-Grabinska, 1939; Kepski, 1991). By 1938 there were already 10,617 children being fostered by 8,447 registered foster families, some of them additionally qualified (and paid) to care for sick or disabled children (Kelm, 1983: 74; Majewska, 1948: 137).

Foster care played a crucial role in the care of war orphans. During both world wars, the lives of thousands of children in Poland were saved when they were placed with foster families. 2,500 Jewish children smuggled from the Warsaw ghetto found refuge with Polish families (Grochowska, 2001). After the war some of the children returned to their families while others found permanent homes with their foster carers (Gladkowska et al., 1995). During that period, foster care continued to be very common: in 1949 there were about 73,000 children in the care of foster families in Poland (Safjan, 1982: 13).

However, with the establishment of the communist state, the policy changed dramatically. The newly-formed Department of Child Welfare was placed under the control of the Ministry of Education. At the beginning of the 1950s all child-care institutions were nationalised. Foster care programmes were no longer encouraged and were replaced by large, state-run children's homes. For many years thereafter, fostering was not an area of interest to those responsible for child welfare in Poland.

An exception was a little foster care programme in Warsaw where the municipal authorities supported efforts by foster care activists within the state-run Friends of Children Society. This support was manifested through an order passed on 9 March 1965 by the Warsaw municipal authorities concerning foster care for children aged 3–7. Foster families were offered an initial sum and a monthly allowance to take in a child. In 1965, the Society began organising care in foster families through Adoption and Fostering Centres (Czaplinska et al., 1975: 265).

It was not until the 1970s that foster care issues gradually became a focus for attention by the government. Starting in 1971, a number of regulations by the Ministry of Education established general rules governing fostering and financial help to foster families (Regulations by the Council of Ministers, 22 November 1971; Order of the Minister of Education, 13 December 1974). Attempts were made to regulate foster care and the supervision of foster families: schoolteachers served as supervisors. Several forms of foster care were proposed, priority being given to kinship care (Regulations by the Council of Ministers, 26 January 1979). Besides kinship care, 'pre-adoptive', 'therapeutic' and 're-socialising' families were proposed (Ziemska, 1979: 59–60).

Since the mid-1970s, the term 'foster family' in Poland has meant the children's next of kin, appointed caregivers or guardians by court order. For years, kinship caregivers received very little help from the state. Typically, the allowance for a child placed in kinship care was only half that for a child placed with non-related caregivers: it was set at 20 per cent of the average salary for kinship caregivers and at 40 per cent for non-related foster families (Safjan, 1982: 193–4).

In addition to kinship foster families, another model of foster care was developed by the Friends of Children Society. 'Family' children's homes (the first came into being in 1958) were run by a married couple, often with their own children. These homes functioned as large foster families, in which one of the parents was employed to organise the home and provide care (Kelm, 1983; Ziemska, 1979). This form of care, intended to provide long-term or permanent placement for six to 10 foster children, was revitalised by new regulations (Order of the Minister of Education, 15 May 1976). In 1984, there were 1,055 children in 155 group-homes of this type (Maciaszkowa, 1986: 108).

The revival of democratic society in Poland after 1989 and the ratification of the Convention on the Rights of the Child in 1991, favoured the rise of child advocacy groups and the deinstitutionalisation movement. The movement began in major cities such as Warsaw, Krakow and Gdansk in 1993, with the aim of influencing the government towards the reform of the child welfare system. The strategies included advising politicians dealing with children's issues at the parliamentary level, responding to consultative documents, and popularising the idea of fostering by educating society at large (Stelmaszuk and Klominek, 1997).

As a result, regulations and policies became gradually much more favourable to foster family care. The 1993 regulations (based on the 1991 Education Act) provided for equal amounts of financial help to be given to both related and non-related caregivers. At the same time, state supervision of foster families, as well as the organisation of supporting services for them, was assured through additional regulations (Regulations by the Ministry of Education concerning foster family care, 21 October 1993; Regulations by the Ministry of Education concerning establishment of Public Adoption and Fostering Centres, 17 August 1993).

The new policies have resulted in great expectations; fostering has come to be seen not only as part of but as 'the future' of child welfare services in Poland (Ministerstwo Edukacji Narodowej, 1994a: 24). A number of newly-developed non-governmental organisations that focus on child welfare have strongly advocated training and support for foster families (Stelmaszuk, 1995). Before the end of the 1990s specialists had begun to discuss the new rules concerning the development of professional foster care services: that is, foster care provided by trained people who were paid for providing it (Stelmaszuk, 1994; Kolankiewicz and Milewska, 1994).

Crucial in this process were contacts with international organisations – IFCO (International Foster Care Organisation) and EUSARF (European Scientific Association for Residential and Foster Care for Children and Adolescents) – which resulted in conferences and publications (e.g. Stelmaszuk 1999; 2001). Another important initiative was the West-East Dialogue in Child Welfare Questions, an Austrian project which brought together representatives from Austria, Germany and the countries of Eastern-Central Europe. This project has resulted in the preparation of the foster care code of ethics, which has been translated into the relevant languages and presented to foster families (Lutter, 1994; Stelmaszuk, 1998).

General child welfare reforms were implemented in the year 2000. Child protection services and the management of child-care institutions were delegated to the social welfare sector. District bureaus for children and family services (*Powiatowe Centrum Pomocy Rodzinie*) were instituted. Funds have been allocated and training programmes have been designed for prospective foster carers. The regulations concerning foster care (Order by Councils of the Ministers, 26 September 2000; Order by the Minister of Labour and Social Policy, 14 September 2000) emphasised the right of children to maintain contact with their families and to have efforts made towards family reunification. Young people were entitled to special assistance, including financial support when leaving care. Initially, all funds were provided from the central budget but gradually subsidies and responsibilities were transferred to local governments. The New Social Welfare Act (*Ustawa o Pomocy Spolecznej*) of 2004 and the associated regulations promote further expansion, professionalisation, and specialisation in foster family care (Wyrwicka, 2004).

Service Provision in Foster Care

The Social Welfare Act of 12 March 2004 delegates responsibility for organising foster family services (as well as other child care services) to the middle level of public administration *(powiat)*. The District Centre for Aid to Families *(Powiatowe Centrum Pomocy Rodzinie)* is responsible for maintaining existing foster families and now is also responsible for the recruitment and training of professional foster carers. The Family Court, however, plays the major role in placement decisions. Preference is given to caregivers who are related to the child. Typically, the Family Court decides whether the child should be placed with a person designated as a foster carer or in residential care (usually, when a foster care option is not available) (Ulanowska, 2004). According to the law, the court must inform the District Centre for Aid to Families about its decision. In an emergency situation, a child can be immediately placed with a licensed stand-by family (known as *Pogotowie rodzinne)* but a court order must be obtained as soon as possible. The District Centre for Aid to Families is obliged to report to the Family Court at least once a year and more often when the situation requires.

The District Centre for Aid to Families provides the foster child with financial support and other help both while in care and when leaving care. It also trains, approves, supervises and supports the foster family. These tasks are carried out by social workers in Adoption and Fostering Centres, of which 49 are public and 38 are non-public, run by the Catholic Church or non-governmental organisations (Ministerstwo Polityki Spolecznej, 2004). Traditionally, the main concern of the Adoption and Fostering Centres has been adoption but, nowadays, more social workers are employed at these centres to work with foster families (Dembe, 2004).

There are currently three types of foster family care settings:

1. **Traditional.** Here, a carer, related or unrelated to the child, cares for no more than three children unless siblings are

being placed together. Most often, this is a kinship or social network placement, usually involving grandparents caring for a child before a court decision has been made. Such foster carers do not receive compensation for the care given and do not need to possess any certificate. The law states that they should be 'prepared' for their role by social workers.

2. **Professional stand-by family.** This foster care setting has only been in place since the year 2000. It is designed to provide short-term care in emergency situations to no more than three young children for no longer than 12 months. A trained foster carer (usually a foster mother), with a certificate, is employed by the local authorities and receives a salary plus an appropriate foster care allowance for as long as she cares for the child.
3. **Family group-homes** (traditionally called 'family children's homes'). Here a married couple lives together with several children, including their own. This type of setting was originally designed as a long-term placement for children deprived of their biological families or for children with special needs. Today it is also expected to serve as a short-term placement. At least one of the parents (required to obtain a foster care certificate) receives a salary equivalent to that of a professional educator, with all costs covered in addition. This type of setting functions like a large foster family but it has its roots in a different tradition and is governed by rules (including financial) that are more similar to the rules of residential care than foster care. This type of care has had its ups and downs, caused by changing policies and requirements on the part of the new administration (Nawrot, 2004; Kowalczyk, 2004). Some authorities strongly encourage this type of care while others view it as too expensive and even problematic since it entails such things as overtime, paid leave, etc. Those who view it as problematic prefer to use foster families (Uliasz, 2004).

In addition to these three types, the current regulations of 2004 propose two new types of professional foster care:

- **Professional 'large'** foster families caring for three to six children, including siblings; and
- **Specialised**, task-centred families caring for not more than three children with special needs (including behavioural problems).

Both these new types of foster families will be employed by local authorities and will be required to complete special training and possess the required qualifications. The training courses will be provided by Adoption and Fostering Centres and also by non-governmental organisations. A licence to train foster carers must be obtained from the Ministry of Social Policy. As of July 25 2004, there are 20 licensed training programmes (including adaptations of American and British programmes), and more than a dozen programmes awaiting registration (Bednarska, 2004).

Children and Young People Placed in Foster Care

In 2003, there were 52,507 children in 39,085 foster families and 1,810 children in 248 family group-homes (Ministerstwo Polityki Spolecznej, 2004). This number might be an overestimation if 'children' is defined as including only persons aged less than 18. Some children remain in their foster family (and sometimes in residential care) beyond the age of 18 if they are still attending school and the available statistics do not separate these out. It is quite common in Poland for young people to live with their parents or grandparents and, if the grandparents happen to also be the foster parents, maintenance of their 'foster care' status will enable them to care for grandchildren whom they might otherwise not financially be able to support.

After some years of economic growth Poland is now facing serious economic difficulties, accompanied by high unemployment. There is an increasing number of children under court supervision and a growing number of young people at risk. Although foster care is being systematically expanded, still large numbers of children are placed in various kinds of residential facilities (see Table 1).

In the past, the vast majority of children in foster care were placed as a result of court intervention. At that time the Family Court was the only institution intervening in family matters and it responded to situations where there were serious problems: predominantly child abuse or neglect, often resulting from alcoholism on the part of the biological parents (Jaworska-Maj, 1990; Stelmaszuk, 1996; Kolankiewicz, 1998). Today it is common for grandparents, who are caring for the child because the biological parents cannot, to go to the court to formalise their status as foster carers.

The majority of foster children live in the major cities while 31 per cent live in rural areas. Out of 3,824 children placed in foster families in 1997, 17 per cent had no mother and 13 per cent had no father (Kolankiewicz 1998: 270, 282). Many children come from families affected by alcohol abuse and related problems. A study by Luczak (1994) reports that, of a representative sample of 100 foster children from the Warsaw area, 46 per cent of their biological parents had substance abuse problems, 34 per cent suffered from alcohol-related disorders, and 37 per cent had committed a crime. Kolankiewicz (1998) and Kusio (1998) have made similar observations. In the Luczak (1994: 14) study, the majority of children entered foster care between the ages of 3 and 7, and spent at least half their lives until they reached majority in care. In the Kolankiewicz (1988) sample, half of the children entering foster care were more than 10 years old (p. 273). For many children, placement with relatives seems to be virtually permanent (Jaworska-Maj, 1990; Kolankiewicz, 1998). Sometimes the child's parents live in the same household as the children and their caregivers (Ministerstwo Edukacji Narodowej, 1994b: 8; Kolankiewicz, 1998: 282).

Table 1: Children and young people in out-of-home care in Poland, 2000–2002

Number of children in care **Forms of care**	**2000**	**2001**	**2002**
Welfare Sector			
Foster Care:			
Foster families (traditional)	58,097	50,164	50,754
Professional foster families	1,246	1,286	1,590
Family group-homes	1,075	1,166	1,275
Residential Care:			
Emergency care centres	3,836	5,337	7,382
Children's homes	18,196	19,744	20,969
Centres for youth with behaviour problems	3,148	3,166	3,449
Care centres for children with disabilities	3,777	3,702	3,660
Education Sector			
Special education centres	31,776	31,482	29,912
Therapeutic-educational centres	3,371	3,843	4,084
Health Sector			
Therapeutic-educational centres	558	273	–
Therapeutic care centres	358	351	505
Homes for the severely disabled	22	54	92
Justice Sector			
Correctional centres	1,622	1,322	1,385

Sources: Statistics of the Ministry of Social Policy, Ministry of National Education and Sport, Ministry of Health, Ministry of Justice, Central Statistical Office

The research shows that among children and young people placed in 'family' children's homes were those who have had great difficulty adapting to life in a traditional residential care institution. Many had no contact with their families of origin and their placement in the group-home was intended to be permanent: they were to be cared for until they were able to live independently (Kelm, 1986; Ziemska, 1979; Telka, 2000).

The new regulations require that the situation of a young person reaching the age of majority (18 years) must be made clear. Young people must choose to either continue their education or enter independent living. Those who continue their education are entitled to receive 30 per cent of a base amount per month up to the age of 25 provided they are still in school. The base amount is currently set at 1,621 Zlotys (USD 428.08) so the young person would receive 486.30 Zlotys (USD 128.42) per month. Those who choose independent living are entitled to receive a lump sum of up to 300 per cent of the base amount (4,863 Zlotys or USD 1,284.23) to give them a start in life. A person with special needs could also receive additional help in kind of a value up to 300 per cent of the base amount. According to statistics, out of 23,969 young people reaching their majority in 2003, 4,913 chose independent living, while 19,056 decided to stay in the foster family and continue their education (Ministerstwo Polityki Spolecznej, 2004).

Foster Care Providers

According to the foster care regulations, a couple or a single person with Polish citizenship and living in Poland can be foster parents, on condition that their parental rights have never been terminated. Other requirements are good health and adequate living conditions, an 'appropriate' age difference between the child and the foster parents, and an agreement by the child to be fostered, provided that the child is able to express an opinion. It is also stipulated that professional foster carers should complete appropriate training and obtain a license, while kinship carers should be 'prepared' for their task on a case-by-case basis by social workers.

The majority of foster family care providers are the children's grandparents, most often grandmothers, who, in Poland, are usually deeply involved in their grandchildren's upbringing and well-being. Under Polish law, relatives — grandparents, step-parents or siblings — are obliged to support their young relatives if the parents cannot provide adequate care (Kodeks Rodzinny i Opiekunczy, art. 132). According to current statistics, 82.6 per cent of foster children are placed with relatives (Ministerstwo Polityki Spolecznej, 2004). Data on the whole population are not available, but research has shown that 65 per cent of the relatives are grandparents while about 10 per cent are older siblings and 20 per cent are other family members. Forty per cent of foster carers are pensioners (20% of female and 24% of male carers are over 60 years old) of relatively low socio-economic status (Kolankiewicz, 1998: 282–7). Moreover, many have serious health problems, and conflicts with the child's parents are frequent (Jaworska-Maj, 1990; Stelmaszuk, 1996). Non-related foster carers, by contrast, are usually much younger, with better health and higher socio-economic status (Luczak, 1994; Dembe, 2004). Similarly, family children's homes' parents have higher socio-economic status and often have professional training (Telka, 2000).

The majority of parents in the new 'professional' families (stand-by families for young children) are young. Often the mother is caring for the foster child together with her own one or two young children. So far their work has been favourably received (Raclaw-Markowska and Legat, 2004; Bartosiewicz, 2004).

Financial Support for Foster Carers

Until the establishment of 'professional' foster care in the year 2000, it was clearly understood that foster parents were not to be compensated for their efforts with the exception of family children's homes, where one or both parents were employed by the state.

Today there is a clear division between two categories of foster family: traditional and professional. Parents in both categories receive the allowance defined as 'financial help for the child' but only 'professional' (trained and licensed) parents also receive a salary. According to the 2004 Social Welfare Act, the allowance for a foster child might be 40, 60 or 80 per cent of a base amount fixed at the national level, i.e. 1,621.00 Zlotys (equivalent to USD 428.03 as of June 2004). Thus the monthly allowance provided for a child may be 40 per cent of 1,621 Zlotys (648.40 Zlotys or USD 171.18), 60 per cent (972.60 Zlotys or USD 256.85) or 80 per cent (1296, 80 Zlotys or USD 342.46), depending on the child's age, health, and special needs. Children under the age of seven years are entitled to an allowance of 60 per cent of the fixed amount, while children with disabilities or special needs receive 80 per cent (see Table 2). All unrelated foster caregivers receive an additional 10 per cent of the fixed amount. For children who receive any kind of income or survivor's benefits, the allowance is reduced by half the amount of the income or benefit, but the child must still receive at least 10 per cent of the base. An allowance (up to 150% of the fixed amount) is earmarked for the accommodation of a new foster child.

According to the 2004 regulations, the payment (salary) offered to a professional foster carer is 120 per cent of the base amount per child per month (equivalent to USD 513.69 as of June 2004). A stand-by family, prepared to receive a child in an emergency situation, receives 80 per cent of the base amount per month (equivalent to USD 342.46), even when they are not currently caring for a child (and 120% when they have a child in their care). Stand-by families are paid extra if they care for more than three children at a time or for a child with special needs. When the foster parents are a couple, only one of them is entitled to a payment.

Major Issues in Foster Family Care

The issues the foster care community in Poland must deal with are:

- Recruiting and preparing prospective foster families.
- Encouraging and supporting those people who are committed to the idea of foster care.
- Educating the public through good quality media campaigns.
- Developing a model for professional foster care, since the idea of professional foster care is new to the Polish culture.

Table 2: Foster family care in Poland in 2003 (as of 31 December)

Category of care/foster care allowance	Number of families	Number of children and young people in care
Kinship foster families	33,967	43,347
allowance 40%		33,625
60%		9,229
80%		507
Non-related foster families*	5,118	9,160
allowance 40%		4,965
60%		3,206
80%		284
including:		
Professional (task-centered)	384	2,281^
allowance 40%		738
60%		1,503
80%		61
Total	39,085	52,507

*family group-homes (1,810 children in 248 families in 2003) are not listed in the foster care statistics
^number of children served during the year
Source: Ministry of Social Policy
Note: There were 8,349,808 persons aged under 18 in Poland as of 31 December 2003

- Recruiting and training child protection specialists and professionals working in the field.
- Coordinating a variety of forms of foster care and establishing their place on the service continuum.
- Developing collaborative strategies between different professional groups, especially 'pedagogues' who have traditionally worked with children, and social workers who are new but powerful actors in the traditionally 'pedagogical' field.
- Providing local social workers with the skills required to allow them to build trust and partnership with families, and to make them more sensitive to the needs of children and families.
- Using local resources, both with respect to the skills of professional child welfare workers and the experience and great tradition of Polish social pedagogy. Since child welfare is new in the social policy sector, there are new activists in the field, often without any professional background, who believe that Poland would do best to import Western social work ideas and Western foster care programmes. The American PRIDE programme is already being used. Although there is never any harm in learning from others, it is important to remember that Poland has its own traditions and local resources.
- Improving the quality of care offered in kinship care.
- Improving placement policies: for example, requiring consultation with child welfare professionals before placement by the court.
- Improving collaboration between the public and non-government sectors, including strategies for sharing responsibility and power.
- Continuing to move towards professionalisation and specialisation in foster family care so that more forms of care become available: for example, respite care to meet the needs of children and families.
- Clarifying the status of parents in family children's homes, who are now fighting to preserve the status of 'residential care workers'.
- Ensuring the professional stability of child welfare specialists who are threatened by changing policies and laws and the interests of different political and professional groups.
- Ensuring professional status and financial stability to professional foster families, including clarification of their mission and obligations.
- Dealing with the complex situations which arise after disclosures of the sexual abuse of children by respected specialists from the child welfare field.
- Building a foster carers' association on the national level. To date, there are many different clubs, groups and organisations but no process for representation at the national level.

Future Trends

Future trends in foster care in Poland may include the following:

- The idea of professional foster care seems to be gaining in popularity, and there is a green light for further professionalisation and specialisation.
- Until recently, reliance has been placed mostly upon kinship carers and they have been given priority when children need to be placed. The ongoing process of recruitment and training of specialised foster families will provide for more options, although kinship care will continue to be valued.
- In addition to long-term/permanent foster care placements, short-term placement and respite care options will become available.
- Support services for foster carers will be organised through the non-governmental sector.
- There will be an increasing interest in working with biological families.

Foster Care Research

Since foster care became a part of the child welfare system, several studies have been conducted, most of them by university researchers. They have, for the most part, been small-scale, descriptive studies, some undertaken for academic theses. They focus on: foster family functioning; foster care providers, their living conditions and motivations for fostering; the social climate; and relationships within the family (Bedkowska, 1979; Jaworska-Maj, 1990; Kelm, 1983; Rozanska and Tynelski, 1981; Kusio, 1998; Przygoda, 1998). The majority of researchers, even though they have been critical about the quality of kinship care and favour non-related caregivers, emphasise the strong emotional bonds between children and their caregivers (Kelm, 1983; Luczak, 1994; Kusio, 1998). They point out that many of those who have left foster care keep in touch with their foster parents more often than with their biological families (Jaworska-Maj, 1990; Przygoda, 1998).

Other studies have focused on the difficulties experienced by foster children and the causes of these difficulties: for example, contacts with biological parents (Safjan, 1982; Stelmaszuk 1996); and performance in school and educational and career plans (Rozanska and Tynelski, 1981; Baran, 1985; Przygoda, 1998;). The studies by Jaworska-Maj (1990) and Przygoda (1998) deal with the perception of foster care by those who have been in care, as well as with the foster family's influence on the educational pursuits and professional plans of foster children. A comparative study by Baran (1985), which describes the life expectations of children from foster and residential care settings, argues that foster care helps develop more optimistic attitudes than residential care. Another study by Luczak (1994) compared health and development in three representative samples (100 children in each group) from foster care, residential care and natural family settings. The best developmental conditions, outside the natural family environment, were found in non-related foster families.

A number of studies on family group-homes conclude that this form of placement is relatively successful, especially for children in need of long-term or permanent placement and for those having special needs (Kelm, 1976; 1986; Ziemska, 1979; Telka, 2000).

Subsequent studies included critical examination of historical developments in foster care, as well as action-research on the development of non-governmental support services for foster families (Stelmaszuk, 1994; 1995). Research assessing possibilities for the family reunification of 300 children placed in three different kinds of settings (residential care, foster family care, and residential school for children with special needs) (Stelmaszuk, 1996) revealed that many child-care specialists and residential educators were trying to prevent children from having contact with their biological families. They were generally negative towards family reunification and contributed to the breaking of links with families. Similarly, specialists working with foster families perceived the foster family to be a substitute family and were opposed to contacts with the biological parents. The research by Przygoda (1998) has confirmed that foster children in care, although strongly attached to their foster family, feel 'caught' between two families and suffer from conflicting loyalties.

The UNICEF sponsored cross-national study, exploring the situation in child-care in Poland at the end of the 1990s, showed that, in many cases, placement was the only option offered to children and families in a difficult situation. Children who were placed were staying in care for far too long and no efforts were being made to change the family's situation or to help the children reunite with their families. The study also noted that the growing number of children in foster care was not accompanied by a decreasing number in residential care placements. It concluded with a suggestion to develop more service options, especially for children with special needs, and it strongly recommended specialised foster care (Kolankiewicz, 1998).

The ongoing process of revolutionary change in the child welfare system has not yet resulted in many research projects. The first published cross-national study was undertaken through the initiative of the Children's Ombudsman by the Institute of Public Affairs (Raclaw-Markowska and Legat, 2004). Overall, the research that has been undertaken documents general acceptance of the reforms and difficulties with implementation. It confirms, however, that specialised foster care is expanding and is perceived as a promising service option by local authorities.

References

Babicki, J.C. and Woytowicz-Grabinska, W. (1939) Opieka spoleczna nad dziecmi i mlodzieza, in *Encyklopedia wychowania*, Vol III. Warsaw: Nasza Ksiegarnia, pp. 531–82.

Baran, B. (1985) 'Wyobrazenia o wlasnej przyszlosci dzieci wychowywanych poza rodzina', in Tyszkowa, M. (Ed.) *Rozwoj dziecka w rodzinie i poza rodzina*, Poznan: Uniwersytet Adama Mickiewicza.

Bartosiewicz Marzena (2004) The head of Child and Family Welfare Section in the Ministry of Social Policy, personal communication, 29 July.

Bedkowska, V. (1979) 'Sytuacja emocjonalna dzieci w rodzinach zastepczych', *Problemy Rodziny*, No. 5.

Bednarska Wanda (2004) Specialist in the Ministry of Social Policy, personal communication, 25 July.

Czajkowski, K. (1957) 'Kazimierz Jezewski', *Dom Dziecka*, No. 2.

Czaplinska, J. et al. (1975) 'Problematyka sieroctwa spolecznego', in: Butrymowicz B. and Gomolka L. (Eds.) *Pedagogika Towarzystwa Przyjaciol Dzieci*. Warsaw: Panstwowe Wydawnictwo Naukowe, pp. 260–97.

Czapinski, J. and Panek, T. (2004) *Social diagnosis 2003. Objective and subjective quality of life in Poland*. Warsaw: University of Finance and Management Press.

Dembe, M. (2004) Head of the Foster Family Section, Adoption and Fostering Centre in Warsaw, personal communication, 20 March.

Gladkowska, M. et al. (1995) *Opieka spoleczna w Warszawie 1923–1947*. Warszawa: Interart.

Glowny Urzad Statystyczny (2003a) *Powierzchnia i ludnosc w przekroju terytorialnym*. Warsaw.

Glowny Urzad Statystyczny (2003b) *Wyznania religijne. Stowarzyszenia narodowosciowe i etniczne w Polsce 2000–2002*. Warsaw.

Glowny Urzad Statystyczny (2004a) *Ludnosc wedlug plci, wieku, wojewodztw, podregionow, miast i gmin*. Warsaw.

Glowny Urzad Statystyczny (2004b) *Zatrudnienie i wynagrodzenie w gospodarce narodowej w I kwartale 2004 roku*. Warsaw.

Grochowska, M. (2001) 'Lista Sendlerowej', *Gazeta Wyborcza*, 9–10 June, pp. 16–7.

Jaworska-Maj, H. (1990) *Sytuacja zyciowa bylych wychowankow rodzin zastepczych*, Warsaw: Instytut Badan Pedagogicznych.

Kelm, A. (Ed.) (1976) *Odzyskane domy rodzinne*. Z *doswiadczen rodzinnych domow dziecka w Polsce Ludowej*, Warsaw: Wydawnictwa Szkolne i Pedagogiczne.

Kelm, A. (Ed.) (1986) *Materialy z ogolnopolskiej konferencji naukowo-pedagogicznej poswieconej doswiadczeniom rodzinnych domow dziecka*, Warsaw: Ministerstwo Oswiaty i Wychowania.

Kelm, A. (1983) *Formy opieki nad dzieckiem w Polsce Ludowej*, Warsaw: Wydawnictwa Szkolne i Pedagogiczne.

Kepski, C. (1991) *Dziecko sieroce i opieka nad nim w Polsce w okresie miedzywojennym*, Lublin: Uniwersytet Marii Curie-Skłodowskiej.

Kodeks rodzinny i opiekunczy. Ustawa z dnia 25 lutego 1964 roku. Dz. U. z dnia 5 marca 1964 roku, nr 9 poz. 59 z pozn. zm.

Kolankiewicz, M. (1993) 'Zarys dziejow Domu Ks. Baudouina', *Kwartalnik Pedagogiczny*, Vol. 38, No., pp.159–175.

Kolankiewicz, M. and Milewska, E. (1994) 'Kontraktowe rodziny zastepcze – nowa forma opieki nad dziecmi', unpublished.

Kolankiewicz M. (1998) (ed) *Zagrozone dziecinstwo. Rodzinne i instytucjonalne formy opieki*. Warszawa: Wydawnictwa Szkolne i Pedagogiczne.

Konstytucja Rzeczypospolitej Polskiej z dnia 2 kwietnia 1997 roku (Dz. U. Nr 78, poz. 483).

Kowalczyk, E. (2004) Foster carer in the family group-home in Wroclaw, personal communication, 24 July.

Kusio U. (1998) *Rodzina zastepcza jako środowisko wychowawcze. Studium socjologiczne na przykładzie Lublina*. Lublin: Uniwersytet Marii Curie-Sklodowskiej.

Luczak, E. (1994) 'Srodowisko wychowawcze rodzin zastepczych', *Opieka-Wychowanie-Terapia*, No. 17, pp. 13–18.

Lutter, E. (1994) 'Foreign Aid by Social Know-How Transfer. Austria-Hungary-Romania. Project', unpublished.

Maciaszkowa, J. (1986) 'Instytucjonalne formy wychowania dzieci pozbawionych naturalnej rodziny. *Problemy Opiekunczo-Wychowawcze* nr 3, pp. 99–111.

Majewska, A. (ed.) (1948) *Rodziny zastepcze Lodzi*, Lodz: Polski Instytut Sluzby Spolecznej.

Ministerstwo Edukacji Narodowej (1994a) 'Glowne kierunki doskonalenia systemu edukacji w Polsce. Materialy na debate sejmowa', unpublished.

Ministerstwo Edukacji Narodowej (1994b) 'Funkcjonowanie placowek opieki calkowitej nad dziecmi i mlodzieza. Materialy na posiedzenie Sejmowej Komisji Edukacji, Nauki i Postepu Technicznego', unpublished.

Ministerstwo Polityki Spolecznej (2004) 'Sprawozdanie polroczne i roczne z udzielonych swiadczen pomocy spolecznej – pienieznych, w naturze i uslugach za styczeń –grudzień 2003, unpublished.

Nawrot, J. (2004) 'W plataninie dwoch szkol reformowania'. *Problemy Opiekunczo-Wychowawcze*, No 3, pp. 22–7.

Przygoda, J. (1998) 'Biografie i start zyciowy usamodzielnianych wychowankow roznych form opieki', in: Kolankiewicz M. (ed) *Zagrozone dziecinstwo. Rodzinne i instytucjonalne formy opieki*. Warszawa: Wydawnictwa Szkolne i Pedagogiczne, pp. 193–220.

Puternicka, J. (1930) 'Umieszczanie dzieci w rodzinach. Dzialalnosc Wydzialu Opieki Spolecznej Magistratu m. Lodzi', *Opieka nad dzieckiem*, No. 1. pp. 1–6.

Raclaw-Markowska, M. and Legat, S. (2004) *Opieka zastepcza nad dzieckiem i mlodzieza – od form instytucjonalnych do rodzinnych*. Warszawa: Instytut spraw Publicznych.

Rozanska, E. and Tynelski, A. (1981) *Rodzina zastepcza jako forma opieki nad dzieckiem*, Kielce: Wyzsza Szkola Pedagogiczna.

Rozporzadzenie Ministerstwa Edukacji Narodowej z dnia 17 sierpnia 1993r. w sprawie osrodkow adopcyjno-opiekunczych (Dz. U. Nr 84, poz. 394).

Rozporzadzenie Rady Ministrow z dnia 21 pazdziernika 1993r. w sprawie rodzin zastepczych (Dz. U. Nr 103, poz. 470, z pozn. zm.).

Rozporzadzenie Rady Ministrow z dnia 29 wrzesnia 2001 r. w sprawie rodzin zastepczych (Dz. U. Z 2001 r. nr 120 poz. 1284).

Rozporzadzenie Ministra Pracy i Polityki Spolecznej z dnia 9 pazdziernika 2001 r. w sprawie udzielania pomocy na usamodzielnienie się, kontynuowanie nauki oraz zagospodarowanie dla pelnoletnich osob z rodzin zastepczych oraz osob opuszczajacych niektore typy placowek opiekunczo-wychowawczych i domow pomocy spolecznej, zaklady poprawcze, schroniska dla nieletnich i specjalne osrodki szkolno-wychowawcze (Dz. U. Z 2001 r. nr 120, poz. 1293).

Rozporzadzenie Ministra Polityki Spolecznej w sprawie rodzin zastepczych. Projekt z dnia 17 czerwca 2004 roku, unpublished.

Safjan, M. (1982) *Instytucja rodzin zastepczych. Problemy prawno-organizacyjne*, Warsaw: Wydawnictwo Prawnicze.

Stelmaszuk, Z.W. (1994) Fostering in Poland. *European Journal of Social Work*. 1: 2, 39–41.

Stelmaszuk, Z.W. (1995) 'Foster Care in Times of Socio-Economic Changes: Expectations and Perspectives. in *Foster Children in a Changing World: Documentation of the European IFCO Conference, Berlin* 1994, Münster: Votum Verlag.

Stelmaszuk, Z.W. (1996) 'Reintegracja rodziny jako cel i efekt opieki zastepczej nad dzieckiem. Raport z badan wykonanych na zlecenie Komitetu Badan Naukowych', unpublished.

Stelmaszuk, Z.W. (1998) 'Kodeks etyczny rodzin zastepczych', *Problemy Opiekunczo –Wychowawcze* nr 8, pp. 21–5.

Stelmaszuk, Z.W. (Ed.) (1999) *Wspolczesne kierunki w opiece nad dzieckiem. Wybor tekstow*. Warszawa: Wydawnictwo Akademickie Zak.

Stelmaszuk, Z.W. (Ed.) (2001) *Zmiany w systemie opieki nad dziecmi i mlodzieza. Perspektywa europejska*. Katowice: Wydawnictwo Slask.

Stelmaszuk, Z.W. and Klominek, W. (1997) Poland. in Colton, M. and Williams, M. (Eds.) *The World of Foster Care. An International Sourcebook on Foster Family Care Systems*. Aldershot: Arena.

Telka, L. (2000) *Rodzinne domy dziecka. Zarys monograficzny*. Lodz: Wydawnictwa Uniwersytetu Lodzkiego.

Ulanowska, L. (2004) Deputy director in the District Centre for the Aid to Families in Warsaw, personal communication, 15 February.

Uliasz, T. (2004) Senior specialist in the Child and Family Welfare Section in the Ministry of Social Policy, personal communication, 19 July.

Ustawa z dnia 29 listopada 1990 roku o pomocy spolecznej (Dz. U. Nr 64, poz. 414 z pozn. zm.).

Ustawa z dnia 7 wrzesnia 1991 roku o systemie oswiaty (Dz. U. Nr 95, poz. 425, z pozn. zm.).

Ustawa z dnia 12 marca 2004 roku o pomocy spolecznej (Dz. U. Nr 64 poz. 593).

Wyrwicka, K. (2004) 'Zmiany i nowe rozwiazania w ustawie o pomocy spolecznej', *Problemy Opiekunczo-Wychowawcze*, No 5, pp. 3–7.

Ziemska, M. (1981) Poland: Foster Family Homes. in Payne, C.J. and White, K.J. (Eds.) *Caring for Deprived Children: International Case Studies of Residential Settings*. London: Croom Helm.

7 South Africa

Wilfried van Delft

Jurisdiction

The Republic of South Africa is an independent country occupying the Southern-most part of the African continent. It is crossed in the north east by the Tropic of Capricorn and is bordered by Zimbabwe, Mozambique, Swaziland, Botswana and Namibia.

The country covers 470,886 square miles or 1,219,090 square kilometres. The total population of 44,819,778 (Statistics South Africa, 2003: 6) comprises four ethnic groups: black 35,416,166 (79.0%) white 4,293,640 (9.6%) coloured 3,994,505 (8.9%) and Indian or Asian 1,115,467 (2.5%). The age distribution for the population is: 0–19 years, 19,347,009 (43%); 20–64 years, 22,064,702 (49%); and 65 years and over, 3,408,373 (8%).

The 0–9 age group is the most vulnerable to abuse and neglect and constitutes 9,303,377 (21%) of the total population (Statistics South Africa, 2003: 27).

The country is divided into nine provinces (populations in brackets): KwaZulu-Natal (9, 426,017); Gauteng (8,837,178); Eastern Cape (6,436, 763); Limpopo (5,273,642); Western Cape (4,524,335); Mpumalanga (3,122,990); Northwest Province (3,669,349); Free State (2,706,775); and Northern Cape (822,727). Completely surrounded by South Africa in the East-central region, lies the independent country of Lesotho.

With respect to religious affiliation, most whites and coloureds as well as 60 per cent of blacks are Christians. Hindus constitute about 60 per cent of the Asian and Indian population, while 2 per cent of the total population is Muslim.

There are 11 official languages. English is the official language for documentation.

Some Historical Pointers

The Dutch East India Company established a settlement on the Cape of Good Hope in 1652 to serve as a depot en route to India and other eastern trading partners. Later, a steady stream of mainly European settlers came to the Cape of Good Hope and, from there, slowly moved northwards in search of better business opportunities, more land and grazing. They gradually settled all over the present South Africa, together with black people who also moved around, fleeing tribal warfare or searching for better land and grazing.

After a number of conflicts between the Dutch and the British after 1795, the Cape was formally ceded to the British in 1814. Slavery was abolished in 1834.

Partly in revolt against British rule, hundreds of Boer families left the Cape in 1836 and started the Great Trek Northward, founding the Republics of Transvaal and the Orange Free State which were later annexed by the British and fell under British rule after the Anglo-Boer war of 1899–1902. In 1910, the two republics were integrated with the colonies of the Cape and Natal to form the Union of South Africa, which became the independent Republic of South Africa in 1961.

Particularly during the period of discovering diamonds in 1866 and gold in 1886, many fortune seekers from all over the world, as well as thousands of blacks native to South Africa, descended on the diamond and gold fields adding to the already large cultural diversity. Settlers and fortune seekers brought with them cultural and religious practices from all corners of the earth. The black nations and tribes in South Africa contribute significantly to the cultural diversity through their history, language and customs. South Africa is indeed a cosmopolitan society.

Significant turning points in the political and social history of South Africa are the Anglo-Boer War (1899–1902), the coming into power of the Nationalist Party (1948) with its racial segregation and later Apartheid policies, the dismantling of Apartheid (early 1990s), and the new democratic political dispensation culminating in the first democratic elections in 1994 with Nelson Mandela as the president.

Organisation of Social Services

Throughout the history of South Africa the development and delivery of social services has been characterised by a partnership between the state and the non-government sector and specifically the churches (Van Delft, 1998: 129).

The National Department of Social Development designs, develops, partly implements and monitors the social welfare policy that steers present day social services in South Africa. The national department also presents the national budget for social services to the cabinet and allocates funds to the provincial departments. Each of the nine provinces has a Department of Social Development, or equivalent department, targeted with the responsibility to deliver and oversee the development and implementation of social services in the province. The provincial departments also partly finance welfare programmes and other social services offered by registered welfare organisations and other acknowledged NGOs.

The South African community, by means of voluntary contributions, donations and fund raising campaigns, is responsible for a large portion of the finances needed to offer services. Foreign governments and foreign private donors also play a significant role in financial aid to social services. In fact, without the significant caritas element prevalent in the South African society, the delivery of social services would be seriously hampered. As it is, the NGO sector is faced with chronic financial shortages.

For all practical purposes the NGOs develop and deliver social services in South Africa. According to Bosman (personal communication), in December 2003, there were 22,493 registered NGOs under the Act on Non-profit Organisations (Act 71 of 1997). However, as it is no longer a legal requirement for all NGOs to register under the Act, it is not possible to present an accurate figure. It is estimated that there are at least 100,000 NGOs in South Africa (Bosman, 2003).

The Social Service Professions Act (Act 74 of 1978 as amended) regulates the social work profession in South Africa. Registration with the South African Council for Social Service Professions (previously known as the SA Council for Social Work) and paying of annual registration fees is compulsory for all practicing social workers. In 2003, there were approximately 10,000 registered social workers—not many given the size of the South African population.

Dominant Political System

The dramatic socio-political changes that have characterised South Africa since 1989 culminated in the release of Nelson Mandela from prison on 11 February 1990, the unbanning of previously banned political parties and the first democratic election in 1994. Through victory at the ballot box, the African National Congress (ANC) came into power with Nelson Mandela becoming the president of the New South Africa. Since coming into power, the ANC, together with other political parties, re-charted the socio-political course of South Africa including the social welfare system.

Politically speaking, black people in South Africa were for all practical purposes marginalised by the rulers of South Africa, including the British, when it came to basic human rights and political participation in the affairs of South Africa. Today, South Africa is a constitutional democracy addressing many racially based injustices of the past through policies and legislation as well as striving towards developing the socio-economic quality of life of all its citizens. In the Human Development Report (HDR), South Africa is classified as a developing country and is ranked 111 on the Human Development Indicators (HDI). The Human Development Report is a publication of the United Nations and gives a measure of human development based on three distinct components: indication of longevity; education; and income per head. The three components are translated into a Human Development Index (HDI) which is a critically important index because issues such as health provision and services, schooling and literacy training, employment patterns and enterprises are linked together as crucial components of development. The challenges to improve on the HDI are demanding.

Freedom of speech and democratic elections are essential ingredients in making South Africa a prosperous country and a leading role player in sub-Saharan Africa. Yet, looming ahead of the widely acclaimed New South Africa lies the immense problem of HIV/AIDS which has taken on epidemic proportions and which has become the single most serious problem facing the entire nation. HIV/AIDS is stretching health and welfare budgets and services to the limits, just in terms of coping with the consequences of HIV/AIDS let alone preventing the disease. HIV/AIDS has become a political 'hot potato' and requires great political will and ability to mobilise national and international financial and human resources to address this problem in a meaningful way.

HIV/AIDS has also changed the face of foster care in South Africa dramatically.

Dominant Welfare System

With the coming of the new political system, a new focus on social welfare emerged, culminating in a **developmental social welfare policy** as outlined in the White Paper for Social Welfare (1997), removing all racial or other discriminatory barriers in social service delivery, and emphasising services to children and youth, persons with disabilities, women, and the aged. The focus is very much on preventative services and less so on therapeutic services, and that the poorest of the poor must receive priority attention in the development and delivery of social services.

The White Paper for Social Welfare also clearly moves away from promoting specialised welfare services in favour of encouraging welfare and other social service organisations to develop and implement comprehensive multi-focused or generic services that address a variety of human problems in one organisation.

Parallel with the White Paper for Social Welfare runs the Financing Policy (1999) which clearly stipulates the conditions that welfare organisations must comply with in order to receive funding from the provincial Department of Social Development.

Although the majority of registered welfare organisations embrace the philosophy, goals and objectives of the White Paper on Social Welfare, the practical implementation is a rather slow process as a significant paradigm shift is required from both social service providers and consumers. One does not easily move away from an historic predominantly institutional model for social welfare towards a developmental model for social welfare that is unique in the world (Midgley 1998, pp. 90–91). Neither does one move away from the Apartheid era that governed South Africa for decades to a democratic dispensation overnight, so to speak.

Van Delft (2002: 18) states that whereas before 1994 social workers reigned supreme in the welfare field, the new developmental model opens up the field to all relevant players.

Van Delft (2000) also suggests that not only will service delivery organisations have to rethink traditional service delivery strategies and content, but universities training entrance level social workers will also have to adapt their curriculae to accommodate the developmental model for social welfare.

The South African social work fraternity by and large accepts the international definition of social work developed by the International Association for Schools of Social Work (IASSW, 2002):

> *The social work profession promotes social change, problem solving in human relationships and the empowerment and liberation of people to enhance well being. Utilising theories of human behaviour and social systems, social work intervenes at the point where people interact with their environment. Principles of human rights and social justice are fundamental to social work.*

This definition complements the developmental approach yet allows sufficient leeway for clinical/therapeutic work where and when it is indicated.

With particular reference to foster care in South Africa it can be stated undeniably that it is the NGO sector that carries the brunt of the responsibilities involved in foster care, with the state playing a legal, monitoring and financial role as will be explained later on.

The HIV/AIDS epidemic has made the practical implementation of the developmental welfare policy as it was originally designed quite challenging. Welfare organisations and other NGOs are so overwhelmed by the immediate HIV/AIDS related needs of people that crisis intervention and basic care overshadow the emphasis on development work on a much broader community level.

History and Origins of Foster Family Care for Children and Youth

In a comprehensive study on foster care, Van Bochove (1965: 125) states that the development of foster care in South Africa cannot be separated from the development of social work in South Africa. Social work has in fact made foster care an issue that merits professional involvement. Although there was legislation dealing with the protection of children as early as 1913 (Child Protection Act) and the Act on Adoption of Children was passed in 1925, the focus on foster care as an alternative to institutional care was only seriously addressed in the Child Care Act of 1937, followed by the New Child Care Act of 1960. Since 1960 several amendments have been made to the Act and at present the Child Care Act (Act 74 of 1983) governs foster care and other matters related to child welfare. The Act is at present under revision.

The entire development of child-focused social work has been significantly influenced by socio-political events impacting on South Africa such as the Anglo-Boer War (1899–1902), the First World War (1914–1918), The Great Depression (1929–1933), and the Second World War (1939–1945). These events saw much action by the South African community to deal with the enormous amount of human deprivation especially amongst children.

However as Potgieter (1998: 21) rightly points out, 'efforts to help focused almost exclusively on the problems amongst poor whites and culminated in an investigation by the Carnegie Commission of Enquiry into the *poor white problem*'. Two of the major recommendations by the Carnegie Commission were the establishment of a state department for welfare to overcome the piecemeal approach to welfare and the training of social workers.

Even though the government of the time established a Department of Social Welfare and Pensions in 1937, private welfare organisations, and especially the churches, responded to the welfare needs of children much earlier (Van Bochove, 1965).

The establishment of the department also paved the way for subsidising social workers who were being trained for the first time during the 1930s. The presence of qualified social workers on the South African welfare scene also prepared the way for better child-care legislation including the recognition and management of foster care.

The whites only general election of 1948 saw a government coming into power that ruled South Africa for 46 years. This government designed and implemented the Apartheid policies and laws which culminated in a system of institutionalised racial discrimination.

Under the Apartheid dispensation, social workers were trained in racially separated universities and colleges and were employed by welfare organisations and government departments serving designated races only. Naturally this segregated education and practice resulted in social workers from different races losing touch with each other as professionals. This segregation was also reflected in diverse social work practices and planning, and a variety of discriminatory foster care rules and regulations. Never was there a national voice and action to address the needs of people irrespective of race.

In November 1993 a national welfare conference was held to debate plans for a new welfare system for a country that was now liberated after the unbanning of selected political parties in 1990 and the release of Nelson Mandela. In 1991 a National Peace Accord was signed while all the remaining discriminatory laws were removed from the statute books (Potgieter, 1998: 23).

True, the political changes in South Africa have liberated many people from oppression, but as far as welfare services to children and young people are concerned, South Africa has not moved much further in addressing the foster care obstacles that were identified by Van Bochove (1965).

The much referred to New South Africa is faced with the rather complicated task of streamlining welfare services, specifically in relation to the realities of child neglect and abuse. In this regard, the South african national council for child and family welfare plays a crucial role, demonstrated by their very relevant and intensive comments on the first and second draft Children's Bill put forward for comments by the Department of Social Development. In its *Quarterly Newsletter* (September 2003), the said Council requests the establishment of minimum norms and standards for foster care, a complete revision of foster care grants, and the clarification of exactly who should be defined as a 'care giver' as it is unacceptable by social work and the community, to regard a seven year old as a care giver and head of a household.

Guidelines for standards and procedures for foster care have been addressed by the Committee of Inquiry into Foster Care of Children (Department of Health Services and Welfare, 1990). This committee was, unfortunately, established by the previous government and as such carries the stigma of the Apartheid government. Yet despite this the report has much to offer when read from a professional point of view.

Mass poverty, unemployment, and the realities of HIV/AIDS impacts millions of children for whom a safe home environment in the form of foster care seems to be the best alternative to being placed in a children's home. South African social workers and welfare leaders will one day be judged by history as to how the profession responded to crises among children in a society that was so harshly criticised by the world regarding its racial policies and disrespect for human rights. The present government is in a position to rectify many injustices from the past—not only Apartheid driven issues. However, the government must also ensure that present welfare issues, and specifically child and youth care issues, receive the much needed priority attention they deserve.

Service Provision in the Area of Foster Care

Foster care services are predominantly provided by registered welfare organisations employing qualified and registered social workers. Provincial governments also employ social workers who will provide foster care services in geographical areas where no welfare organisation provides them or where there is a need for reasons such as staff shortage or work load. However, governments do not play a major role in direct service delivery in the field of foster care though they do contribute to the costs involved.

Before the new developmental approach, as outlined in the White Paper for Social Welfare, started to drive social services, foster care was the special focus of child and family welfare organisations. Today this service may be provided by any welfare organisation that has qualified social workers in its employ. Although foster care is therefore not the exclusive domain of child and family welfare organisations anymore, it is evident that these organisations still carry the brunt of foster care services. It is also evident from observation and discussions with social workers that foster care is regarded as a specialised service that is preferably rendered by experienced social workers and organisations in this field.

As in the past, churches still play a major role in the development and maintenance of social welfare services in South Africa. Whereas in the past church or religious-driven welfare organisations predominantly rendered services, including foster care services, to individuals and families belonging to a specific denomination, the new welfare policy stipulates that all church or religious welfare organisations must render services to all people irrespective of religious affiliation should these organisations wish to be financed by the government. With a few exceptions, churches in general have responded positively to the new policy and in the field of foster care have in fact become leaders in developing services for all races, denominations and non-religious persons.

In South Africa there is no licensing mechanism for rendering foster care services. The great demand and need for foster care services especially in view of the HIV/AIDS related problems, and the huge rural population often served by the so called one-person-welfare-offices delivering a wide variety of services (Schenck, 2002), would make such licensing unpractical. There is also quite a high turnover of social workers in the welfare organisations which are mandated to render foster care and other child and family welfare services. The developmental welfare policy is aiming at empowering as many welfare organisations as possible to render a so called 'one stop service', including foster care, instead of endorsing specialisation through licensing and, by so doing, contravening the policy.

Foster care workers are cognisant of the cultural and religious diversity of South African society and respect the unique cultural heritage and rights of all persons involved in foster care. This translates into culturally sensitive selection of foster parents and families, and placement of children and youth in culturally appropriate foster care homes wherever possible. The Child Care Act (Act 74 of 1983) in fact makes legal provision to place a child in a foster home that complements the child's language, culture and religion. The ever increasing demand for foster care, especially due to HIV/AIDS, but also due to the general increase in child neglect and abuse (Child Welfare Statistical Data, 2003) is of course placing this culturally sensitive practice under great pressure. Parallel to the increasing demand for foster care runs the equal demand for suitable foster care parents and families as there is a chronic shortage of foster parents. This state of affairs forces social workers to place children first and foremost where they will be safe and cared for appropriately. Therefore it is the case, for example, that white foster parents or families will take in a black foster child irrespective of whether the cultures and languages complement each other.

South African foster care statistics are not centralised and processed by government according to different variables such as age, gender, duration of stay in foster care, etc. Such a refined data base is urgently required for welfare and related planning purposes.

However, government and welfare organisations do provide general statistical data on foster care. According to Vasinti Pillay (personal communication, December 2003) from the National Department of Social Development, it is estimated that there were approximately 170,150 children in foster care in 2003, calculated in terms of the number of foster care grants being paid to foster parents.

Data collected from 174 organisations affiliated with the South African National Council for Child and Family Welfare show that during 2000–2002 (Child Welfare Statistics, 2003 : 2) the number of orphaned children reached epidemic proportions. In this period the number of orphans doubled from approximately 2,100 to 5,100. Orphaned children constituted 12 per cent of the case loads of the participating affiliated organisations and comprise triple the number of orphaned children for the period 1997–1999.

In a press release on 14 September 2000, the minister of Social Development, Dr Zola Skweyiya, stated that in 2000 there were 250,000 known orphans in the welfare system of which an estimated 35 per cent were cared for in foster care (Mosese, 2003: 9).

The number of orphaned children given by the South African National Council for Child and Family Welfare (5,100) and by the minister of Social Development (250,000) are quite different. However, the National Council only comments on the active cases social workers deal with at its affiliated organisations. The minister, on the other hand, comments on the estimated figure for the entire country based on demographical statistics and these orphans are not necessarily officially on the caseloads of registered welfare organisations. Most of the children are taken care of by family through ad hoc arrangements and may be reported to welfare organisations only when circumstances change. The statistics indicate, on the one hand, how welfare organisations are experiencing the problem and, on the other hand, what the estimated position is for the country. An exact figure is not available as not all family or other people caring for orphans come forward to apply for a foster care grant.

As calculated by the South African National Council for Child and Family Welfare (Mosese, 2003: 9), South Africa will be confronted with 2.6 million HIV/AIDS orphans by 2010. The above data clearly illustrate the demand that is being made on the government and communities of South Africa to care for children, and foster care is an option that cannot be overlooked.

Children and Young People placed in Foster Families

Although, under the Child Care Act, all children and youth can theoretically be cared for by foster parents, relatively few children with mental or physical disabilities are placed in foster care. The majority of special needs children who require alternative care are cared for in children's homes, or in shelters in the case of many street children, or in institutions for seriously handicapped children and youth. There are, of course, foster families that do care for special needs children but they are few relative to the great need that exists for foster homes. The HIV/AIDS problem is mobilising many individuals, couples and families to foster babies and children who have tested HIV positive and whose parents either cannot care for the children due to their HIV/AIDS related ill health and lack of income, or have died and left their children orphaned.

In terms of the Child Care Act, all children in foster care as well as the foster parents and families should receive social work services.

In fact the law stipulates that the biological parents of the foster child should also be involved in reconstruction services with the aim of a possible reunification of the foster child with its biological parents. The Commissioner of Child Welfare must also be provided with regular updates by a social worker on the progress made with reconstruction services. Should the biological parents not achieve sufficient improvement to warrant reunification, the social worker can recommend permanent foster care placement of the child. A child in foster care may also be adopted when the biological parents have abandoned the child.

As pointed out by Van Delft (1995), reconstruction is often a difficult task as many biological parents experience serious psycho-social handicaps that impact on their parenting skills and abilities as well as on their overall social functioning.

Programs for foster families and reconstruction services are not developed on a national basis. Each welfare organisation is at liberty to develop and implement its own programme, and these programmes are not accredited in any way. The government (Financing Policy, 1999) does however stipulate that foster care programs, like any other programme for a specific target group, must be in place before the organisation will be considered for financial support from the state. Broad criteria for programmes do exist but are not sufficiently specific to take account of the uniqueness of foster care.

A number of organisations, for example the Christian Social Council-North (duToit, 2002a; 2002b; 2002c; 2002d; 2002e) and the South African National Council for Child and Family Welfare (1987), have published guidelines for foster care services but these are not necessarily used by all organisations delivering foster care services. Due to high caseloads, the foster care services delivered are often the minimum necessary to satisfy certain legal requirements, such as periodic progress reports to the judicial system needed to extend the foster care placement. High caseloads and a large turnover of social workers impact negatively on the quality of the psychosocial dimension of services rendered to foster parents, foster children and biological parents.

There are many possible reasons for the high turnover of social workers. First, some 90 per cent of foster care work in child and family organisations is done by young women who often leave to start their own families after a few years in practice. Second, financially rewarding career paths for social workers in the domain of private welfare organisations are very scarce. Men, who are usually looking for more lucrative positions, are reluctant to enter such organisations and turn instead to government departments of welfare where foster care is not a key (specialisation) function. In May, 2004, there were 11, 217 registered social workers in South Africa of whom only 1,183 were men. This huge imbalance tells its own story.

Family Care Providers

As previously outlined, foster care services are delivered primarily by registered family welfare organisations which also deliver a wide variety of other social work activities including community development and poverty alleviation. Foster families and the social worker form the basic team together with an occasional other professional such as a clinical psychologist. Most social workers recognise the principle that foster parents are equal partners in the foster care process, but to say that this value is put into practice routinely would be stretching the point. The high incidence of kinship placements, in particular among black families, adds another dimension to this issue. The child is often fostered by grandparents who take ownership of the child, and social work intervention often centres around dealing with practical issues, such as financial matters. Despite much effort being put into involving foster parents in the entire process, starting with the selection and training of foster parents and siblings in the (prospective) foster family, there is still a long way to go in the quest to develop a real, solid partnership.

Urban foster parents have access to a number of supportive services to deal with problems related to foster care. Foster parents in rural areas however are generally speaking severely under-serviced and support services are often non-existent, totally over-booked, or too expensive for many foster parents to access. As pointed out by Schenck (2002) social workers in small towns or rural areas must deal with all the challenges and problems accompanying foster care as well as performing a wide variety of other social work tasks.

Financial Support for Foster Carers

Financial support for foster parents (carers) is pathetic to say the least. All foster parents qualify for a monthly foster care grant of R500 (USD 70) for each child placed in their care under the Child Care Act. This is the only direct monetary contribution made by the state towards foster care expenditure. Foster children do not have to pay school fees in regular schools and have access to free medical and dental treatment provided by state medical services. Should a foster child experience learning problems or demonstrate exceptional talents that ought to be developed, the foster parents must finance such services out of their own pockets. In some instances state remedial educational services, for example, do exist but are either so over-booked or inconveniently geographically located that access becomes a big problem. Some foster parents do have medical insurance and can register their foster children as beneficiaries. But this is not the case with all medical insurances. Foster parents therefore run the risk of significant medical and other therapeutic expenses if they cannot for some reason or other utilise the already over-burdened state services. Fortunate indeed are the foster children who are placed with financially well-off foster parents.

In view of the significant increase in HIV/AIDS related orphans and the expectation of government that the community will care for many, if not the majority, of these children, it is clear that government is facing an ever-increasing financial dilemma in the near future. In South Africa where the cost of living is constantly rising and poverty and unemployment are endemic, foster care may become a source of extra cash flow for many families who at present struggle financially. The quality of care provided to up to six foster children in an already financially overstretched household is debatable if foster care is supposed to offer more than a shelter and a plate of food. The already huge demand and anticipated increase for foster care created by HIV/AIDS, as well as the lack of sufficient numbers of children's homes as an alternative, is going to impact very negatively on the quality of foster care.

Should a child be placed in a children's home the government will contribute R910 (USD 130) per month per child. As in the case of foster care, the children's home must finance all special needs services out of their own funds raised by donations and other activities.

Major Issues in Foster Care

Finding and training foster parents for an increasing number of children as well as developing a sound and sufficient financial support system for foster care should be a top priority of government. It can be argued that many children, especially orphans, should be adopted rather than being placed in foster care. As South Africa has no system of subsidised adoptions, foster care at least provides some financial compensation and is at the moment the only alternative. The development of appropriate legislation for child and youth care which includes foster care, is long overdue and urgently needed. The adoption of children in foster care must be addressed in legislation much more vigorously and financial support for parents who adopt children should also be negotiated.

As emphasised by van Delft (1995: 188) the capacity of the biological parents to care for their children must be very well assessed and placing a child back with the biological parent should not become an experiment to determine the success of reconstruction services to biological parents.

Legislation and legal procedures should enable social workers to ensure permanency for children within well functioning foster families without foster parents constantly having to fear the day the foster child will be forcefully returned to the biological parents when the latter have made but minor improvements in their social functioning but are exerting constant (legal) pressure on the social worker to have their child returned.

Within the diverse South African cultural context, the issues of cross-cultural and trans-racial foster care placements require a sensitive approach. Post Apartheid South Africa, like many other countries in the world, including first world countries in Western Europe (Leistra, 2003), is still confronted with racial and cultural prejudice which naturally also impacts on interpersonal harmony and the willingness to care, for others who do not share similar views and values on many issues of life. Foster care, as a very significant demonstration of caring for others, is also subjected to racial and cultural prejudice. Where possible, children are placed with foster families who share similar customs and beliefs and are of the same race. Embarking on an ongoing programme to find and train sufficient numbers of foster parents representing the racial and cultural diversity in South Africa is mandatory. It goes without saying, however, that the fostering of racial and cultural harmony and tolerance of diversity amongst all South Africans is an ongoing necessity and challenge.

Future Trends in Foster Family Care

Permanent foster care with grandparents is becoming more common by the day for children whose HIV/AIDS parents cannot take care of them anymore or have died. Grandparents themselves are often frail and experience financial hardships which makes child-care responsibilities a burdensome and stressful task indeed. This is specifically so amongst many black South Africans. The support of these fostering grandparents is becoming a specialised task and contingency care is constantly being addressed. Young children being cared for by their ageing grandparents are at great risk of being moved to other foster care placements should the grandparents or other family not be able to continue the caring task.

The increasing number of child headed households where both parents are either incapacitated due to HIV/AIDS or are deceased, may require the development of an entirely new foster care system whereby a foster parent moves into the family home and replaces the biological parents. This is a very drastic alternative and will require a very well planned and supervised system. In fact there are many child headed families in rural areas where concerned adults from the community render assistance to these households in a number of ways, preventing the children from being removed and placed in alternative care.

Foster Care Research

As would be expected, the HIV/AIDS pandemic is also impacting on foster care research. Issues related to this pandemic and foster care in the South African context are addressed by a number of researchers, including: Booyens, 1982; Clark, 2000; Diederiks, 2000; Foster, 2001; Halkett, 1999; Loenig-Voysey, 2002; Mona, 1997; Pillay, 2003; Swanepoel, 1999: Szabo and Ritchken, 2002; Wild, 2001, and Wilson, Loenig-Voysey and Loffell, 2001. As can be seen from the dates of the publications, research on foster care and related matters has been and is at present, an ongoing concern in South Africa.

The NEXUS-database of current and completed research provides a detailed and up-to-date overview of the South African research scenario. The Index to South African Periodicals (ISAP) as well as the Index to South African Thesis and Dissertations provides up-to-date information on research into foster care and related matters.

Conclusion

South Africa has indeed astonished and impressed the world with its relatively smooth political transition from an Apartheid to a democratic socio-political dispensation where the rights and dignity of all people are entrenched in a human rights driven constitution, reflecting and guiding the values and attitudes of people towards creating a more just society.

Within this new democracy, child-care is of the utmost importance to ensure a stable and prosperous future South Africa. Amongst the many factors that impact negatively on child-care, the direct consequences for child-care and mental health of the HIV/AIDS pandemic now challenges the values and attitudes of South Africans on more practical levels than just having a positive attitude. Many thousands of children, victims of HIV/AIDS and others, growing up in the post Apartheid New South Africa face a grim future either as orphans or as abandoned, displaced children.

The mobilisation of the hearts and minds of South Africans, as well as government policies and procedures that culminate in concrete assistance and proper financial support towards ensuring a better future for children lacking proper parental support and guidance, should be a top priority on the social welfare agenda of South Africa.

Professional ability to guide the foster care process and the political will of government to co-provide for the requirements of children in need of care, in partnership with the community, is essential to address the evolving child-care crises in South Africa.

References

Bosman, H. (2003) Senior administrative officer. Non-Profit Organisation Sector. Pretoria: Department of Social Development.

Booyens, M. (1982) *'n Evaluering van die pleegsorgplasing van kinders wat tussen die ouderdom van 13 tot 18 jaar sorgbehoewend bevind is.* Unpublished MA thesis. Department of Social Work. University of Pretoria.

Child Welfare Statistical Data (2002) Johannesburg, South African national Council for Child and Family Welfare.

Child Welfare Statistical Data (2003) Johannesburg, South African National Council for Child and Family Welfare.

Clark, B. (2000) The Duty of the State to Support Children in Need. *South African Law Journal.*117: 2, 342–61.

Department of Health Services and Welfare: House of Assembly (1990) *Committee of Inquiry into the Foster Care of Children.* Pretoria: Government Printer.

Diederiks, A.M. (2000) *An Eco-Systemic Reappraisal of Foster Care Services.* Unpublished MA thesis. Department of Social Work: University of South Africa.

Du Toit, R. (2002a) *Pleegsorg beleid en prosedure.* Pretoria: Christian Social Council.

Du Toit, R. (2002b) *Help for Foster Parents.* Pretoria: Christian Social Council.

Du Toit, R. (2002c) *Millenium ouers.* Pretoria: Christian Social Council.

Du Toit, R. (2002d) *Parental Guidance: A Series for Social Workers.* Pretoria: Christian Social Council.

Du Toit, R. (2002e) *Hulp vir pleegouers.* Pretoria: Christian Social Council.

Financing policy: developmental social welfare services (1999). *Government Gazette 405 (1988): 26 March.* Pretoria: Government Printer.

Foster, G. (2001) Proliferation of Community Initiatives for Orphans and Vulnerable Children: Aids and Orphans. *Aids Analysis Africa.*12: 1, 4–5.

Human Development Report (2003) New York: United Nations Development Program.

Halkett, R. (1999) *HIV/AIDS and the Care for Children.* Johannesburg: South African National Council for Child and Family Welfare.

International Association of Schools of Social Work (2002) July Montpellier conference, France.

Loenig-Voysey, H. (2002) HIV/AIDS in South Africa: Caring for Vulnerable Children. *African Journal of AIDS Research.* 1: 2, 103–10.

Leistra, G. (2003) De macho's van West. *Elsevier.* 1 November. 30–1.

Midgley, J. (1998) Social Development and Social Welfare: South Africa in an International Context. *Social work/maatskaplike werk.* 34: 1, 90–8.

Mona, T.P. (1997) *A Sociological Study of Transracial Placements of Children in Foster Care and Adoption In the Pietermaritsburg Area.* Unpublished MA thesis. School of Social Sciences and Development: University of Durban-Westville.

Mosese, G.P. (2003) *Assessment of an HIV/AIDS Programme.* Unpublished 4th year research project. Department of Social Work: University of South Africa.

Pillay, V. (2003) Assistant director. Pretoria: Department of Social Development.

Potgieter, M.C. (1998) *The Social Work Process: Development to Empower.* Johannesburg: Prentice Hall.

National Council for Child and Family Welfare (2003) *Quarterly Newsletter of SANC for Child and Family Welfare.* September. Johannesburg.

Schenck, C.J. (2002) *Rural Social Work in South Africa: Perceptions of Practitioners.* Unpublished research report. Department of Social Work: University of South Africa.

South African National Council for Child and Family Welfare (1987) *A Guide to Foster Care Practice in South Africa.* Johannesburg: South African National Council for Child and Family Welfare.

Statistics South Africa (2003) *Census in Brief.* Pretoria: Statistics South Africa.

Swanepoel, J.M. (1999) *Experiences of Kinship Foster Parents.* Unpublished MA thesis. Department of Social Work: Rhodes University.

Szabo, C.P. and Ritchken, D.A. (2002) Race and Family Placements; A Case Report Review. *South African Journal of Psychology.* 32: 4, 60–3.

Van Bochove, J.M. (1965) *Pleegsorg.* Unpublished DPhil dissertation. Department of Social Work: University of Pretoria.

Van Delft, W.F. (1995) Variables Influencing Foster Care Reconstruction Services. *The Social Work Practitioner-Researcher.* 8: 3, 186–98.

Van Delft, W.F. (1998) Social Stability and the Strategic Relevance of Health and Welfare in South Africa. *Social Work/maatskaplike werk.* 34: 1, 124–33.

Van Delft, W.F. (2000) A Mutually Empowering Partnership Between Social Welfare Organisations and Universities in South Africa: A New Challenge. *The Social Work Practitioner/Researcher.* 12: 3, 155–65.

Van Delft, W.F. (2002) Social Work Research Within the Context of the New Welfare Policy of South Africa. *Africanus.* 32: 2, 7–26.

White Paper for Social Welfare (1997) Department of Social Development. Pretoria: Government Printer.

Wild, L. (2001) The Psychosocial Adjustment of Children Orphaned by AIDS. *Southern African Journal for Child and Adolescent Mental Health.* 13: 1,3–22.

Wilson, T., Loenig-Voysey, H. and Loffell, J.M. (2001) Approaches to Caring for HIV/AIDS Orphaned and Vulnerable Children: Essential Elements for a Quality Service. *Southern African Journal of Child and Adolescent Mental Health.* 14: 2, 21–2.

8 Sweden

Ingrid Hojer

Jurisdiction

Sweden occupies the eastern part of the Scandinavian Peninsula, sharing borders with Norway to the west and Finland to the north east. Although it has a land area of some 450,000 square kilometres, it is sparsely populated, with the population concentrated mostly in the urban areas. Thus, about half of the nation's nine million inhabitants live in just three per cent of the country's area (Hessle and Vinnerljung, 2000).

Sweden used to be an ethnically homogenous society but over the last few decades this situation has changed. Today about 18 per cent of the Swedish population have family roots in other countries, either because they were born outside Sweden, or because one or both of their parents are of non-Swedish origin (Hessle and Vinnerljung, 2000). In the 1960s and 1970s, most immigrants came from southern Europe to work in the expanding industrial sector. In the 1980s and 1990s immigrants mainly came from non-European countries, often as refugees from war or oppression. During the first seven years of the 1990s, the number of people of non-European origin increased by 40 per cent (SOU, 2000: 3).

Organisation of Social Services

Sweden has three levels of democratic government: Parliament at the national level, county councils at the regional level and municipalities at the local level. There are 21 county councils and 289 municipalities. County councils and municipalities have their own decision-making powers. They are run by elected bodies, known as county council and municipal assemblies respectively. These assemblies consist of politicians who are directly elected in general elections held every four years.

Municipalities in Sweden have a high level of local self-government. There is no special Children's Act in Sweden. The equivalent of child welfare law is found in two Acts: the Social Services Act (revised 2001), which is a 'framing' or overarching law and regulates different areas of social support; and the Care of Young Persons Act 1990 which regulates taking children and young people into care without the parents' or children's consent. As long as the basic standards of the Social Services Act are respected, local authorities can organise their child welfare in any way they find most suitable (Hessle and Vinnerljung, 2000).

The Welfare System in Sweden

Along with other Nordic countries, Sweden can be defined as an institutional welfare state with general, and not selective, means-tested benefits. The Social Democratic Party has dominated the political scene for many decades. Their social policy is very much in accordance with the system of the institutional welfare state (Bäck-Wiklund, 2003). Hinnfors (1991) classifies this system as 'generous institutionalism', and describes it as 'A system which includes all public contributions, with high standards, directed towards the whole population. It offers services outside the market place and aims at security based on economic and social needs' (Hinnfors, 1991: 17).

Swedish Family Policy

Modern family policy was introduced in the beginning of the 1930s. At that time, Sweden experienced an economic recession, and birth rates were low. This was a major concern for the Swedish government, and several measures were taken to improve conditions for families; for example, child allowances. The ideas of Alva and Gunnar Myrdal formed the basis for many reforms that aimed at state responsibility for the health and well being of children and families. The Myrdals were eager pursuers of public child care and support to mothers and children, with respect to both health and economic issues (Hessle and Vinnerljung, 2000; Bäck-Wiklund, 2003).

In the majority of families with children, both fathers and mothers are gainfully employed, as are most single parents. The Swedish welfare state with its extensive system of support to individuals and families has made it possible for both men and women to find a balance between their professional and family lives (Bäck-Wiklund, 2003).

History and Origins of Foster Family Care

The placing of children in foster care as opposed to institutional care has long been the tradition in Sweden. The first national decree around foster care dates from 1785 and even in those days foster care was preferred to institutional care, principally due to the fact that care given in foster homes was less costly.

In cases where parents lack the ability to take proper care of their children, the prevailing notion in Sweden all through the 20th century has been that children and young people under the age of 18 should be cared for in foster families, not in institutions.

A Historical Perspective of Child Welfare Laws

At the beginning of the 20th century the Swedish state was criticised for ignoring the hardship of orphans and children in poor and/or dysfunctional families. Debaters highlighted the need for laws that could regulate placements of children and could provide opportunities for authorities to take children into custody when their situation was unsatisfactory (Ohrlander, 1992). The first two laws concerning child welfare were designed to meet these needs and were passed in 1902.

In 1924, the next law was instituted. This was the first law that gave authorities the power to take children into custody against the will of their parents. Responsibility for administration and enforcement was given to special child welfare committees in the municipalities and not, as in other countries, to special family or youth courts (Lundström, 1993).

The next child welfare law was instituted in 1960 and focused more on means of assessment and administrative procedures than did its predecessor. Nevertheless, all these laws were based on the idea that it was possible to predict the future of children by looking at the conduct of their parents and the circumstances in which they were brought up (Lundström, 1993). This notion was questioned in the next law, which was instituted in 1980. It is still in force, although with some changes. What makes this law different from the others is that legislators were no longer as convinced as before of the absolute connection between a 'problematic childhood' and bad future prospects for the child.

Present Situation

Compared to other countries, the legislation for the protection of children in non-parental care in Sweden is rather strict. Unregulated *private foster care* is illegal (Hessle and Vinnerljung, 2000). On every occasion when a child lives, on more than a temporary basis, with someone who does not have custody, child welfare authorities have to give their formal consent. This means that if parents choose to place their child with another family (for example, with grandparents) or if the child or young person chooses to live with another family, the placement has to be formally approved by the child welfare authorities. Such 'private placements' have to submit to regular inspections in the same way as they would if they were formal foster placements, accommodating a child under the auspices of the child welfare authorities. The difference between private placements and placements initiated by the Child Welfare Committee is that 'private' carers do not receive any allowances and they do not have the same access to support from social services.

According to the County Council in West Sweden, the rate of private placements has decreased. When advising social services, the County Council makes it a policy to recommend them *not* to encourage private placements of children and young people. Their reason for this is that, in their experience, even a private placement is usually due to some problem in the family. Thus, the children, parents and guardians concerned are probably in need of the support and supervision provided by social services. The County Council is especially aware of immigrant children who come to Sweden without their parents. In many cases, these children live with a relative by private arrangement. Since such children could be in need of special support and help to adjust to their new families and to Swedish society, the County Council strongly recommends that these placements be made under the auspices of the child welfare authority. In this way, the children and their guardians can receive adequate support and financial help.

In the Swedish child welfare system there is no permanency planning. Usually there are no time limits to placements. Children stay in care for as long as this is deemed the best alternative. Adoption without the parents' consent does not exist, and children in care are not 'free for adoption' as they are in some other countries, for example the United States, and the UK. Biological parents still have custody of their children, even though the children are in care (Andersson, 1999b; Hessle and Vinnerljung, 2000). One consequence of this is that childless couples often turn to international sources in order to adopt.

Over the last few decades the importance of contact between children in care, their natural parents and other members of their private network has been emphasised. The idea of foster care as 'substitute parenthood' has changed to the idea of foster care as 'supplementary parenthood'. Foster carers nowadays are expected to be a part of a working team around the foster child, together with the biological parents and professionals such as social workers and psychologists. The task of foster carers involves both caring for the foster child and helping the child to maintain relationships with biological parents and other relatives.

Municipalities which have the economic and organisational means to do so, often organise their foster care staff into specialised units where each social worker works exclusively in a particular area such as recruitment or education. However, in most municipalities, social workers in foster care units would all be engaged in the recruitment, education and supervision of foster carers. Most social workers in such units also have responsibility for the well being of the foster child. The law requires semi-annual reviews of the placement of children in foster care, regardless of whether the child is placed in foster care with or without the parents' consent (Andersson, 1999b). These reviews are performed by case workers from the social services in the municipalities. The law also regulates the general supervision of placements and it is made very clear that each placement should be followed carefully by case workers.

However, when Parliamentary Auditors undertook an investigation of foster care at the beginning of the 1990s, it became obvious that the state had insufficient measures in place with respect to foster care. The Auditors found that foster carers were lacking the support, education and supervision they needed to provide good care (Riksdagens Revisorer, 1991). In 2001 the Swedish Parliament decided to begin another investigation into foster care. The investigation has been thorough. Enquiries were made in 151 of Sweden's 289 municipalities and interviews were conducted with social workers. The results of the investigation highlighted new knowledge of current practices and important issues for social workers working in foster care. The Parliament Auditors particularly emphasised the importance of a more stable and secure employment situation for foster carers, the need for better recruitment methods, and also the need to enhance and improve the general public's knowledge of foster care (Riksdagen Revisorer, 2001).

Service Provision in the Area of Foster Care

The local social welfare committee in each municipality is responsible for the placement of children in foster care. Each committee has to exercise its own judgement about what characterises high quality foster care. The work of the committees is supervised at the national level by the National Board of Health and Welfare, and at the regional level by the County Administrative Board, which links national with regional and local interests. The County Administrative Boards are not responsible for the supervision of each foster home, but should ensure that each municipality manages and organises foster care according to existing laws and regulations.

The actual number of active foster homes in Sweden is unknown. There are two major organisations for foster carers, Familjehemmens Riksförbund with 600 members, and Familjevårdens Centralorganisation with 1,200 members. According to estimates made by Familjehemmens Riksförbund, there are about 8,000 active foster homes in Sweden (Riksdagen Revisorer, 2001).

Private agencies

A new feature in Swedish foster care is the occurrence of private agencies which provide specialised and strengthened foster care. There are 10–15 private agencies in Sweden that sell extended foster care to the social boards. Such agencies write special contracts with skilled foster carers (Riksdagen Revisorer, 2001). The agencies provide supervision, counselling and education to foster carers, but the social boards are still responsible for all legal procedures for each placement. The services of these private agencies are mostly used when the social boards need to place children who are especially demanding or in need of specialised foster care. These placements are generally more costly than placements made in foster homes recruited by the social services in the municipalities. Nevertheless, the services of these private agencies are frequently used, and are in many cases considered to be a preferable alternative to institutional care.

Small residential 'family-like' units

Residential care in Sweden today is mainly represented by small, privately run units. Seventy three per cent of residential care units house nine children or fewer (Hessle and Vinnerljung, 2000; Sallnäs, 2000). Before starting a private care facility, a licence must first be obtained from the County Administrative Board.

Some of the new private residential units would probably be defined as 'specialist foster care' in another context. More than half of the owners have experience of fostering, and many of the units describe their establishment as 'family like'. In fact, they can be described as 'hybrid units' – a cross between residential care and foster care (Hessle and Vinnerljung, 2000; Sallnäs, 2000).

Homes for special supervision

Youth justice is included in Swedish child welfare, and therefore criminal and drug abusing youth make up a substantial part of children in care. For several decades special residential care has been used for this group. These *homes for special supervision* have facilities for incarcerating youth. There are 30 residential units of this kind, and since 1994 they have been monitored by a national government agency. Thus, these special homes cannot be private. Local authorities apply for placement and are obliged to pay for the care (Hessle and Vinnerljung, 2000).

Costs for foster care and residential care

According to statistics from the National Board of Health and Welfare, the median cost for foster care was 600 SEK (USD 82) per day in the year 2000. This figure includes payment to foster carers, recruitment costs, and support and supervision of placements. The corresponding figure for residential care was 2,800 SEK (USD 383) (Riksdagens Revisorer, 2001).

Children and Young People in Foster Family Care

In Sweden, around three per cent of all 18 year olds born between 1976 and 1980 have, at some time during their childhood, been placed in out-of-home care. Every other placement occurred after the young person was 13 years old, which implies that care given outside of home before the teenage years affects only 1.6 per cent of children (SOU 2000: 7).

According to the statistics for children and young people subjected to measures under the Social Services Act and the Care of Young people Act, about 18,500 children (0.85% of children 0–17 years old) were in care with a placement outside their own home *at some time* during 2001. About 14,000 received care according to the (voluntary) Social Services Act and about 6,500 received care according to the (compulsory) Care of Young persons Act. About 73 per cent (13,500) of these children were placed in foster homes (Socialtjänst, 2002: 7).

About 65 per cent of all children and young people in out-of-home care in Sweden are in care for three years or less and 20 per cent are in care for more than five years. A few, 10 per cent, have been in out-of-home care for more than 10 years, and a very small group (5%) have spent their entire childhood in care (SOU 2000: 7). Few children alternate between their home and placements. In a register study of 16,000 children, only eight per cent had experienced more than three placements in care before their 18th birthday (Vinnerljung et al., 2000).

Immigrant children

Statistics show that about 40 per cent of children in care in 2000 had one or both parents of non-Swedish origin. In a survey carried out by the Parliament Auditors (Riksdagen Revisorer, 2001) a questionnaire was sent to social workers and heads of social services in 160 municipalities. Almost 40 per cent of respondents reported difficulties in finding foster homes for this group of children and young people.

Characteristics of the Parents of Children in Care

A study by Hessle (1988) showed that parents who had their children placed in foster care also had social problems: 84 per cent were single parents, mainly single mothers, 50 per cent were unemployed and 72 per cent had no vocational training. The majority had drug or alcohol problems, or psychological problems. This picture of socially marginalised people is also salient in other studies of foster children and their parents. Parents of children in care are usually marginalised both economically and socially. They are poorly educated and they have never found their way into the labour market. In many cases they have a weak or even destructive social network, which leaves them with no support or poor support as parents (Lundström 1993; Egelund 1997). There is a clear connection between class and children in care. Child welfare has never really been part of the social welfare state: rather it has been a measure for use with those who are marginalised in the social welfare system (Lundström and Sallnäs, 2003).

Kinship Placements

In the 1950s, about 50 per cent of placements in foster care were kinship placements. Gradually, kinship placements were reduced until, in the beginning of the 1990s, they only represented 16 per cent of all placements (Vinnerljung, 1996a). According to Vinnerljung (1993), this change might be ascribed to the professionalisation of social work, which resulted in social workers preferring foster homes recruited by social services. Wåhlander (1994) stated that social workers seldom contacted relatives when they searched for possible foster homes for a child. This situation was criticised, both by relatives of children in care, and by the National Board of Health and Welfare. Consequently, in the year 1999, there was an amendment to the Social Services Act which stated that the possibility of kinship placements should be considered in every case when a child was taken into care. Twenty per cent of children who were placed in foster care in the year 2000 were placed in kinship homes (Socialtjänst, 2002: 7).

Foster Family Care Providers

The general picture is that a majority of foster carers belong to the working class (Vinnerljung, 1996a). In a survey where 366 foster carers (174 men and 192 women) answered a questionnaire (Höjer, 2001) 61 per cent of carers were working class, 26 per cent were categorised as middle class, and only 13 per cent were from the upper classes. The majority of foster carers in Sweden live in small villages or in rural areas (Kälvesten, 1974; Wåhlander, 1990; Höjer, 2001). Foster carers are usually older than parents with only natural children. In Höjer's (2001) study, the median age for foster mothers was 45 years and for foster fathers 48 years.

Foster parents usually live in stable marriages, with a high level of emotional satisfaction and harmony between the spouses. They often have a traditional way of organising their everyday life, with the woman taking the major responsibility for housework and caring for the children (Kälvesten, 1974; Höjer, 2001). It is usually the women who introduce the idea of fostering to the family. In the survey referred to above (Höjer, 2001), 40 per cent of women and six per cent of men stated that fostering was their idea (one third said it was a mutual idea, and the rest were requested to become foster parents in different ways).

Höjer (2001) also found that 65 per cent of foster mothers worked outside the home, full-time or part-time. About 20 per cent were solely engaged in housework and caring for children at home. Ninety per cent of foster fathers were gainfully employed: only Three per cent had housework and caring for children at home as their only source of income. In 1992, when the survey was undertaken, 82 per cent of women and 85 per cent of men with children under the age of 18 were working outside the home. Apparently, foster mothers were more often working at home than mothers without foster children, but there was no such difference between foster fathers and fathers with no foster children (SCB, 1998).

In the survey mentioned above (Höjer, 2001) 60 per cent of carers described their relationship with the foster child as very close and equivalent to their relationship with their natural children. Carers were usually very committed, and found fostering to be a demanding but at the same time rewarding assignment.

Assessment of Foster Carers

In Sweden, there are mainly two methods used for the assessment of foster carers. The oldest one has been in use for more than 20 years. It is a semi-structured interview, where the foster father and foster mother are interviewed separately about important aspects of their family life, their relationships to parents, partner and children. It is based on a method introduced by Anna-Lisa Kälvesten (Kälvesten and Meldahl, 1982) but many local social services have revised the original interview method, adapting it to current knowledge about children and families. The second method is called PRIDE (Parents Resources for Information, Development and Education) and can be described as a combination of an assessment method and a study circle. A group of people, usually couples, interested in becoming foster carers, meet on 10 occasions under the supervision of one social worker and one experienced foster carer. The prospective foster carers are given information about fostering and have the opportunity to discuss the impact fostering can have on themselves and their families. After the 10 meetings, the participatants decide if fostering is a possibility for them. Then it is up to the child welfare committee in the municipality to decide if they will be accepted as foster carers. Social services in some municipalities combine these two methods when assessing future foster families.

Financial Support for Foster Carers

Foster carers are paid for the work they do. Payment is divided into two parts. One part is remuneration for the caring work performed by the foster carers. It is based on the age of the child and is connected to the needs of the child so that carers with more demanding foster children receive a higher payment. Table 1 shows the range of remuneration according to the child's age.

The other part of the payment is viewed as remuneration for 'board and lodging', and is usually not taxable. Table 2 shows remuneration for board and lodging according to the child's age.

Table 1: Remuneration to foster carers for their caring work with the foster child according to recommendations from the national organisations of municipalities (Kommunförbundet, 2003)

Age of foster child	Basic fee	Increased fee
0–12 years old	3,961 SEK/month 298 GBP 546 USD	6,318–8,885 SEK/month 476–669 GBP 870–1,224 USD
13–19 years old	5,137 SEK/month 387 GBP 708 USD	6,318–8,885 SEK/month 476–669 GBP 870–1,224 USD

Table 2: Remuneration to foster carers for 'board and lodging' of foster child according to recommendations from the national organisations of municipalities (Kommunförbundet, 2003)

Age of foster child	Remuneration for board and lodging	Highest non-taxable sum
0–12 years old	3,439 SEK/month 259 GBP 474 USD	4,913 SEK/month 370 GBP 677 USD
13–19 years old	3,930 SEK/month 296 GBP 541 USD	5,568 SEK/month 419 GBP 767 USD

If the child needs so much attention that one of the carers has to stay at home, the carer can be compensated up to a fee of 13,840 SEK/month (USD 1,907). This type of fee is seen as compensation for lost employment income (Kommunförbundet, 2003).

Most foster carers engaged by social services in the municipalities are paid according to the figures shown above. Foster carers engaged by private agencies usually receive higher fees. For example, one of the agencies in the southwest region of Sweden provides a basic fee of 8,850 SEK/month (USD 1,220) to its foster carers: this figure does not include remuneration for board and lodging.

The remuneration for the caring work is taxable and is also considered to be pensionable income. However, foster carers are not *employed* by the social services: they have what can be called a *paid commission*. As foster carers are not employed, they do not receive any unemployment benefits, a state of affairs that places foster carers in an unfortunate and unfair position. Their assignment as foster carers can be terminated at a very short notice, which means that all payments will cease. This can be especially difficult if carers have been fostering a child with high needs, where the fostering assignment has demanded a full-time fostering effort from one foster carer, who thus can find themself deprived of their only regular income. The Swedish government has acknowledged this insecure situation for foster carers and has made it an issue for further investigation (Riksdagens Revisorer, 2001).

Höjer (2001) found that 95 per cent (n = 366) of foster carers felt that they were entitled to the payment they got. Twenty eight per cent of carers saw the level of payment as fair, based on their achievements, while 50 per cent thought it was too low and 22 per cent had no opinion. Some carers had ambivalent feelings towards the payment. They were afraid that people (including case workers) would regard them as greedy, and that their foster children would suspect that they were looked after for the sake of money, not out of personal commitment.

Current Major Issues in Foster Care

One of the most important issues in contemporary Swedish foster care is the shortage of foster homes. Finding new foster homes is becoming increasingly difficult in most municipalities. At the same time as social workers are experiencing difficulties in finding suitable foster homes, the number of children placed in foster care is increasing: this number has increased by 20 per cent between 1993 and 2000 (Riksdagens Revisorer, 2001). Social workers generally try to solve the problem by placing more children in the same foster home and also by being more active in searching for placements within the child's biological family and social network. Nevertheless, 41 per cent of social services in the survey undertaken by the Parliament Auditors have had experience of placing children and young people in institutional care because a foster care placement could not be found. Another negative effect of the recruitment difficulties is placement of children far away from their birth families because social services cannot find a local foster carer (Riksdagens Revisorer, 2001).

Other important issues are connected to the quality of foster care. In a study conducted by Vinnerljung et al. (2001) between 40 and 50 per cent of all placements of teenagers (13 to 18 years of age) ended in breakdown. It is also true that children placed in foster care have problems in school and problems establishing themselves in the labour market when they leave care (Vinnerljung, 1996b).

The Parliament Auditors came to the conclusion that the problems faced by foster care were due to insufficient interest shown by government for this specific form of care. Their recommendation was that the state should take the initiative to formulate a national strategy for foster care (Riksdagen Revisorer, 2001).

Future Trends in Foster Family Care

The Swedish welfare state system is built on economic and gender equality but, at the same time, it is also built on work: that is to say, you need to be employed or self-employed to have the opportunity of enjoying general state support. Without a job, you run the risk of being marginalised. Therefore, it is true to say that parenthood in contemporary Sweden is viewed as a project that needs to be carefully planned in order not to risk the prospective parent's professional position. Today Sweden has the lowest birth rate ever, and the average age of first-time mothers is beginning to reach 30. The decision to become parents is greatly influenced by long-range changes in the economy (Bäck-Wiklund, 2003).

In a situation like this, where young couples postpone parenthood and both men and women must focus on developing their careers, 'traditional' foster homes, where fostering is undertaken by housewives with no employment outside the home, will be very hard to find. Social services will have to find ways to make fostering attractive for modern Swedish families where both parents have a professional career.

The Parliament Auditors suggest that work as a foster carer should be made more similar to 'regular' employment on the labour market. Foster carers should have the same benefits and the same rights as other employees. Another suggested strategy is to enhance public knowledge of fostering and thus to make the general perception of work as a foster carer more positive (Riksdagens Revisorer, 2001).

When thinking about the demands of foster care in the future, it might be a good idea to start with the carers' motives. Foster carers have a social conscience. They want to do a good job and to make a difference in the life of a child with high needs (Triseliotis et al., 2000; Höjer, 2001). One way to make fostering attractive is to give foster carers high quality support and supervision, and thus to give them the prerequisites they need to succeed with this demanding task. To make fostering a well supported, highly appreciated assignment might be the most efficient way to recruit new foster homes. An increase in the payment for fostering will not be a sufficient measure (Riksdagens Revisorer, 2001). Both Kirton (2001) and Höjer (2001) found payment to be of little importance compared with other motivations to foster.

Foster Care Research

The following provides a brief description of research within the area of foster care in Sweden. It is not to be considered as a complete account of Swedish foster care research.

A study of children in care performed in the beginning of the 1980s had a great impact on Swedish child welfare in general. The study included 89 children, 0–16 years of age who were placed in care in the city of Malmö (Swedens' third city) in 1981–1982 (Vinnerljung, 1996a). The results focused on different aspects of child welfare:

- Kerstin Vinterhed (Vinterhed, 1985) focused on foster carers.
- Sven Hessle (Hessle, 1988) focused on the biological parents of children taken into care.
- Bengt Börjesson and Håkan Håkanson (Börjesson and Håkansson, 1990) focused on the social workers and the foster children.
- Anita Cederström (Cederström, 1990) focused on foster children.
- Gunilla Lindén (Lindén, 1998) focused on teenagers in care.

Although the results are some 15 years old, they are still relevant, and are still referred to by both researchers and social workers.

The work of Gunvor Andersson (University of Lund) has been of great importance for child welfare and foster care. Some of her research is based on a group of small children taken into care when they were 0–4 years of age.

The children were followed up over the years, and the results are presented in three books (Andersson, 1984; 1988; 1995). Andersson has also undertaken research on foster children and their experiences of fostering. Results from this study and from other research projects have been published in various journals (see, for example, Andersson, 1998; 1999a; 1999b; 2001; 2002).

Bo Vinnerljung (National Board of Health and Social Welfare) has published articles, reports and books within the area of foster care. His work is mainly concentrated on outcomes of care, and presents an important contribution to child welfare (Vinnerljung 1993; 1996a; 1996b; Hessle and Vinnerljung, 2000, Vinnerljung et al., 2000; 2001).

The publications of Ingrid Höjer (University of Göteborg) focus mainly on the impact of fostering on the foster family and its members (Höjer 2000; 2001; 2002; 2003; 2004a). An ongoing study focuses particularly on the natural children of foster carers and the impact of fostering on their lives (Höjer and Nordenfors, 2003; Höjer, 2004b).

Conclusion

In Sweden, foster care is well used and highly regarded for children in care. Family patterns have changed, but it is still a fact that close and warm relationships and care given within a family setting is vitally important to the well being of men, women and children (Silva and Smart, 1999). Andersson (1998) found that living in a family was important for foster children. Being part of a family made their everyday lives equivalent to the everyday lives of their peers, and even though they missed their natural parents they appreciated the familial context, the structure of life and the care given in their foster family. Foster care is an important part of child welfare as it gives children who cannot live with their natural parents for various reasons a chance to live in a family and benefit from familial care.

References

Andersson, G. (1984) *Små barn på barnhem.* Diss. Malmö: Liber.

Andersson, G. (1988) *En uppföljning av barn som skilts från sina föräldrar.* Lund: Meddelanden från Socialhögskolan, 1988:1.

Andersson, G. (1995) *Barn i samhällsvård.* Lund: Studentlitteratur.

Andersson, G. (1998) Föräldrakontakt och familjetillhörighet ur fosterbarns perspektiv. *Socialvetenskaplig Tidskrift,* nr. 1, s 3–23.

Andersson, G. (1999a) Children in Residential and Foster Care: A Swedish Example. *International Journal of Social Welfare.* 8: 253–66.

Andersson, G. (1999b) Children in Permanent Foster Care in Sweden. *Child and Family Social Work.* Aug, 4: 3, 175.

Andersson, G. (2001) The Motives of Foster Parents, Their Family and Work Circumstances. *British Journal of Social Work.* 31, 235–48.

Andersson, G. (2002) Fosterbarn ur ett könsperspektiv. *Nordisk Socialt Arbeid* nr.1.

Bäck-Wiklund, M. (2003) Familj och Modernitet. In Bäck-Wiklund, M. and Johansson, T. (Eds.) *Nätverksfamiljen.* Stockholm: Natur and Kultur.

Börjeson, B. and Håkansson, H. (1990) *Hotade - försummade - övergivna.* Stockholm: Rabén och Sjögren.

Cederström, A. (1990) *Fosterbarns anpassning - en relationsproblematik.* Doktorsavhandling. Stockholms universitet, Pedagogiska institutionen.

Egelund, T. (1997) *Beskyttelse av barndomen.* Köpenhamn: Hans Reitzels Forlag.

Hessle, S. (1988) *Familjer i sönderfall.* Göteborg: Norstedts.

Hessle, S. and Vinnerljung, B. (2000) *Child Welfare in Sweden: An Overview.* Stockholm Studies in Social Work, 15. Stockholm University, Department of Social Work.

Hinnfors, J. (1991) *Familjepolitik: Samhällsförändring och partistrategier 1960–1990.* Göteborgs universitet: Studies in Politics, 26.

Höjer, I. (2000) Exploring the Inner Life of the Foster Family. A Study of Family Relations in Families Who Foster. *Book of Proceedings,* IFCO European Foster Care Conference, Ireland.

Höjer, I. (2001) Fosterfamiljens inre liv. Diss. University of Göteborg.

Höjer, I. (2002) Den belönade utmaningen. *Nordiskt Socialt Arbeid* nr. 2 2002. Oslo.

Höjer, I. (2003) Fosterfamiljen. In Bäck-Wiklund, M. and Johansson, T. (Eds.) *Nätverksfamiljen.* Stockholm: Natur och Kultur.

Höjer, I (2004) What Happens in the Foster Family? *Adoption and Fostering.* 28: 1, Spring.

Höjer, I. and Nordenfors, M. (2003) Growing Up With Foster Siblings. In *Childhoods in Late Modern Society.* Göteborg University, Skriftserien.

Höjer, I. and Nordenfors, M. (2004) Living With Foster Siblings: What Impact Has Fostering on the Biological Children of Foster Carers? In Eriksson, H.G. and Tjelflaat, T. (Eds.) *Residential Care, Horizons for the New Century.* Ashgate.

Kälvesten, A-L. (1974) *40 fosterfamiljer med Skåbarn.* Stockholm: Almqvist och Wiksell Förlag AB.

Kälvesten, A-L.and Meldahl, G. (1982) *Familjepsykologi; En handledning I intervu- och tolkningsmetodig.* Stockholm: Liber.

Kirton, D. (2001) Love and Money: Payment, Motivation and the Fostering Task. *Child and Family Social Work.* 6, 199–208.

Kommunförbundet (2003) *Ersättningar till familjehem för barn och vuxna samt kontaktfamiljer för år 2004.* Cirkulär 2003:90.

Lindén, G. (1998) *Att bli fosterbarn i tonåren. Om frigörelsen från internaliserade föräldraobjekt.* Diss. Stockholm: Almqvist och Wiksell International.

Lundström, T. (1993) *Tvångsomhändertagande av barn. En studie av lagarna, professionerna och praktiken under 1900-talet.* Diss. Stockholms Universitet: Socialhögskolan, Rapport i Socialt Arbete, nr 61.

Lundström, T. and Sallnäs, M. (2003) Klass, kön och etnicitet i den sociala barnavården. *Socialvetenskaplig tidskrift,* nummer 2–3.

Ohrlander, K. (1992) *I barnens och nationens intressen; Socialliberal reformpolitik 1903–1930.* Stockholm: Almqvist och Wiksell.

Riksdagens Revisorer (1991) *Familjehemsvård för barn och unga.* Stockholm, Förslag 1991/92:21.

Riksdagens Revisorer (2001) *Familjehemsvården.* Stockholm, Rapport 2001/02:16.

Sallnäs, M. (2000) *Barnavårdens institutioner.* Diss. Stockholms universitet, institutionen för socialt arbete.

SCB (1998) *Levnadsförhållanden. Sysselsättning, arbetstider och arbetsmiljö 1994 - 95.* Rapport nr 92. Stockholm: Statistiska Centralbyrån.

Silva, E. and Smart, C. (Eds.) (1999) *The New Family?* London: Sage.

Socialtjänst (2002) 7. *Statistik.* Stockholm: Socialstyrelsen.

SOU (2000) 3 *Välfärd vid vägskäl.* Delbetänkande av kommittén för välfärdsbokslut. Stockholm: Socialdepartementet.

SOU (2000) 77 *Omhändertagen. Samhällets ansvar för utsatta barn och unga. Betänkande av LVU-utredningen.* Stockholm: Socialdepartementet.

Triseliotis, J., Borland, M. and Hill, M. (2000) *Delivering Foster Care.* London: BAAF.

Vinnerljung, B. (1993) Släktingplaceringar i fosterbarnsvården. *Socionomens Forskningssupplement,* nr 3, Socionomen. 6, 3–10.

Vinnerljung, B. (1996a) *Svensk forskning om fosterbarnsvård.* Stockholm: CUS och Liber utbildning.

Vinnerljung, B. (1996b): *Fosterbarn som vuxna.* Diss. Lund, Arkiv.

Vinnerljung, B. and Langlet, P. and Zaar, A-K. and Gunnarsson, T. (2000) Prevalens av långa vårdtider mm. bland barn som placererats i dygnsvård – en kohortstudie. In SOU 2000:77 *Omhändertagen. Samhällets ansvar för utsatta barn och unga. Betänkande av LVU-utredningen.* Stockholm: Socialdepartementet.

Vinnerljung B. and Sallnäs, M. and Kyhle-Westermark, P. (2001) *Sammanbrott i dygnsvården.* Stockholm: Centrum för utvärdering av socialt arbete.

Vinterhed, K. (1985) *De andra föräldrarna.* Stockholm: Skeab.

Wåhlander, E. (1990) *Familjehem - stöd och hjälp.* Stockholm: FOU-rapport nr 133.

Wåhlander, E. (1994) *Att allsidigt belysa barns sociala situation.* Stockholm, Socialtjänsten, FoU-rapport 3.

9 United Kingdom

Clive Sellick

Jurisdiction

The United Kingdom of Great Britain and Northern Ireland (UK) comprises four countries: England, Northern Ireland, Scotland and Wales. Legal and administrative systems vary throughout these four parts of the UK. Scotland has a quite different legal system from the others. All, except England have their own regional governments namely the Scottish Parliament, the Northern Ireland Assembly and the National Assembly for Wales. The most recent 10 yearly census of 2001 collected information about ethnicity and religious identity in the UK. Although the British people are more culturally diverse than ever before, almost 70 per cent describe themselves as white Christians. Most black Britons and those from mixed ethnic backgrounds also described themselves as Christian (71 and 52% respectively). Among other faiths the largest groups were Pakistani Muslims (658,000) and Indian Hindus (467,000) followed by Indian Sikhs (301,000), Bangladeshi Muslims (260,000) and white Jews (252,000). Overall, 15 per cent of the English and Welsh population reported having no religion. There are 21,660,475 households in England and Wales according to the 2001 Census and 30 per cent of these (6.5 million) are one-person households. Almost half of these are one-pensioner only households and three-quarters of these (2,366,000) are occupied by a woman living on her own (Office of National Statistics, 2001).

Social work and social care services in the UK including fostering are delivered at local authority level except in Northern Ireland where these services are provided by the National Health Service. England has the largest number of local authorities (150), representing its population of 49,138, 831 people; Scotland has 32 local authorities for a population of 5,062, 011 people, Wales has 22 local authorities for a population of 2,903,085 people and Northern Ireland has four specialist Health and Social Services Boards made up of 18 Trusts 11 of which provide social services for a population of 1,685,267 people (Office of National Statistics, 2001). Until recently social services departments in England and Wales were distinct from other welfare agencies such as health and education. Recent developments have occurred which will bring together children's services at local level in respect of education, social work and some health care. Children's Trusts are planned to be in place in England by 2006 with multi-agency teams based in schools and children's centres delivering integrated children's services (DoH, 2003a). In Scotland social work departments have included criminal justice including probation functions. In Northern Ireland Health and Social Services Boards have functioned jointly at local authority level for many years with social work including fostering services being delivered by local trusts. Each country in the UK receives regular government scrutiny and details of policy and practice reviews and inspections of fostering and other child care services are publicly available (see for example, Department for Education and Skills, 2003; National Assembly for Wales, 2003; NIDHSSPS, 2003; and Scottish Executive, 2003). The many similarities and differences in the way in which social services are organised and delivered in the UK have been studied extensively and specialist publications are available which allow detailed comparisons to be made (see for example Payne and Shardlow, 2002).

Dominant Political System

The UK has a democratic government structure with a constitutional monarchy. The Queen is the head of state occupying a largely ceremonial position whilst the prime minister is the head of government comprising the prevailing political party of which they are a member. Britain has been governed by one of two major political parties for almost a century. In the recent past the Conservative Party had an unbroken period of power between 1979 and 1997. Since then the Labour Party has been in power having won three consecutive election victories in 1997, 2001 and 2005. Considerable constitutional and political reform has taken place since 1997. Power has been devolved to a lesser or greater degree to the populations of Northern Ireland, Scotland and Wales. Britain, which has the fourth strongest economy in the world, is a member of the European Union which currently comprises 25 countries.

Dominant Welfare System

The shape and substance of Britain's welfare system have shifted from the neo-liberal approach of the Thatcher and post-Thatcher Conservative years (Clarke and Langan, 1994; Pringle, 1998) to a more mixed economy of care since the election of a Labour government. Described by friends and critics alike as 'New Labour' there has not been a clear leftward shift in direction for Britain's welfare services. Rather the government 'has championed a 'third way' between state monopoly welfare and private market provision' (Alcock and Craig, 2001: 125). This is particularly well illustrated by the government's intention that local authorities should commission fostering services from non-governmental organisations (NGOs) including those in the private sector. A government initiative, *Choice Protects* (Department of Health, 2003b) has provided £113 million (USD 193 million) to help local authorities improve services for looked after children. The money has been used to expand and strengthen fostering services in 2003–4, including the support of foster carers to develop their skills and retain their services and the commissioning of placements and related health and educational services for fostered children.

History and Origins of Foster Family Care for Children and Youth

Foster care in its current form has been available in the UK since the middle of the last century, principally following the end of the Second World War. For many years before this time early forms of fostering were found for abandoned or orphaned babies who were cared for by 'wet nurses' and older children who were 'boarded out' (a term which was commonly used until the implementation of the Children Act 1989) as apprentices or domestic servants (Triseliotis et al., 1995; Hendrick, 1997). The 1948 Children Act, which introduced local government based professional social work departments for children and families in England and Wales, emphasised the importance of foster care over residential care for children separated from their families. As a result by 1956 45 per cent of children in care were fostered, from a figure of 35 per cent in 1949 (Thoburn, 1999). This figure has continued to grow and has stabilised in England over the past several years to the current figure of 68 per cent (Department for Education and Skills, 2003).

Service Provision in the Area of Foster Care

Foster family care in the UK is provided by governmental and non-governmental fostering agencies. The former belong to public sector local authorities and the latter to not-for-profit voluntary child-care organisations and private not-for-profit independent fostering providers (IFPs). A small proportion of fostering agencies in the NGO sector have a religious, generally Christian, ethos but most of these are secular based agencies. Considerable legal and policy guidance exists to direct foster care practice. The British government has introduced *National Minimum Standards* for fostering as a part of its statutory regulations (DoH, 2002). These regulations relate to the assessment, training, approval and supervision of foster carers and to the conduct and organisation of fostering agencies across the public, private and independent sectors. All fostering agencies are inspected each year and judged against agreed standards which are set out in these regulations. Fostering in Britain has received considerable research scrutiny and the Social Care Institute for Excellence has recently published a research and practice review of innovative fostering in all sectors across the UK (Sellick and Howell, 2003).

The public sector remains the major provider of foster care placements in Britain. However British local authorities have experienced a major shortage in the supply of public sector foster carers and this has had a major impact on the lack of placement choice. Only 20 per cent of English local authorities reported that they could always offer a foster placement of choice for children aged under 10 years and only three per cent for children over that age (Waterhouse, 1997). In Scotland almost 30 per cent of children could not be placed and a further 14 per cent were not in a foster placement of first choice (Triseliotis et al, 2000).

As a result of the crisis in recruiting and retaining local authority foster carers the NGO fostering sector has grown rapidly since the early 1990s. A survey of IFPs in 2001 found that there are now almost as many of these agencies, the majority of which are in England, as there are English local authorities and that at that time approximately 11 per cent of fostered children were placed with IFP foster carers (Sellick and Connolly, 2002). This figure is likely to have grown since then. IFPs provide foster placements to local authorities when these are not available within the public sector. The financial costs are considerably greater, often three times as much, than local authority placements but IFP placements often provide additional therapeutic and educational services to children many of whom have complex and specialist needs. IFPs also provide a range of support services to foster carers which are associated in the research with foster carer satisfaction and retention (Bebbington and Miles, 1990; Sellick, 1992, 1999 and 2002; and Kirton et al., 2003). As a result of increased British government investment since 1997 fostering services for children and their foster carers in the public sector have also developed significantly (Sellick and Howell, 2004).

Children and Young People Placed in Foster Family Care

Foster care has replaced residential care in the UK as the principal placement of choice for children and young people in public care. In a review of research which looks at foster care effectiveness (Sellick et al., 2004) the authors found that placement patterns differ across the UK. In England 65 per cent, in Northern Ireland 63 per cent and in Wales 74 per cent of children in care are fostered but in Scotland this figure is only 28 per cent. In Scotland children living with their parents under social work supervision from the local authority are included in the official statistics and these make up 45 per cent of the total number of 'looked after' children. Of these a number are young offenders and these are recorded differently elsewhere in the UK. A growing number of children, officially in public care are placed in kinship placements or what are known as 'family and friends' foster care. In Northern Ireland 20 per cent of children on court imposed care orders are placed with their parents as compared with 11 per cent in England and Wales. Four countries with different ways of defining and recording children in foster care makes for complexity but the overall patterns and trends are clear. Most children in public care in the UK are fostered and most of these are with local authority approved non-related or 'stranger' foster carers. However more children are being officially fostered by relatives and as we saw above growing numbers of children are being placed with stranger foster carers in the non-governmental IFPs.

The majority of looked after children in England and Wales (64%), including those who are fostered, are subject to court imposed care orders related to parental abuse or neglect. More boys than girls are in public care: 56 as opposed to 44 per cent. Most children are white, with only 18 per cent of looked after children in England and Wales being described as black or Asian. Of these almost half are of mixed ethnicity (Department for Education and Skills, 2003). As the actual number of children in public care has decreased over the past 25 years a far greater proportion of these have been fostered and the old notion that children are 'unfosterable' has been challenged. A significant proportion of children in foster care in all sectors display the kind of behavioural and emotional difficulties which place considerable demands upon their foster families and agencies. In an extensive study of fostering in seven English local authorities the researchers found that over half of the children referred for placement were said by their social workers to present emotional or behavioural problems and a further 10 per cent had a disability or health problem. As these researchers put it foster children:

> *... might steal, lie, break things, have tantrums, refuse to eat, smear walls, wet their beds, refuse to bath, continually defy their carers, set light to their bedding, take overdoses, make sexual advances to other children, expose themselves in public, make false allegations, attack others, truant, take drugs or get into trouble with the police.*
>
> (Sinclair et al., 2000: 3)

Children are staying longer in foster care and this is related to the degree of difficulty which they have experienced as well as the often lengthy and complex legal and psychosocial assessments which they receive. Detailed information about the length of time spent in care and the number of placements experienced is available only for children in England. Of these a quarter had been in the same placement for a year or less but a further quarter had been in placements for five years or longer (Sellick et al., 2004). In a recent review of fostering practice in the UK the authors came across many fostering programmes in all sectors which have been established as alternatives to residential placements. There are for example fostering schemes for young people who sexually abuse others, children with significant disabilities and health problems and unaccompanied asylum seekers (Sellick and Howell, 2003). There have also been significant developments in foster care for young offenders including fostering for those on remand from the courts (Lipscombe, 2003) and those who might otherwise be in secure care (Walker at al., 2002). These approaches to caring for young people in trouble with the law provide significant social, emotional, physical and psychological advantages for many children and young people, particularly when compared with the potentially damaging effects of incarceration.

Foster Family Care Providers

The characteristics of British foster carers have changed very little in the past 40 or so years even though the nature of their tasks and the types and needs of children have changed significantly. Most foster carers are in long-term heterosexual partnerships and the majority of these are married. Most are described as white British and have children of their own. Many have traditional life styles where the male partner has a full-time job outside the home and the female partner works either part-time or as a full-time foster carer (Sinclair et al., 2000; Triseliotis et al., 2000). The traditional profile of foster carers is as true of the independent sector as it is of the local authority sector. In their survey of IFPs in England, Scotland and Wales the researchers found that of the 1,819 foster households (including both couple and single foster carers) 1,416 were in heterosexual partnerships of whom 1,269 were married (Sellick and Connolly, 2002). However these researchers also discovered that the high percentage of foster carer couples 'almost certainly conceals the large number of men who provide a joint service (and are occasionally the principal carer) with their female partners' in the IFP sector (Sellick and Connolly, 2002: 112). Kinship foster carers are estimated to be in the region of 18 per cent of foster carers in the UK (Richards and Tapsfield, 2003). The majority are grandparents, older, poorer, more likely to be headed by single women and with greater health needs than 'stranger' foster carers (Flynn, 2002).

The practice of approving foster carers follows similar guidelines and procedures across public, private and independent fostering agencies. Research messages are available to social workers about the effective recruitment, assessment and training of potential foster carers and the support and further training of approved foster carers (see for example Triseliotis et al., 1995 and 2000 and Sellick et al., 2004). Foster carers are licensed only after thorough assessments of their suitability have taken place via a home study and various health and police checks. Most fostering agencies have moved towards a competence based, strengths-focused approach where potential carers are well informed and prepared before seeking approval by a panel of local experts.

Financial Support for Foster Carers

Although the present UK government has introduced a minimum wage, currently there is no equivalent standard minimum income for foster carers. Payments for foster carers are in two parts. All foster carers receive an allowance which is calculated to cover the costs of the children's care such as their clothing, food, sports, cultural and leisure activities and birthday and other gifts. A growing number of agencies in the public sector and almost all in the non-governmental sector pay foster carers a fee which acknowledges the occupational nature of fostering. Fees and allowances vary considerably across the UK and in their study of IFAs Sellick and Connolly (2002) found wide discrepancies between agencies. Until recently allowances were non-taxable and fees were taxable. However the Inland Revenue has introduced rules aimed at simplifying and standardising the tax burden for foster carers in Britain. Foster carers can now earn a fixed amount (£10,000 or USD 17,000 for the year 2003–4) and an amount per week per child (currently £200-£250 per week or the equivalent of USD 340 to 425) depending on the child's age before incurring tax liability (Inland Revenue, 2002). As fostering is now considered a 'home responsibility' foster carers are entitled to receive state pensions.

Major Issues in Foster Family Care Serving Children and Youth

Contemporary foster care in Britain is facing several challenges which have both policy and psychosocial implications. For example:

- More children require longer term placements when they cannot safely return home or be found adoptive parents. These placements need to be found, resourced and supported to provide young people with a real sense of permanence and belonging.
- Children and young people, especially those with early experiences of abuse and neglect require a range of assistance and therapy over time in foster care.
- Foster care providers across sectors need to work together to maximise foster carer recruitment and placement choice when these are in short supply.
- There is a need to recognise and balance the two wings of foster care: a vocational activity motivated by the wish to nurture children and a professional occupation delivered by well trained foster carers in collaboration with social work, education and health care professionals.
- Although fostered children and their carers are more involved in appraising and influencing policy and practice, the parents and other birth relatives of fostered children are not (Sellick and Howell, 2004).

Future Trends in Foster Family Care

Foster care in the UK is no longer a predominantly public sector activity. In the past few years there has been a rapid and significant expansion in the use of kinship placements and in the commissioning of non-governmental independent fostering providers. Britain now has, and is very likely to retain, a mixed economy of foster care provision. As a result fostering agencies are entering into partnership or service level agreements usually in small regional clusters which determine issues such as the levels of fees and other costs which local authorities are charged by the IFPs, the numbers and types of placements and the provision of associated education, health and other services.

The professionalisation of foster care is also likely to gather pace. The acceptance that the children placed are more challenging and difficult and that foster care requires trained and supervised carers to function effectively will support the move towards a better paid and recognised career of foster care. Fostering agencies are likely to continue to increase their support services to foster carers both to develop their practice in this demanding field and to retain their services.

Foster Care Research

Foster care research is both extensive and well established in the UK as the following summary of relevant, published studies shows:

- Aldgate and Bradley (1999) investigated the use of short-term fostering as a family support service to prevent long-term family breakdown. Service arrangements and provision were studied in four local authorities and the progress of 60 children was measured by exploring the views of social workers, carers, parents and the children themselves.
- Padbury and Frost (2002: 3) examined how 'young people in foster care are listened to and involved - ranging from day to day decisions to wider decisions involving policy making'. A total of 169 interviews took place and more than one-third of these were with fostered children and young people between the ages of eight and 18.
- Pithouse et al. (2000) used national census data on 'looked after' children to provide a snapshot of foster care in Wales. More recently, Perez-del Aguila et al. (2003) examined key service elements likely to

promote effective outcomes in relation to stability and continuity of fostering placements in Wales.

- Schofield (2003) conducted a qualitative study of 40 adults who grew up in long-term foster care. Schofield and her colleagues are also conducting a longitudinal study of children currently growing up in long-term foster care placements (Schofield et al., 2000; Beek and Schofield, 2004). These studies have demonstrated the diversity of experience and social work practice, but have emphasised the way in which foster families can provide a family for life and that both close attachment relationships and family membership contribute to good outcomes.
- Sellick (1999), Sellick and Connolly (2002) and Sellick and Howell (2004) conducted three related studies. The first evaluated one large Independent Fostering Agency from the perspectives of local authority social workers and the agency's foster carers. Emerging from this a survey of 55 IFAs in England, Scotland and Wales explored this sector's services, costs, size and staffing as well as the needs and characteristics of the children placed. The third study examined multi-sectoral fostering services across the U.K.
- Sinclair et al. (2000) conducted extensive research which included information on over 1,500 foster carers from seven English local authorities and 500 placements. The research comprised three linked studies which focused on the experience of foster carers and their need for support, foster placements and their outcomes and what happened to foster children over a three year period.
- Triseliotis et al. (2000) conducted an extensive foster care study in two parts which took place in all 32 Scottish local authorities and one voluntary organisation between 1996 and 1998. Its major aims were to establish the characteristics, motives, social circumstances and experiences of foster carers and to identify and assess departmental fostering policies, structures and services.

The following three publications provide further information on foster care in Britain:

Sellick, C. and Howell, D. (2004) A Description and Analysis of Multi-Sectoral Fostering in the United Kingdom. *British Journal of Social Work*. 34: 4, 481–99.

Sellick, C., Thoburn, J. and Philpot, T. (2004) *What Works in Adoption and Foster Care?* London. Barnardo's.

Sinclair, I., Wilson, K. and Gibbs, I. (2004) *Foster Placements: Why They Succeed and Why They Fail*. London: Jessica Kingsley Publishers.

Conclusion

Foster care remains a significant and much developed tool of social policy in the UK for children and young people in state care. However, although fostering in the British Isles has traditionally been an almost exclusively public sector activity, this is no longer the case. Likewise, children are not simply cared for by unrelated stranger foster carers. In the past few years, there has been a rapid and significant expansion in the commissioning of non-governmental independent fostering agencies or providers and in the use of kinship placements. Britain now has, and is very likely to retain, a mixed economy of foster care provision.

References

Alcock, P. and Craig, G (2001) The United Kingdom: Rolling back the Welfare State? In Alcock, P. and Craig, G (Eds.) *International Social Policy: Welfare Regimes in the Developed World*. Basingstoke: Palgrave.

Aldgate, J. and Bradley, M. (1999) *Supporting Families through Short Term Fostering*. London. The Stationary Office.

Bebbington, A. and Miles, J. (1990) The Supply of Foster Families for Children in Care. *British Journal of Social Work*. 20: 283–307.

Beek, M. and Schofield, G. (2004) *Providing a Secure Base in Foster Care*. London. BAAF.

Clarke, J. and Langan, M. (1994) Restructuring Welfare: The British Welfare Regime in the 1980s. In Cochrane, A. and Clarke, J. (Eds) *Comparing Welfare States: Britain in International Context*. London: Sage Publications.

DfES (2003) *Children Looked After in England: 2002–2003*. Issue No 06/03. November.

DoH (2002) *Fostering Service Regulations: National Minimum Standards*. London. The Stationary Office.

DoH (2003a) *Children's Trusts*. www.doh.gov.uk/childrenstrusts/index

DoH (2003b) *Choice Protects.* www.doh.gov.uk/choiceprotects.

Flynn, R. (2002) Kinship Foster Care: Research Review. *Child and Family Social Work.* 7: 4, 311–21.

Hendrick, H. (1997) *Children, Childhood and English Society 1880–1990.* Cambridge University Press.

Inland Revenue (2002) *Foster Care Relief.* www.inlandrevenue.gov.uk/local.

Kirton, D., Ogilvie, K. and Beecham, J. (2003) *Remuneration and Performance in Foster Care.* University of Kent at Canterbury.

Lipscombe, J. 2003 Another Side of Life: Foster Care for Young People on Remand. *Youth Justice.* 3: 1, 34–48.

National Assembly for Wales. (2003) *Improving Placement Choice and Stability for Children and Young People Looked After: Strategic Framework.* Cardiff. National Assembly for Wales.

NIDHSSPS (2003) *Community Statistics, 1 April 2000 – 31 March 2001.* Belfast. Northern Ireland Department of Health, Social Services and Public Safety.

Office of National Statistics (2001) *Census 2001.* www.statistics.gov.uk/census 2001/pyramids.

Padbury, P. and Frost, N. (2002) *Solving Problems in Foster Care.* The Children's Society.

Payne, M. and Shardlow, S. (2002) *Social Work in the British Isles.* London. Jessica Kingsley Publishers.

Perez-del-Aguila, R. et al. (2003) *Overview and Survey of Effectiveness of Interventions to Promote Stability and Continuity of Care for Looked After Children.* Cardiff University School of Social Sciences.

Pithouse, A. et al. (2000) *A Study of the placement of Looked After Children in Wales.* Cardiff University.

Pringle, K. (1998) *Children and Social Welfare in Europe.* Buckingham: Open University Press.

Richards, A. and Tapsfield, R. (2003) *Funding Family and Friends Care: the way forward.* London: Family Rights Group.

Schofield, G. (2003) *Part of the Family: Pathways Through Foster Care.* London. BAAF.

Schofield, G., Beek, M., Sargent, K. and Thoburn, J. (2000) *Growing up in Foster Care.* London. BAAF.

Scottish Executive (2003) *Children Looked After in the Year to 31 March 2001.* Edinburgh. Scottish Executive.

Sellick, C. (1992) *Supporting Short Term Foster Carers.* Aldershot: Avebury.

Sellick, C. (1999) Independent Fostering Agencies: Providing High Quality Services to Children and Carers? *Adoption and Fostering.* 23: 4, 7–14.

Sellick, C. (2002) The aims and Principles of Independent Fostering Agencies: A View From the Inside. *Adoption and Fostering.* 26: 1, 56–63.

Sellick, C. and Connolly, J. (2002) Independent Fostering Agencies Uncovered: the Findings of a National Study. *Child and Family Social Work.* 7: 2, 107–20.

Sellick, C. and Howell, D. (2003) *Innovative, Tried and Tested: A Review of Good Practice in Fostering.* Social Care Institute for Excellence. Bristol: Policy Press.

Sellick, C. and Howell, D. (2004) A Description and Analysis of Multi-Sectoral Fostering in the United Kingdom. *British Journal of Social Work.* 34: 4, 481–99.

Sellick, C., Thoburn, J. and Philpot, T. (2004) *What Works in Adoption and Foster Care?* London: Barnardo's.

Sinclair, I., Wilson, K. and Gibbs, I. (2000) *Supporting Foster Placements. Reports 1, 2 and 3.* University of York. (www.york.ac.uk/inst/swrdu/fosterplacements).

Thoburn, J. (1999) Trends in Foster Care and Adoption. In Stevenson, O. (Ed.) *Child Welfare in the United Kingdom 1948–1998.* Oxford: Blackwell Science.

Triseliotis, J., Borland, M. and Hill, M. (2000) *Delivering Foster Care.* London: BAAF.

Triseliotis, J., Sellick, C, and Short, R. (1995) *Foster Care: Theory and Practice.* London: Batsford.

Walker, M., Hill, M. and Triseliotis, J. (2002) *Testing the Limits of Foster Care: Fostering as an Alternative to Secure Accommodation.* London: BAAF.

Waterhouse, S. (1997) *The Organisation of Fostering Services: A Study of the Arrangements for Delivery of Fostering Services in England.* London: NFCA.

10 United States

Kathryn Wehrmann, Yvonne Unrau and Judy Martin

Introduction

The US family foster care system is embedded in a complex child welfare system that encompasses governmental agencies at the federal, state, and local level; juvenile and family courts; and private social service agencies. The belief that children have a right to a permanent place to grow up underpins child welfare practice and is the ideological basis for current legislation that specifies timeframes within which children are to be returned to their families or placed with an adoptive family or other option considered appropriate to their age and needs. Despite the positive intent underlying this policy, family foster care in the US and its effectiveness on behalf of children and families is greatly affected by judicial oversight, availability of services, and a social context in which families have needs that extend beyond those that the child welfare system can fully address.

Jurisdiction

With 9.6 million square kilometres of land, the US is nearly 2.5 times larger than Western Europe and half the size of Russia (CIA, 2002). It is home to over 281 million people, 69 per cent of whom self-identify as being white, 13 per cent Hispanic or Latino, 12 per cent black or African-American, four per cent Asian, less than one per cent American Indian or Alaskan Native, and less than one per cent of another race (US Census, 2000). These percentages take into account the fact that individuals responding to the census could choose more than one racial category, which was a new option in the most recent census. The Bureau of Census projects that minority groups will account for almost half the US population by 2050. The changing population is explained in part by immigration (including refugees) of Asian and Hispanic peoples and declining fertility rates among Caucasians (United States Information Agency, 1999).

The US has high rates of poverty despite being one of the richest nations in the world. The official measure of poverty is set by the US Census Bureau which declares a money threshold that varies by family size. For example, a three-person household with one child under the age of 18 years earning less than USD 14,480 per year is defined as living in poverty. The threshold for a three-person household with two children is USD 14,494 (Proctor and Dalaker, 2003). In 2002 the US poverty rate was 12.1 per cent, with 34.6 million people living in poverty (Proctor and Dalaker, 2003). The rate was higher among African-Americans (23.9 to 24.1%), Hispanics (21.8%), female headed households with no husband (26.5%), and families with children under the age of 18 years (16.3%) or under six years (18.5%) (Proctor and Dalaker, 2003). Shamefully, many US families living in poverty are employed in the labor market. The government provides a 'safety net' of social and economic services for families; however, it is not sufficient to meet basic needs.

Publicly funded social services in the United States are primarily organised by the federal government, which has responsibility for issuing service guidelines, eligibility criteria for funding (federal reimbursement), and accountability mechanisms. In turn, states and counties individually translate federal statutes by either further stipulating service guidelines or delineating statewide practice policies within their jurisdictions (Segal and Brzuzy, 1998; Stein, 1998). While the amount of federal assistance given to each state varies, on average, it accounts for an estimated 43 per cent of state operating funds (Stein, 1998). The majority of social service delivery is offered by the state or county public agencies or by private sector agencies that rely partially or wholly on state funds to operate.

Dominant Political System

The United States is a constitution-based federal republic with a strong democratic tradition (CIA, 2002). Democratic ideals in the United States draw from four key elements: (1) people are the ultimate source of the government's authority, (2) representative government, (3) checks and balances, and (4) federalism (i.e. division of authority between the states and the national government to avoid abuse of power by either level). These elements sustain a government that is comprised of federal, state, and local laws, bodies, and agencies that carry out the operations of the United States.

Congruent with democratic ideals, the economy of the United States is based on principles of capitalism whereby citizens and residents are expected to participate in the marketplace to earn their living. To make it possible for people without sufficient resources to participate in the capitalist economy and to maintain order, 'the government plays a key role in maintaining society's social well being' (Segal and Brzuzy, 1998: 10). Franklin Delano Roosevelt's *New Deal*, a set of government policies and programmes designed to respond to widespread poverty in The Great Depression of the 1930s, created a greatly expanded role for government in the provision of welfare services. Since then public social welfare programmes have become more numerous and more widely accepted, as the country experienced continuous improvement in social conditions and economic prosperity.

Dominant Welfare System

The system of welfare in the United States is a product of two competing ideologies: individualism and institutionalism (Segal and Brzuzy, 1998). The ideology of individualism holds that the individual is responsible for dealing with human difficulties. It argues for a residual approach to governmental intervention whereby welfare services should only be offered when the normal resources of the family and marketplace break down, after problems have been identified. In contrast, the societal or institutional approach holds that society as a whole is responsible for dealing with difficulties. It argues that welfare programmes should be built into the basic social structure and considered an entitlement. With its focus on prevention and collective responsibility, the institutional approach accepts that any citizen might need the assistance of welfare services at some point in life.

US public policy is, in fact, the product of conflicts between these two approaches. Welfare policies emerge incrementally out of debates among policy makers who deliberate existing policies, programmes and expenditures. This approach keeps discussion narrow and diminishes the likelihood of major policy shifts (DiNitto, 2000). Overall, the residual approach has prevailed in policy debates, as evidenced by a categorically-defined welfare system; that is, services are classified by explicit criteria that determine who qualifies for service and how much service the eligible candidate will receive. Most public services are available only to those who demonstrate a need, and the burden of proof typically rests on the individual in need.

Federal welfare systems that provide out-of-home care for children include: child welfare (serving dependent and maltreated children), mental health (serving children with emotional and psychiatric needs), and juvenile justice (serving children who have violated the law). Each system is operated by a separate division of government. Foster care is a core service in child welfare, accounting for USD 9.1 billion of the total USD 20 billion spent on child welfare services in fiscal year 2000. In contrast, the mental health and juvenile justice systems have only experimented with family foster care, and more commonly rely on institutional care facilities. Many children face issues that are addressed by multiple systems. However, in keeping with a categorical system of services set by government, the general rule is that children may be served by only one system at a time. For example, in some states a child in foster care who is sentenced to a juvenile detention centre for an extended length of time will be discharged from the child welfare system. Two major problems faced by the separation of these systems is spillover of children from one system to another as resources wax and wane, and children who fall between the gaps when system transfer fails.

History and Origins of Foster Family Care for Children and Youth

The beginnings of the present day foster family care in the United States trace back to the mid-1850s as part of a church effort when Reverend Charles Loring Brace began the 'Placing Out System' of the New York Children's Aid Society in an effort to rescue children who were either orphaned or whose parents were considered inadequate. Between 1854 and1929 approximately 100,000 children, many of whom were immigrants, were transferred by train — 'orphan trains' — from the streets of New York to the Midwestern, Western, and Southern states. Children were placed with families who agreed to raise them in exchange for their labor. In 1874, New York was the first state to pass legislation designed to protect and safeguard the rights of children, and, by 1886 Charles Birtwell of the Boston Children's Aid Society pioneered use of foster family care as a means of reuniting children with their biological families.

The federal government entered the child welfare scene in 1909 with the first White House Conference on Children, which established the goal of providing a 'secure and loving home for each child,' and signaled the beginning of an American child welfare system that would include both public (government) and private (e.g., church) agencies. In 1912 the US Children's Bureau was established under the auspices of the federal government to 'plan, integrate, and advocate national programs on behalf of children' (National Association of Social Workers, 1999).

Present day policies that directly affect foster family care were stimulated by the work of Dr. C. Henry Kempe, Elizabeth Elmer, and others who in the 1960s publicly documented incidents of severe physical child abuse; a phenomenon that eventually came to be known as the 'battered child syndrome.' A growing body of medical evidence prompted policy debate that eventually produced the Child Abuse and Prevention Act of 1974, which introduced mandated reporting of child abuse and neglect by health care professionals and resulted in an increased number of children entering foster care. Table 1 summarises key federal legislation impacting foster family care over the past 30 years. Each new law was created as policy makers debated contentious issues such as, the overrepresentation of children of colour in care, transracial placements, returning children to their families (reunification), and the preparedness of foster youth aging out of care.

Service Provision in the Area of Foster Care

The major types of organisations involved in the delivery of foster family care in the United States are characterised as rational or bureaucratic. Although federal and state government influences every level of program services, the variation in foster care programmes across states complicates any discussion of a 'national' programme (Courtney, 1995). While most states are organised such that the public child welfare agency relies on separate private agencies to deliver foster care services (Bess et al., 2002), there is variation in the degree to which contracted (private) providers are used to deliver foster care services across the states. For example, Texas rejected the idea of contracting services after a pilot project determined that privatised services were not cost-effective (Bess et al., 2002). In contrast, Illinois, with approximately 70 per cent of its foster children placed in the care of private agency foster homes, recognise contracted providers as a 'major program partner in delivering foster care' (Illinois Department of Children and Family Services, 2003). In all states, either the state or its designated county child welfare agency is responsible for monitoring private contracts.

While there is a substantial and growing amount of research and administrative data on family foster care in the US, none specifically targets the study of organisations providing foster family care. However, it can be said that most organisations (public or private) that deliver foster family care are private, non-profit, and multifunctional. While private organisations exist separate from public or state departments, they are not necessarily independent of the state since public monies are a major source of their funding. As multifunctional agencies, they offer a variety of social services (e.g., foster care, residential care, in-home family support services) so that if funding for one type of service is cut, the organisation can still survive (Bellini, 2003).

Data describing the extent to which private organisations delivering foster care are

Table 1: Federal Legislation Pertaining to Foster Family Care in the United States

Federal Legislation	Emphasis
Child Abuse Prevention and Treatment Act of 1974 Public Law (P.L.) 93–247	Made financial assistance available for prevention and treatment programs, and established the National Center on Child Abuse and Neglect. Financial incentives were offered to states that passed laws that mandated health care professionals to report suspected cases of child abuse and neglect. All states in the US currently have such laws.
Indian Child Welfare Act (ICWA) of 1978 P.L. 95–608	Stipulated the order of placement considerations for Native American children who came to the attention of child welfare. The emphasis was to keep children with extended family and within tribal communities, and to recognise tribal courts as having jurisdiction in child welfare issues involving Native Americans.
Adoption Assistance and Child Welfare Act of 1980 P.L. 96–272	Offered states financial incentives (under Section 427 of the Social Security Act, Title IV-B) to curtail 'foster care drift' or the length of time that children were spending in foster care, and to make 'reasonable efforts' to reunite children with their families of origin, and failing reunification to seek other permanent placements outside the foster care system. Mandated case reviews every six months, and court hearing every 18 months to monitor progress on permanency planning for each child.
Multiethnic Placement Act (MEPA) of 1994 P.L.103–82	Prohibited racial or ethnic discrimination in making placement decisions but permitted agencies to consider race, color, or national origin of children and prospective parents when deciding on a suitable foster home. Required states to recruit a racially and ethnically diverse pool of eligible foster parents to match the needs of children in care.
Interethnic Placement Act (IEPA) of 1996 P.L. 104–188	The provision in MEPA that permitted consideration of race, color, and national origin as a factor in child placement decisions was repealed. Prohibited any organisations making a foster care placement to 'delay' or 'deny' a child's placement based on the race, colour, or national origin of either the child or prospective parent. Financial penalties were imposed with any violations.
Adoption and Safe Families Act (ASFA) of 1997 P.L. 105–89	Required states to develop standards for monitoring children's health and safety while in foster care. ASFA also introduced more specific (and less stringent) criteria and timelines for terminating parental rights and ensuring that every child's case is periodically reviewed by the state and the courts. Provided states with financial incentives to increase the number of adoptions of foster children. Since ASFA's enactment, the number of adoptions of children in foster care has greatly increased. Most of the adoptions of children in foster care have been by children's former foster parents.
The Foster Care Independence Act of 1999 P.L. 106–169	Ensured that foster care agencies address personal, social, financial, and health care needs of young men and women (age 18 to 21) that moved out of foster care to live on their own. The focus was to achieve better outcomes in areas such as education, employment, and adequate housing, as well as reducing problems such as early parenthood and incarceration.

religiously oriented also were not available. However, as previously mentioned, churches have had a central role in foster family care since the mid-1800s. In more recent times, the trend has been for faith-based social service organisations to rely more on public funds versus private contributions (Degeneffe, 2003). Since public funds are a source of more predictable revenues (Kingma, 1993), it is likely that this trend will continue.

There is no formal mechanism for licensing organisations that provide foster family care; however, we identify five interrelated nationwide processes that act as regulatory mechanisms by shaping how foster family care is delivered throughout the United States:

- *Federal legislation* (see Table 1) stipulates programme parameters and priorities designed to influence 'policy-preferred' action among states in practice areas such as placement decision making, children's well-being, family reunification, and other avenues for exiting foster care to permanent placements (Pecora et al., 2000).
- *Federal reimbursement* is the mechanism by which states receive repayment of funds spent in accordance with specific federal legislation. Overall, reimbursement is set up to give states incentives to develop 'policy-preferred' programmes advocated for in legislation or, in some cases, penalties are issued for non-compliance.
- *Federal reporting* is inextricably linked to federal reimbursement. For instance, maintenance funds are paid quarterly (four times per year), which places a huge administrative burden on the states (Geen, 2000). Furthermore, states are required to maintain records for audit purposes (Catolog of Federal Domestic Assistance, 2003).
- *Federal lawsuits* play a function in shaping foster care service delivery. For example, in 1979 the Supreme Court of the United States (the highest court in the land) ruled that kin (or relatives) of foster children are entitled to receive the same Federal financial support for providing foster care as non-kin (*Miller vs. Youakim*, 440 US 125). The ruling effectively changed the pool of eligible foster parents that could care for children in state custody.
- *Accreditation* is increasingly being relied on by the federal government in an effort to have objective bodies give official endorsement that organisations have complied with stated standards of practice. The Council on Accreditation (COA) founded by the Child Welfare League of America is presently the major player in this regard. The presence and impact of COA varies across states. For example, two states (Illinois and Michigan) each have more than 100 social service organisations accredited by COA, while 24 states have less than 10. Although the COA has accredited 268 organisations in the United States that provide foster (and kinship) care, they state 'with great certainty [COA] does not accredit the majority of agencies that provide foster care [in the US]' (Joseph Seoane, personal communication, 2003).

Children and Young People Placed in Foster Family Care

The population for which US foster family care is intended is children that have been abused or neglected. While some states only provide services to abused and neglected children, others also serve delinquent, homeless, or runaway youth (Bess et al., 2002). Nationally, the focus on serving abused and neglected children has become more intense over time. In 1977, 45 per cent of child welfare cases received social services because of abuse and neglect, compared to 80 per cent in 1994 (US DHHS, 1997).

National data and other research (Wulczyn, Hislop, and Goerge, 2000) have consistently reported that children of colour are overrepresented in the foster care system. (See Table 2.) Race, poverty, and single parenthood are entwined when considering the plight of children (and families) of colour and foster care placement because single parenthood and poverty also disproportionately affect children of colour (Proctor and Dalaker, 2003).

Table 3 shows that on 30 September 2001 three out of four children in out-of-home placements in the US were in foster care settings, and one in five was placed in group home (typically with six beds) or institutional settings (can house hundreds of children but are usually subdivided into grouped living quarters of six to 12 beds). For half of children in care, the plan was to reunify with parents or live with other relatives (Table 3). These figures underestimate the total number of children in care during the year, since a substantial number experience stays in care of less than one year (Martin, 2000). Also underestimated is the total number of children served by the broader child welfare system (e.g., children that are monitored by the state but permitted to remain at home with the receipt of in-home services).

Although research comparing children served by in-home services, foster care services, and group or institutional care is somewhat fragmented, there appears to be a continuum of

Table 2: Population of Children in Foster Care and in the United States by Race

	Children in foster care AFCARS 2001[a]	Children in US census 2000[b]	Ratio: # of children in foster care-to- # of children in US population		
	$N = 542{,}000$	$N = 72{,}293{,}812$			
Race of Children	**Per cent**	**Per cent**			
Some other race alone	3	<1	3	-to-	1
Black or African American alone	38	15	2.5	-to-	1
American Indian/Alaska Native alone	2	1	2	-to-	1
Hispanic or Latino	17	17	1	-to-	1
Native Hawaiian/Other Pacific Islander alone	0[c]	<1	1	-to-	1
Asian alone	1	3	1	-to-	3
White alone	37	61	1	-to-	1.6
Two or more races Non-Hispanic	2	3	1	-to-	1.5

[a] *The AFCARS REPORT: Preliminary FY 2001 Estimates as of March 2003 (8)* US Department of Health and Human Services, (2003).
[b] Source: 2000 Census of Population and Housing, SF3 Data Set, Table P4.
[c] Interpreted as <1.

services related to children's need. Specifically, children who receive in-home services as an alternative to out of home placement have fewer problems on average than children who are placed. Among children in out of home care, those with the least severe problems are placed in traditional foster care, which provides food, shelter, and basic care needs available in a family setting. Children who exhibit emotional or behavioural problems, or who have special medical needs are more often placed in treatment foster care where foster parents are trained to care for children's special needs. Finally, children presenting severe problems that cannot safely be managed in family settings are placed in group care or institutional settings, which are considered the most restrictive placement for out of home care in the US. Children served in group care tend to be older, more seriously disturbed (emotionally and behaviourally), and struggle more with issues of acculturation and racism compared to children in treatment foster homes. In addition, children infected with HIV/AIDS (a relatively small number in the US) are most likely to be placed in group settings (Berrick, Courtney, and Barth, 1993).

Foster Family Care Providers

In the United States, three types of foster care providers are available to children: kinship foster homes (selected because the providers have an ongoing, close relationship to the foster child), non-kin homes (selected because the providers are qualified and licensed to care for the child), and treatment foster homes (selected because the child's physical or psychological challenges require more extensive and intensive care). In Table 3, the numbers of children placed in treatment foster care are counted as foster family placements.

Children in foster care may be placed in homes recruited and licensed by the public child welfare agency or by a private agency. Private agencies may have religious or secular roots. Private agency placements are supported by

Table 3: Placement Settings and Case Goals of Foster Children in the United States on September 30, 2001 (N = 542,000)

Placement Settings	**Per cent**	**Case Goals**	**Per cent**
Pre-adoptive home	4	Reunify with parents/principal caretakers	44
Foster family home (relative)	24	Live with other relatives	5
Foster family home (non-relative)	48	Adoption	22
Group home	8	Long term foster care	8
Institution	10	Emancipation	6
Supervised independent living	1	Guardianship	3
Runaway	2	Case goal not yet established	11
Trial home visit	3		

Data Source: The Adoption and Foster Care Analysis and Reporting System (AFCARS), mandated by the US Congress, requires states to collect case-specific data on all children in foster care for whom the state child welfare agency has responsibility for placement, care, or supervision. States also collect and report data on all children adopted with the involvement of public child welfare agencies. These data support program management and policy formulation at the federal, state, and local levels.

public funds through a purchase-of-service arrangement. Homes receiving public funds must meet licensing standards that are set by each of the 50 states. Typically, these standards include verification that the foster parents' home has adequate space for a child and meets sanitary and safety standards, verification that the applicants are healthy enough and have sufficient income to meet basic family needs, verification that the parents have no history of child maltreatment, and assessment of the applicants' parenting abilities and standards. In kinship placements, some or all of these standards may be waived. An Urban Institute analysis (2003) reported that only 15 states have the same requirements for kin and non-kin homes. Twenty states 'have a separate, less stringent licensing process for kin' (See also Leos-Urbel, Bess and Geen, 2002).

The licensing process involves a series of interviews between the child welfare worker and the prospective foster family, home visits, contacts with family references, and completion of required paperwork. In most states, parents are also required to complete pre-service training, which typically includes an overview of the child welfare agency and its foster care policies, material on the causes and consequences of child maltreatment, common adjustment reactions of foster families when foster children move into the home, and some material on preferred child rearing approaches (Martin 2000: 54; see also Rhodes, Orme and Buehler, 2001).

Ideally, the licensing process is one in which the worker facilitates the family's self-evaluation and determination of whether or not fostering is an appropriate choice (Buehler, Cox and Cuddeback, 2003). However, the agency has the final authority to decide whether to license a foster home, and applicants have no right to appeal this decision outside the agency.

In-depth information about the characteristics of foster parents is surprisingly difficult to obtain. Non-kin foster care providers have traditionally come from blue collar or lower middle class backgrounds (James Bell Associates, 1993; Fanshel, 1982). Today, a substantial proportion of these care providers have both parents working outside the home. A comprehensive review of empirical research on the functioning of foster children (Orme and Buehler, 2001) found that approximately 85 per cent of foster parents were considered to have adequate parenting skills.

Kinship caretakers are more likely to be female (grandmothers or aunts of the foster children), non-white, and 'poorer, older, and less well educated' than non-kin foster mothers (Martin 2000: 46; see also Scannapieco and

Hegar, 2002; Ehrle, Geen and Clark, 2001; Orme and Buehler, 2001). Kinship caretakers are more likely to struggle with financial and health issues but are less likely than non-kin caretakers to receive child welfare support in addressing these difficulties.

Financial Support for Foster Parents

In the United States, there has been a great deal of ambivalence about providing financial support for foster parents. In the past, professionals have argued that providing payments might lead foster parents to care for children 'for the money' rather than for more appropriate altruistic motives. This mind-set continues to influence the level of reimbursement provided to foster parents, who are not compensated sufficiently for the costs of maintaining children in their care. Individual states determine the monthly rates paid to foster families, and these rates vary widely. The CWLA's 2001 Agency Survey revealed monthly payment ranges between $216 and $760, with a national average of $418. In the state of Alaska, it is expected that this payment will cover all the basic costs of care, which 'in addition to room and board, clothing, and daily supervision' include 'personal items and grooming care, school supplies and regular school activities, games, toys, etc.' (CWLA, 2000: 4). There are similar expectations in the other states. Foster parents may be provided with additional funds if the children come into care without clothing, if the parents must travel unusual distances to help children receive appropriate medical, educational, or mental health care, if the family needs child-care or respite care services, and when the child is considered sufficiently challenged so as to require treatment foster care services. Over the years, foster parents have voiced insistent concern about the low level of these payments and have noted that foster children are prevented from engaging in educational, recreational, or other activities because foster families simply do not have the funds to pay for them (US DHHS, 2002).

As limited as the level of support is for foster parents in general, the picture is even bleaker for kinship caretakers. Kin foster parents who are not licensed by the child welfare agency are not eligible for foster care payments. Kinship caretakers may be ineligible because they cannot meet licensing standards (when, for example, the caretaker's home is considered too small or does not meet safety standards or when the caretaker's criminal record or child abuse history would preclude licensing). They may also be unlicensed because a state has decided to provide only limited funds to support kinship foster care and they must go on a waiting list and hope to eventually receive funding. Kinship caretakers may be directed to apply for some type of welfare support or may be left on their own to find ways to financially support the children in their care. This is an especially critical issue since approximately 40 per cent of kin caretakers have family incomes that fall below the federal poverty level (Ehrle, Geen and Clark, 2001: 4). Using data from the 1997 National Survey of American Families, the authors found that 'only 53 per cent of all children in kinship care received Medicaid,' despite the fact that all of the children in this type of care are categorically eligible to receive this support. The authors conclude that 'children in all kinship care environments face substantial socioeconomic risk' (5).

Major Issues in Foster Family Care Serving Children and Youth

The development of the US foster care system in the 20th century produced a sophisticated framework for policy and practice of protecting children and aiding families. While the bureaucratic structure of foster care provides a solid organising framework, the system of service delivery remains both complex and vulnerable to social, economic, and political trends. The major issues facing the system lie in the details of service implementation. First, more is known about 'input' (e.g. number of foster homes, children coming into care) and 'output' (e.g., length of stay, discharge placement) than about what goes on during care – or the actual process of fostering. Cultural competence and responsiveness of services for children of colour is an issue of particular importance. A second issue relates to foster parents having the least amount of influence in deciding the needs or fate of foster children, as they are often overlooked in professional decision-making processes. Finally, foster care research, policy, and practice are often vetted through a myopic lens that ignores the reality of foster care, which is situated at a crossroad of multiple systems (education, judicial, mental health, criminal), is straddled across several tiers of bureaucracy, and is expected to address a quagmire of social problems (economic, socio-psychological, interpersonal, racial), all with limited fiscal resources.

Future Trends in Foster Family Care

The devolution of federal responsibility for foster care programming and services to state and local levels is a major trend in the US. Furthermore, federal directives are increasingly focused on 'cost-saving' and less on improving quality of service. However, there are independent research efforts underway to study the impact of foster care on children that grow up in the care of the system (e.g., Pecora et al., 2003). A second and related trend is the focus on obtaining data that account for characteristics of foster children and their exit placement from foster care (outcome) to monitor foster care across the nation. Although considerable funds have been devoted to this effort, these data add little if anything to our understanding of foster children's well-being. It is important to note, however, that in 2000, the Administration for Children and Families Bureau initiated Child and Family Services Reviews intended to assess the effectiveness of state child welfare programmes and implement standards to ensure that children in foster care are provided quality services that protect the safety and health of children (Administration for Children, Youth and Family, 2000). A key component of the review process is the development of programme improvement plans to address identified areas of concern.

Finally, another disconcerting trend in foster care relates to broader welfare reform efforts. In sum, in 1996, public welfare laws were changed to restrict the length of time that families can receive financial and medical benefits. Researchers in foster care believe that as the number of families losing income increases, the number of children entering foster care will increase (Courtney, 1995; Malm et al., 2001).

Foster Care Research

There are many layers of resources that contain research on foster care in the US. Classic research studies by Mass and Engler (1959), Fanshel and Shinn (1978), and Shyne and Schroeder, (1978) exist in published print, as does Martin's (2000) recent writing on the theory and practice of foster family care. In addition to peer-review journals, many commissioned and private research studies can be obtained through national clearing houses and private organisations. The US Children's Bureau has played a major role in facilitating access to these findings.

Conclusion

The US foster family care system is shaped by federal legislation that emphasises permanency for children through reunification with parents, permanent placement with a relative, or adoption. Juvenile courts in each state play a significant role in directing and monitoring the efforts of the vast network of public and private agencies that provide the foster care services that are intended to achieve permanency. Federal policies directing foster care practice are directly linked to identification of 'battered child syndrome' in the 1960s. The development of more recent legislation has occurred as a result of issues including over lengthy stays in foster care, overrepresentation of children of colour in the system, and difficulty in effectively transitioning foster youth to independence as young adults.

Although they generally adhere to the framework created by federal legislation, each state enacts its own legislation dealing with foster care, which leads to variation in how foster care practice is carried out throughout the country. States are free to determine how much of foster care service is provided by public agencies and how much is contracted for from private agencies using tax monies. Each state also determines how private foster care organisations are to be approved or licensed. States also determine the level of reimbursement that both kin and non-kin providers receive.

There are a number of challenges facing the foster care system in the US today. Included among them is the concern that the system is overwhelmed by social problems that affect many of the families that the foster care system is attempting to serve. Most notable among these problems are poverty and substance abuse. It is also worthwhile to note that welfare services of all kinds including foster care are also highly vulnerable to changing agendas depending on the prevailing political philosophy.

References

Administration for Children and Families, Department of Health and Human Services (2000) *Preparing for the Child and Family Service Reviews*. Retrieved November 20, 2003. http://mUSkie.USm.maine.edu/helpkids/pubstext/process.html#Anchor-Preparing-49575.

Barbell, K. and Freundlich, M. (2001) *Foster Care Today*. Washington, DC: Casey Family Programs. Retrieved December 3, 2003. http://www.casey.org/cnc/policy_issues/foster_care_today.htm.

Bellini, G.A. (2003) Insuring Nonprofit and Social Service Organisations. *American Agent and Broker*. 75.

Berrick, J.D., Courtney, M. and Barth, R.P. (1993) Specialised Foster Care and Group Home Care: Similarities and Differences in the Characteristics of Children in Care. *Children and Youth Services Review*. 15, 453–73.

Bess, R. et al. (2002) *The Cost of Protecting Vulnerable Children II: What Factors Affect States' Fiscal Decision*. Occasional Paper Number 61. The Urban Institute: Washington, DC. Retrieved September 5. http://www.urban.org/Template.cfm?NavMenuID = 24andtemplate = /TaggedContent/View Publication.cfmandPublicationID = 8054.

Buehler, C., Cox, M.E. and Cuddeback, G. (2003) Foster Parents' Perceptions of Factors That Promote or Inhibit Successful Fostering. *Qualitative Social Work*. 2, 61–83.

Catalog of Federal Domestic Assistance (2003) *93.568: Foster Care Title IV-E*. Retrieved December 3. http://www.cfda.gov/.

Child Welfare League of America (2000) *Foster Care Basic Monthly Maintenance Rates for Children Ages* 2, 9, and 1. Retrieved August 21.

CIA (2002) *The World Factbook*. Retrieved December 3 http://www.cia.gov/cia/publications/factbook/.

Courtney, M. (1995) The Foster Care Crisis and Welfare Reform. *Public Welfare*. 53, 26–35.

Degeneffe, C.E. (2003) What is Catholic About Catholic Charities? *Social Work*. 48, 374–83.

DiNitto, D. (2000) *Social Welfare: Politics and Public Policy*. 5th edn. Needham Heights, MA: Allyn and Bacon.

Ehrle, J., Geen, R. and Clark, R. (2001) Children Cared for by Relatives: Who Are They and How are They Faring? *New Federalism. B-28*, 1–7. Washington, DC: The Urban Institute.

Fanshel, D. (1982) *On the Road to Permanency: An Expanded Data Base for Service to Children in Foster Care*. New York: Columbia University Press.

Fanshel, D. and Shinn, E. (1978) *Children in Foster Care: A Longitudinal Investigation*. New York: Columbia University Press.

Geen, R. (2000) *Hearing on Flexible Funding for Child Welfare: Testimony Before the House Committee of Ways and Means, Subcommittee on Human Resources*. Retrieved September 5, 2003. http://www.urban.org/Template.cfm?Section = ResearchandNavMenuID = 141andtemplate = /TaggedContent/ViewPublication.cfmandPublicationID = 6856.

Illinois Department of Children and Family Services (2003) *Foster Care Brochure*. Springfield, IL: Retrieved August 12. http://www.state.il.US/dcfs/FCBRO.HTM.

James Bell and Associates (1993) *The National Survey of Current and Former Foster Parents*. Report to the US Department of Health and Human Services, Administration for Children and Families.

Kingma, B.R. (1993) Portfolio Theory and Nonprofit Financial Stability. *Nonprofit and Voluntary Sector Quarterly*. 22.

Leos-Urbel, J., Bess, R., and Geen, R. (2002) The Evolution of Federal and State Policies for Assessing and Supporting Kinship Caregivers. *Children and Youth Services Review*. 24, 37–52.

Malm, K. et al. (2001) *Running to Keep in Place: The Continued Evolution of Our Nation's Child Welfare System*. Washington, DC: The Urban Institute. http://www.urban.org/url.cfm?ID = 310358.

Mass, H. and Engler, R. (1959) *Children in Need of Parents*. New York: Columbia University Press.

Martin, J. (2000) *Foster Family Care: Theory and Practice*. Needham Heights, MA: Allyn and Bacon.

National Association of Social Workers (1999) *The Social Work Dictionary*. 4th edn. Washington, DC: NASW Press.

Orme, J.G. and Buehler, C. (2001) Foster Family Characteristics and Behavioral and Emotional Problems of Foster Children: A Narrative Review. *Family Relations*. 50: 1, 3–15.

Pecora, P.J. et al. (2000) *The Child Welfare Challenge: Policy, Practice, and Research*. Hawthorne, NY: Aldine de Gruyter.

Pecora, P.J. et al. (2003) *Assessing the Effects of Foster Care: Early Results From the Casey National Alumni Study*. Seattle, WA: Casey Family Programs. Retrieved December 10. http://www.casey.org/Resources/Projects/AlumniStudy/.

Proctor, B.D. and Dalaker, J. (2003) *Poverty in the United States: 2002*. US Census Bureau, Current Population Reports, P60–222. Washington, DC: US Government Printing Office. Retrieved September, 29, 2003. http://www.censUS.gov/hhes/www/poverty 02.html.

Rhodes, K., Orme, J. and Buehler, C. (2001) A Comparison of Family Foster Parents Who Quit, Consider Quitting, and Plan to Continue Fostering. *Social Services Review*. 37, 84–114.

Scannapieco, M. and Hegar, M. (2002) Kinship Care Providers: Designing an Array of Supportive Services. *Child and Adolescent Social Work Journal.* 19, 315–27.

Segal, E.A. and Brzuzy, S. (1998) *Social Welfare Policy, Programs, and Practice.* Itasca, IL: F.E. Peacock.

Shyne, A.W. and Schroeder, A.G. (1978) *National Study of Social Services to Children and Their Families.* Washington, DC: Department of Health and Human Services, US Children's Bureau (DHEW Publications No. 78–30150).

Stein T.J. (1998) *Child Welfare and the Law.* Washington, DC: Child Welfare League of America.

Urban Institute (2003) State Kinship Foster Care Licensing and Payment Policies. Retrieved August 29. http://www.urban.org/UploadedPDF/900611.pdf.

US Census Bureau (2000) *Profile of General Demographic Characteristics: 2000. Data set: Census 2000 summary file 1 100-percent data.* http: www.factfinder. censUS.gov Retrieved August 29, 2003.

US Department of Health and Human Services. (2002) *Retaining Foster Parents.* Washington, DC: US Government Printing Office.

US Department of Health and Human Services, Administration for Children and Families (2003) *The AFCARS Report: Preliminary FY 2001 Estimates as of September 20, 2001 (8)* Retrieved August 11, 2003. www.acf.hhs.gov/programs/cb/dis/afcars/publications/afcars.htm.

US Department of Health and Human Services, Children's Bureau. (1997) *National Study of Protective, Preventive and Reunification Services Delivered to Children and Their Families.* Washington, DC: US Government Printing Office.

US Department of Health and Human Services (2003) *The AFCARS report: Preliminary FY 2001 estimates as of March 2003 (8)* Retrieved August 11, 2003. www.acf.hhs.gov/programs/cb/dis/afcars/publications/afcars.htm.

US Information Agency (1999) Changing America: The United States Population in Transition. *U. S. Society and Values.* 4, (2). http://USinfo.state.gov./jounrals/itsv/0699/ijse/toc.htm.

Wulczyn, F.H., Hislop, K.B. and Goerge, R.M. (2000) *Foster Care Dynamics 1983–1998: A Report From the Multistate Foster Care Data Archive.* Chicago, IL: Chapin Hall Center for Children at the University of Chicago.

11 Overview and Conclusions

Matthew Colton and Margaret Williams

Introduction

Most readers will already be familiar with the issues raised in the preceding chapters. The countries selected for inclusion in this book represent very different traditions, regimes and cultures but they are all struggling with essentially the same difficulties in their efforts to use foster care to the best advantage of children and families. Since the ways in which they cope with these difficulties are sometimes very different, it will be worthwhile in this chapter to both summarise the issues and explore the factors that influence coping and decision-making strategies in the various countries.

The first issue (taking an 'issue' to mean something vital and still unresolved) is how 'foster care' ought to be defined. *The World of Foster Care* (Colton and Williams, 1997: 292) summarised data on foster family systems provided by authors from 21 countries and used five criteria, drawn from the data, to develop a definition of foster care. The definition developed reads as follows:

> *Foster care is: 'care provided in the carers' home, on a temporary or permanent basis, through the mediation of a recognised authority, by specific carers, who may be relatives or not, to a child (differently defined in different countries) who may or may not be officially resident with them.*

This somewhat cumbersome definition took into account the provision, in Italy, of 'daytime' foster care, provided to a child who is still resident in their own home, for the purpose of preventing the child's removal from home. The idea that 'foster care' may be provided for a child still living at home runs counter to the generally accepted notion that 'foster care' entails the relocation of children from the homes of their biological parents to the homes of foster parents. However, this rather narrow notion precludes prevention as one of the purposes of foster care. Since purpose, whether explicit or assumed, drives service delivery systems and determines to whom foster care will be provided, by whom, under what circumstances, it is as well to begin by exploring the different purposes foster care serves in the 10 countries represented in this book.

The rest of this chapter will examine the most obvious issues emerging from the previous chapters. These are identified as follows:

- minority children
- children with special needs
- stigma
- foster care systems
- standards for kin and unrelated foster carers
- kinship care
- contact and reunification with birth families
- recruitment and retention of foster carers
- foster care and adoption
- love versus money
- outcomes in foster care

This list is by no means exhaustive and readers may well identify other important issues during their own perusal of the chapters.

It should be noted that there is a high degree of inter-relation among the indentified issues, and as a result material related to one issue may appear in a secton devoted to another. Such interweaving reinforces the idea that, while no issue can be resolved separately, efforts to address one will have an impact on all the others. Let us begin with a discussion of the purpose of foster care.

The Purpose of Foster Care

In all countries, the primary purpose is what it has always been: to care for abandoned, abused and neglected children. In Argentina, foster care is also explicitly intended as an expression of solidarity towards families in need within local communities. 'The concept of solidarity within a community does not denote political customers or paternalistic ideas about protection or residualistic notions of charitable assistance to the unfortunate. Instead, solidarity confirms the right of families in need to receive assistance. The exercise of that right results in a foster care system where preparation, training and support is provided to both birth and foster families as a matter of course.'

The language of 'rights' is increasingly embodied in child welfare laws in most countries. In India, for example the shift in focus, from a 'needs' to a 'rights' approach has been paralleled by a shift from an institutional to a family-oriented, community-based approach. The result has been a large number of initiatives in foster care under the auspices of NGOs and the various levels of government. Signatories to the United Nations Convention on the Rights of the Child have an obligation to protect the child's rights through laws and services, and the best interests of the child is invariably a primary consideration.

In theory, the interests of the child can best be served by addressing the interests of the natural family. The current emphasis on continued contact between the child and the natural family and on reunification where possible reflects a change in the traditional purpose of foster care – to find substitute homes for children in difficult circumstances – to a new purpose – to make the original home fit for the child to live in. In theory as well, this new purpose is fulfilled by providing training and support to birth parents and by encouraging foster parents to accept that one of their duties is to work closely with birth parents. The idea of rights as they pertain to the natural family is most explicitly outlined by the author from Argentina who notes that Fundación Emmanuel is promoting a National Law on Family Rights in Foster Care.

However, in the majority of countries represented in this volume, it seems that there exists a definite ambivalence in attitudes towards the birth family. On the one hand, there is recognition that the birth family deserves to be served and, indeed, needs to be served if efforts at reunification are to have any chance of success. On the other hand, there is a sense of shame and failure associated with having a child in foster care which results in a reluctance on the part of both social workers and foster parents to work with the birth family and feelings of stigma and marginalisation on the part of the birth parents. We will return to the stigma associated with receiving child welfare services – and in some cases to providing child welfare services – later on in the chapter. Meanwhile, we should not forget that fostering and adoption have, in the past, been used for political rather than welfare purposes and that purpose still echoes in legislation pertaining to the consideration of race, colour and ethnic origin in the placement of children.

For example, Table 1 in chapter 10 on the United States cites three laws, all addressing cultural considerations in placement decisions but with very different emphases.The first, The Indian Child Welfare Act of 1978 emphasises **not** placing Native American children with non-Native foster parents. Aboriginal peoples in North America have long viewed 'child stealing' by welfare authorities as a form of genocide and point to the loss of language and culture experienced by almost a whole generation of children who were removed from their homes and placed in residential institutions in the 1960s. People from other minority cultures tend to share the suspicion that placing their children with foster parents from the dominant culture is a way of undermining, perhaps destroying, their own cultures.

The second law is the Multiethnic Placement Act of 1994. This Act attempts to tread a middle road, encouraging agencies to consider ethnic origin when making placement decisions but emphasising that no child should be denied a placement solely on the grounds that the child and prospective foster parents come from different ethnic backgrounds. The third law, the Interethnic Placement Act of 1996, repeals the first part of the second law – the part about considering ethnic origin – and places its entire emphasis on finding the child a placement regardless of cultural considerations.

These three laws reflect the struggles of child welfare authorities in North America to move between a rock and a hard place. If they deny a child a placement on the grounds of ethnic mis-match, they are accused of racial discrimination: if they place the child, there are rumblings of genocide. The solution, of course, is to recruit a sufficient pool of ethnically diverse foster parents to enable a match to be made on every occasion, but – as we discuss below – difficulties in recruiting and retaining foster parents are evident in every nation.

Political purposes in foster care cannot be discounted. The different ideologies of political parties are reflected in legislation, in the various systems through which foster care services are provided – health-care, education, social welfare, the judiciary – and in funding sources and financial penalties or incentives for doing this or that. The process of providing foster care is highly political and it is inevitable that foster care goals should sometimes reflect political agendas.

For example, the welfare system in the United States has emerged from two competing ideologies: individualism and institutionalism (Segal and Brzuzy, 1998). Individualism argues for a residual approach to governmental intervention whereby welfare services should only be offered when the normal resources of the family and marketplace break down. In contrast, the institutional approach holds that society as a whole is responsible for dealing with the difficulties encountered by individuals and, thus, welfare programmes should be built into the basic social structure and considered an entitlement.

US public policy is, in fact, the product of conflicts between these two approaches. Welfare policies emerge incrementally out of debates among policy makers who deliberate existing policies, programmes and expenditures. This approach keeps discussion narrow and diminishes the likelihood of major policy shifts (DiNitto, 2000). Overall, the residual approach has prevailed in policy debates, as evidenced by a categorically-defined welfare system; that is, services are classified by explicit criteria that determine who qualifies for service and how much service the eligible candidate will receive. Most public services are available only to those who demonstrate a need, and the burden of proof typically rests on the individual in need.

Usually, the need is associated with poverty. Poverty is a political issue and it is certainly an issue in foster care since, historically, it is the children of the poor who have been removed from their parents and placed in foster or adoptive homes. Our Swedish author cites a study by Hessle (1988) which showed that parents with children in foster care had social problems: single parenthood, unemployment, poor education, drug or alcohol addiction, and psychological issues. This picture of birth parents who are marginalised both economically and socially has been reflected in countless studies and the apprehension of the children of the poor is as much an issue today as it was in England in the Victorian era. 'There is a clear connection between class and children in care. Child welfare has never really been part of the social welfare state: rather, it has been a measure for use with those who are marginalised in the social welfare system (Lundström and Sallnäs,2003).'

In the United Kingdom in the Victorian era, an explicit purpose of apprehending children was to save them from unfit parents. Today, no government or non-governmental organisation would admit to such a purpose but perhaps it is not stretching the imagination too far to suggest that one of the purposes of foster care is still to inculcate into 'lower-class' children the preferred values of the middle class to which the majority of non-related foster parents belong. Such a purpose may be furthered through the deliberate use of stigma as an instrument of social policy and by the emergence of stigma as an unintended consequence of child welfare service delivery (Colton et al., 1997). If the teaching of class values is not a purpose, it becomes a problem since children who form a bond with their foster parents are very likely to absorb from them a class-related value system which may be quite different from the value system of the biological parents. To some degree, this class conflict might be mitigated through the recruitment of foster parents from the child's extended family. It might also be mitigated if the birth parents were included as part of a team, consisting of themselves, the child, the social worker and the foster parents, all dedicated to serving the best interests of the child. In many places, this sort of teamwork is still a distant dream, made more distant by the fact that the majority of social workers, also, are middle class. In this respect the Fundación Emmanuel in Argentina, with its emphases on the right of birth parents and the dissociation between stigma and poverty, comes as a breath of fresh air.

For minority children, as we have seen, the issue is not so much class values as the fear that foster parents from a different ethnic background might instil into the child cultural values and practices that conflict with those of the birth parents: that the child might grow up ignorant of their own culture or, worse yet, ashamed of it, and the culture itself might be lost to the dominant system.

Minority Children

We have already identified ethnic matching as an issue in the placement of children. Obviously, it is more of an issue in countries where there is a significant degree of ethnic and cultural diversity such as the United Kingdom, France, and the United States, where around 30 per cent of people self-identify as being non-white. The people of Argentina are descended from both South-American Natives and from European immigrants. In post-Apartheid South Africa, there are 11 official languages. Even in Sweden, which used to be an ethnically homogenous society, some 18 per cent of the population now have their family roots in other countries, either because they were born outside Sweden or because one or both of their parents are of non-Swedish origin. Of the children in public care in Sweden, roughly 40 per cent are of non-Swedish origin and difficulties in finding placements for such children are commonplace.

In the United Kingdom and other Western European countries, black people experience disadvantage and deprivation through racism and discrimination that permeate many areas of life. They are more likely than white people to be unemployed or on low pay and to lack access to decent housing. Disproportionate numbers of black children are placed in public care, and they have less chance than white children of being reunited with their parents or of being matched with foster parents from the same cultural background. Likewise, national data and other research in the United States have consistently reported that children of colour are over represented in the foster care system. Poverty and single parenthood are inter-related factors underlying entry to foster care and both of these factors disproportionately affect minority children.

Under Apartheid, social workers in South Africa were trained in racially separated universities and colleges and were employed by welfare organisations and government departments serving designated races only. All racial and other discriminatory barriers in service delivery have since been removed and foster care workers do their best to be sensitive to the issues of cross-cultural and trans-racial foster care placements, achieving an appropriate match whenever possible. However, like many so-called first world countries in Western Europe, South Africa is still confronted with racial and cultural prejudice. This, together with the ever-increasing demand for foster care, especially due to HIV/AIDS, but also due to the general increase in recorded levels of child abuse and neglect, is placing culturally sensitive practice under great pressure. Indeed, our South African author suggests that the increasing number of child headed households where both parents are either incapacitated due to HIV/AIDS or are deceased, may require the development of an entirely new foster care system whereby a foster parent moves into the family home and replaces the biological parents.

Children with Special Needs

Children with disabilities represent another major group of children who are denied social justice and whose human rights are routinely violated. The World Health Authority defines disability as a restriction or lack of ability to perform normal activities, resulting from impairment to the structure or function of the body or mind. Such children face considerable discrimination, including lack of access to buildings, transport, health and social care, and restricted opportunities with respect to education, training and work. They are also subject to abuse and social stigma (Colton et al., 2001).

Some attempt has been made to widen access to family placements for children with disabilities. In the United Kingdom, for example, many fostering programmes have been established as alternatives to residential care for children with significant disabilities and health problems. In France, where there is a tradition of foster care for adults with mental illness, physically and mentally challenged children have been placed with foster families for many years. In China, children with disabilities can be placed in long-term foster care and it has been found that children with serious learning difficulties at placement have later made significant progress.

Despite these efforts, it is clear that more needs to be done to widen access to foster care. Children with severe handicaps or severe behavioural problems in France are not placed in foster care. Similarly, our contributor on China notes that attention still needs to be paid to the placement of 'hard to place' children with more serious disabilities. In India, foster family care is restricted to the placement of children who do not have special needs. Qualification criteria exclude Indian children who are disabled or delinquent and this may be due to a lack of conviction on the part of stakeholders that foster care is a realistic option for such children.

In South Africa, too, relatively few children with mental or physical disabilities are placed in foster care. The majority of special needs children who require alternative care are placed in children's homes – or shelters, in the case of street children – or in institutions for seriously handicapped children and youth.

Access to foster care is also restricted for other groups of children with special needs, even in the world's richest countries. In the United States, children presenting severe emotional and behavioural problems, those who struggle with issues of acculturation and racism, and children infected with HIV/AIDS are far more likely to be placed in residential group care than in family foster care.

Stigma

The stigma associated with receiving child welfare services is a theme that runs through all the chapters in this book. Social stigma has been broadly defined as an attribute of 'human conditions which roughly corresponds to some feeling of their unacceptability in the wider community' (Davies and Morris, 1993, p. 109). In a residualistic (individualistic) welfare system such as that in the United States – and, to a lesser extent, the United Kingdom — child welfare is conceived largely in terms of child protection. The privacy of the family is of great importance, intrusion into the family is permitted only when parents fail to maintain minimum standards of child-care, and the intrusion must be authorised through an adversarial judicial system. In such countries, an authorised intrusion by child welfare services is an obvious indicator that the parents have failed in their child-raising task. They have not performed their function in a way that is acceptable to the wider community and so they are stigmatised by definition. Colton et al. (1997) note that recipients of child welfare services in the United Kingdom have reported strong and enduring feelings of being stigmatised as a result of their engagements with the child welfare services. Social workers have reported the same sense of stigma, doubtless due to being identified with their clients in the popular view.

However, in countries which adopt a more institutional approach to welfare – for example, France and Sweden – the focus is on service to the natural family, through which the goal of child protection is expected to be accomplished. Principles of social solidarity and community responsibility for child-care are emphasised, and it is not necessary to demonstrate that a child is 'at-risk' before assistance is offered. The legal system provides mediation through mandated officials and the aim is to reach consensual agreements with families. In such countries, one would expect that there would be much less stigma associated with receiving child welfare services. This seems not to be the case in Sweden, perhaps because the child welfare system is divorced from other social welfare systems. In France, it seems not to be the case either. Michel Corbillon (chapter 3) notes that importance is placed on maintaining the full responsibility of families who are temporarily unable to care for their children via the provision of information about their rights and duties, and by involving them in decisions made in respect of their children. However, parents often feel that they are seen as 'bad parents' because another family has shown itself better able to care for the child.

Corbillon also notes that the last 20 years have seen a weakening of the long-standing ideological differences between the major political parties and frequent transfers of power between right-wing (individualistic) and left-wing (institutional) parties. In most democratic countries, transfers of power occur routinely and it is difficult to categorise one country as 'individualistic' and another as 'institutional' because both positions exist in a continuing state of tension.

Nevertheless, within even the most individualistic of countries, community care models are unfolding which rely, for the protection of children, on consultations with natural parents, extended family and the local community. The examples of community care models given in the literature are largely drawn from the experiences of Aboriginal peoples in the United States, Canada and New Zealand. Because of the devastating effects of colonialism on these peoples, the model emphasises the connection between caring for children and healing whole communities. Individual ties to family, community, place, history and spirit are seen as central to child welfare in the same way as they are central to the health of the community. There is no blame attached to natural parents with problems and thus no stigma results. This ideal is compromised by the fact that community care systems often function within countries which take the child protection approach already discussed. Child welfare activities true to the model may thus be constrained by the adversarial orientation of the dominant systems.

In this volume, Fundación Emmanuel in Argentina seems to present an example of a community care model being successfully implemented. The most striking difference between the Argentinian experience and practice in Aboriginal communities is the emphasis, in Aboriginal communities, on placing children with members of their extended families. Fundación Emmanuel, by contrast, has involved non-related foster parents in the community effort. Implementation of the model in this way is probably facilitated by the fact that Argentina has a tradition of community help and the economic depression, which has affected so many, is obviously outside the control of people newly thrown into poverty. There is therefore little sense of personal deficiency – one of the pre-requisites of stigma – attached to parents who cannot care for their children due to poverty.

In Japan, by contrast, the stigma attached to having one's child cared for by non-related foster parents is so high that birth parents often prefer to have their children placed in residential institutions rather than in foster care. Empirical comparative research confirms that some birth parents in other countries also prefer to have their children placed in residential care rather than foster care because, with residential care, there is no feeling that another family succeeded where the birth family failed (Colton et al., 1997).

The stigma associated with feelings of parental failure may be ameliorated somewhat in countries where kinship care predominates, such as India, Poland and South Africa. As previously noted, India has seen a shift from needs to rights-based foster care, and from an institutional to a family-oriented, community-based approach. Priority has accordingly been given to the placement of children with their own immediate or extended kin. This has met with some success, though the placement of children with disabilities and other special needs is still difficult. The Indian authors do not speculate as to whether parents feel more stigmatised or less when their child is placed with kin rather than with an unrelated foster parent. There seems to be little in the literature on the relative stigma associated with kin and non-kin placements respectively. In the absence of data, one might make a link with the increasing professionalisation of foster parents in many countries. The success of a trained, professional foster parent, for example, might be less shameful to the birth parent than the success of Aunt Maisie, whose ability to raise the child where the birth parent failed can only rest on her personal qualities since environmental factors are presumably much the same. On the other hand, in countries where ancestral ties are particularly important, the shame of Aunt Maisie's superiority may pale before the shame of having a child placed outside the family.

Fostered children themselves often bear the burden of social stigma, carrying labels such as 'troublesome' and 'troubled'. It is noteworthy that in the United Kingdom and the United States there is increasing discourse around the emotional and behavioural problems of children placed in foster care. This can be viewed positively as reflecting the increased attention that is now being paid to meeting the particular needs of the children and young people concerned. There is a danger, however, that highlighting the problems presented by children in foster care can represent a form of 'victim blaming'. Being 'in care' and living with an unrelated family may carry a stigma for children and young people, marking them out as different from their peers and diminishing their sense of self-worth. Children who are visibly different from their foster parents – for example, children of colour placed with white foster parents – may carry an additional stigma. Similarly, the feeling of difference – and often of shame – associated with having a disability is exacerbated if the child is also 'in care'. Even gender can carry a stigma: in China, for example, it is usually female children who come into foster care after being abandoned as a consequence of the 'one child only' approach to population control.

The stigma associated with child welfare services may be exacerbated or ameliorated depending on the systems through which the services are delivered. As previously noted, child welfare in Sweden has never really been part of the social welfare state: rather it has been a measure for use with people marginalised in the social welfare system (Lundström and Sallnäs, 2003). One can only speculate that integration of the child and social welfare systems in Sweden would result in the lower level of child welfare associated stigma theoretically expected in a country with an institutional approach to welfare.

Foster Care Systems

As our Argentinian author notes, 'social welfare programs are useful in supporting the populations eligible to receive their benefits but they are not useful at all in reducing poverty and inequality. Income concentration tends to reinforce the concentration of political power and, thus, to perpetuate and increase poverty and inequality. This highlights the relevance of the political dimension of poverty since the voice and power of people below the poverty line tend to be reduced even in democratic political systems. At present, in Argentina, there is a proliferation of different social programs addressing different problems at different levels of government. These overlap and thus create barriers to efficient coverage and implementation. Political manipulation is reflected in a lack of transparency in allocating funding, and there is a conflictive State-society relationship in the implementation of programs.'

Argentina is not alone in any of this. In all countries, improvement of the foster care system would be greatly facilitated if there were such a system. Instead, there is a complex web of public and private agencies that share responsibility for providing services, payment, decisions and regulation. Our American authors comment on 'the reality of foster care which is situated at a crossroad of multiple systems (education, judicial, mental health, criminal), is straddled across several tiers of bureaucracy, and is expected to address a quagmire of social problems (economic, socio-psychological, interpersonal, racial), all with limited fiscal resources.' Many readers will share these authors' evident frustration.

Decentralisation of the various systems is a thrust common to most industrialised countries, running in parallel to the move towards community-based services and perhaps reflective of the do-it-yourself attitude of people who are losing faith in their governing systems and representatives. There are obvious advantages and disadvantages to decentralisation. In France, the Justice Ministry has assumed more power in the area of child protection, at the expense of the Ministry of Social Affairs, as a result of decentralisation, and the Education Ministry is hardly represented at all in child protection decision-making. Perhaps decentralisation cannot be blamed for the non-involvement of the education system in services to children for whom poor school performance is a major area of difficulty. However, there is no doubt that devolution of control from state to local governments does involve shifts in the balance of power between the different systems serving children and families. And different systems have different values and traditions in the matter of child placement.

In the United States, systems providing out-of-home care for children include: child welfare (serving dependent and maltreated children), mental health (serving children with emotional and psychiatric needs), and juvenile justice (serving children who have violated the law). Each system is operated by a separate division of government. Within the child welfare system, foster care is a core service but the mental health and juvenile justice systems, by contrast, have only experimented with family foster care, and more commonly rely on institutional care facilities.

Many children face issues that are addressed by multiple systems. However, in keeping with a categorical system of services set by government, the general rule is that children may be served by only one system at a time. For example, in some states a child in foster care who is sentenced to a juvenile detention centre for an extended length of time will be discharged from the child welfare system. Two major problems faced by the separation of these systems is spillover of children from one system to another as resources wax and wane, and children who fall between the gaps when system transfer fails.

In the United States, the separation of systems gives rise to difficulties. South Africa has avoided these difficulties by creating a one-stop-shop. Here, the 1997 White Paper for Social Welfare has moved away from promoting specialised welfare services in favour of encouraging welfare organisations and other social service organisations to develop and implement comprehensive multi-focused or generic services that address a variety of human problems in one organisation. Foster care in South Africa is no longer the exclusive domain of child and family welfare organisations as it was prior to 1997. Today foster care services may be provided by any welfare organisation that has qualified social workers in its employ.

There are parallels here with the drive towards service integration which is occurring in North America. Leatt, Pink and Naylor (1996: 55) define service integration as 'a network of organisations that provides or arranges to provide a coordinated continuum of services to a defined population'. For example, people with substance abuse problems would have a single access point to services provided by a number of organisations. A drug-addicted youth might receive foster care without prior involvement with the child welfare system.

The shift to service integration has occurred for a number of reasons. First, as Short and Talley (1999: 195) remark, 'Recent writing and policy ... view clients as whole units, with interrelated needs and strengths that are not easily divided at the bureaucratic and professional boundaries that have been imposed on them.' Similarly, Waldfogel (1997) notes that 'categorical services' cannot meet the complex needs of people and that mismatching of client and service results in less effective service delivery. Another reason for the shift is the belief that service integration is cost effective. 'In times of budget cutbacks, service integration may be viewed as a means for preserving existing services by eliminating duplication and waste' (Hassett and Austin, 1997: 13). Martinson (1999) concurs that integration of services is thought to reduce costs.

In a decentralised structure, it is usually the case that the central government issues general directives, including eligibility criteria for funding and accountability mechanisms, and local authorities are responsible for translating these directives into specific guidelines for service provision. Our American authors remark that federal directives are increasingly focused on 'cost-saving' and less on improving the quality of service. Be that as it may, the actual provision of services is entrusted to various public and private agencies, including church-based organisations.

In South Africa, churches still play a major role in the development and maintenance of social welfare services. Whereas in the past, churches predominantly rendered services, including foster care services, to individuals and families belonging to their own denomination, the new welfare policy stipulates that all church or religious welfare organisations must render services to all people irrespective of religious affiliation should these organisations wish to be financed by the government. With a few exceptions, churches in general have responded positively to the new policy and in the field of foster care have in fact become leaders in developing services for all races, denominations and non-religious persons. By contrast, one of the reasons cited by our Japanese author for the decline of foster care in Japan is that 'there are no religious traditions, like Christianity in Europe, which inspire interest in social care.'

Standards for Kin and Unrelated Foster Carers

Licensing of foster care services varies enormously, from South Africa where there is no licensing mechanism for rendering foster care services to Sweden where regulations are strict. In South Africa, the great need for foster care services especially in view of the HIV/AIDS related problems, and the huge rural population served makes licensing impractical. In Sweden, by contrast, unlicensed foster care is illegal and all placements, including placements with kin, have to submit to regular inspections.

A contentious issue in foster care is the distinction between kin and unrelated foster parents in terms of such things as training, standards, accountability and remuneration. Even when all placements must be licensed, as in Sweden, the licensing standards for kin and unrelated foster parents are not necessarily identical. Indeed, in the United States, only 15 states have identical standards whereas 20 states have separate and less stringent requirements for kinship placements. In Japan, a condition that applies to unrelated foster parents, namely that they be financially comfortable, is waived in the case of kinship foster parents.

Failure of the kinship home to meet licensing standards often does not mean that the child cannot be placed there: it only means that the kin carers will not receive foster care allowances or payments. Cash-strapped authorities can thus have it both ways. On the one hand, they are serving the best interests of the child through compliance with the accepted idea that children are best cared for by their own families. In addition, they are upholding standards by denying funding to families who fail to meet those standards.

One may envisage bureaucrats who have found a cheap placement option rubbing their hands with glee, however, there are genuine difficulties associated with reimbursement and standards which are exacerbated by the current move to increase professionalisation among foster parents. Professionals accept that one of the prerequisites for becoming a professional is training. Conversely, kinship carers, who are often grandparents, do not see why they need to be trained to raise a child when they have already spent many years raising their own children. Such training may be viewed as not only unnecessary but as patronising and intrusive.

A second attribute associated with professionalism is demonstration of competence. Professional foster parents accept that they will be expected to co-operate with child welfare authorities in documenting the child's progress and implementing the child-care strategies that will contribute to that progress. In other words, they expect to be held accountable for what they do. Kinship carers have often not chosen to care for a child in the same way that unrelated carers have. Instead, they are performing a duty, imposed on them by circumstance – a duty which may compromise their own well-being – and they do not see why they should be accountable to anyone.

It may be argued simplistically that people in the general population in all countries receive money for one of two reasons: either because they exist or because they contribute to the labour market. Existence money is provided, often grudgingly, through various welfare systems. Contribution money depends on the perceived level of the contribution which is related to training and accountability. Work outside the labour market, such as child-rearing and housework, predominantly still performed by women, is not viewed as a contribution worthy of reimbursement; and, hence, those who perform such work must rely for support either on a partner who does contribute to the labour market or on welfare payments. One might argue that unrelated foster parents fall into the 'contribution' category whereas kin carers, largely untrained and unaccountable, are relegated to the lesser category of existence. Our American authors remark that kin carers may be obliged to apply for some form of welfare support or be left to fend for themselves financially, and that some 40 per cent of kin carers fall below the federal poverty level.

The obvious solution here is to pay kin carers for their work – in addition to payment for the child's keep — and thus raise them from the existence to the contribution category. To some extent progress has been made in this regard and, in some countries, kin carers are paid, even if at abysmal levels, or at least provision has been made in law that would allow them to be paid. In Poland, for example, regulations passed in 1993 allow equal financial help for related and non-related carers. However, kinship carers need to have their status as foster carers formalised by a court order before they are eligible to receive any financial help. Similarly, in the United States, kinship carers who are not licensed by the child welfare agency are not eligible to receive payments, and many cannot meet the licensing standards because of factors directly related to poverty.

It does not seem unreasonable to expect that kinship foster carers must be formally recognised as foster carers before they can be paid for providing foster care. Neither is it unreasonable, on the face of it, to expect that 'formal recognition' will involve the reaching of some standard other than proof that foster child and kinship carer both exist and are living together. However, it does seem that regulations are designed to prevent many – perhaps the majority – of kinship carers from receiving the benefits that would allow them to offer their foster children adequate developmental opportunities and a better hope for success in later life.

It could be argued that paying kinship carers at the same rate as unrelated carers would contravene three of the basic tenets that underpin most industrialised societies: first, all work is not equal and different types of work must be rewarded based on the level of training required to perform them; second, work is not work unless it falls within the purview of the labour market; and, third, raising one's own children is an act of love which ought not to be contaminated by commercial interests. The combination of these tenets has succeeded in foiling all efforts to pay a salary and benefits to ordinary parents outside the foster care system who choose to stay at home to raise their children, and the same combination dictates that kinship carers – who, after all, have a moral obligation towards their family members – should not be paid either.

The conflict between raising children and pursuing a career is having major impacts, both in the area of foster care where recruitment is affected, and in the increasing numbers of young adults who are choosing to have children later in life or not at all. Ingrid Hojek remarks that the Swedish welfare system is built on work: that is to say, people need to be employed in order to enjoy state support and people without a job are marginalised. Thus, parenthood in Sweden needs to be carefully planned in order not to risk the prospective parent's professional position. Contemporary Sweden has the lowest birth rate ever, and the average age of first-time mothers is beginning to reach 30. Similarly, in Japan, the birth rate in 2005 was at an all-time low, partly due to the reluctance of young women to sacrifice promising careers in order to stay at home with children. It need hardly be said that women reluctant to stay at home with their own children are even less likely to be willing to stay at home with a foster child. This obvious impact on the recruitment of unrelated foster carers means that the recruitment and support of kin carers is even more essential. Nevertheless, it seems that foster care systems in the majority of countries remain mired in the same circular argument: kin carers living in poverty need to be paid in order to reach the required standards; but they also need to reach the required standards before they can be paid. The accepted solution seems to be an unfortunate compromise on both counts: standards are reduced or waived; and payment is minimal or withheld altogether.

The chapters of this book reveal a well defined pattern in relation to the profile of kinship carers. The latter are more likely to be older (often grandparents), poorer, less well educated and to suffer ill-health than their non-related counterparts. The over-representation of minority children in the child welfare populations of many countries also means that a similar over-representation will occur among kinship carers. Cultural considerations may thus complicate already contentious issues around the training, licensing, accountability and reimbursement of kinship carers.

Kinship Care

Kinship care plays an important role in the foster care systems of many countries around the world, including most of the countries represented in this volume. For example in India and Poland it is traditionally expected that relatives will provide care, and kinship care represents the lion's share of foster placements. In Poland, the term 'foster family care' essentially means care by the child's next of kin and over 80 per cent of foster children are placed with relatives. In Maharashtra, India, the authorities first try to place children with relatives, neighbours or close acquaintances whether married or single. It is only where this is not possible that a child is placed with unrelated or unknown foster carers.

South Africa is another country where there is a high incidence of kinship placements, particularly among black families. Because of parental death due to HIV/AIDS, permanent foster care placements with grandparents are increasingly common. Since financial support to all South African foster carers is extremely limited, many grandparents find their caring role an onerous one. Young children looked after by their ageing grandparents are at considerable risk of being moved to alternative foster care placements in the event that their grandparents become unable to provide adequate care.

Other countries have seen an increase in kinship care due to wider acceptance of the idea that children are best served by keeping them in their own communities and within their extended families wherever possible. In the United Kingdom, it is estimated that kinship care accounts for 18 per cent of all foster care placements and in Sweden the figure is 20 per cent. In France, priority is given to placing the child with relatives, geographically close to the birth parents so that the birth parents have a better opportunity to exercise their continuing responsibility towards the child. In Buenos Aires, Argentina, legislation has been passed to enable children who cannot live with their birth parents to be looked after by extended family members or other people they know in their local community.

In China, by contrast, formal kinship care is largely unknown. One of the unintended consequences of strict family planning controls introduced in China during the 1970s was an increase in the number of children entering care via abandonment because of their disability or gender. These children have no contact with their birth families and are often adopted by their foster parents a few years after placement.

In Japan, kinship foster care is only approved if the child is unable to live with his parents because the latter are dead, incarcerated, or missing. The kin foster parents must be related to the child within the third degree of kinship: that is, they must be grandparents, aunts or uncles.

Sweden saw a decline in kin placements from 50 per cent of all foster care placements in the 1950s to only 16 per cent at the beginning of the 1990s. Vinnerljung (1993) ascribes this decline to the professionalisation of social work, and it does seem reasonable that social workers, newly arrived at professional status themselves, would prefer to work with unrelated foster parents who have been recruited, trained and made accountable through due agency process rather than with kinship carers who are often less amenable to agency protocols. In other countries, the professionalisation of social work has occurred at different rates, sometimes in fits and starts, so it is difficult to try to draw any correlation between this and change in kinship placements. However, the professionalisation of social workers has been paralleled to some extent by the professionalisation of unrelated foster parents and both have occurred in the context of the movement towards maintaining children in their own communities and families.

Contact and Reunification with Birth Families

Professional responsibility on the part of both social workers and foster parents now includes a duty to work with the child's birth family and extended kin so that the child can maintain familial and community ties. This is a major shift since foster parents, and often social workers as well, have traditionally experienced difficulty in working with natural parents, who were probably the ones who neglected or abused the child and contributed to the apprehension in the first place. As tends to be the case with major shifts in policy, the letter might be followed but the spirit appears to be lagging quite a way behind.

It is only in Argentina, for example, that birth parents are perceived as having rights, that foster care is conceived as a response to a family in need. In other countries, the child might have rights – first, to be protected and, second, to maintain family bonds – but the birth parents are often seen as vehicles through which the child's rights might be upheld, and as rather rusty and recalcitrant vehicles at that. In the United Kingdom, the value of maintaining contact between children and their birth parents, irrespective of whether or not reunification is the goal, has been emphasised for many years. However, whilst initiatives have been taken to ensure that fostered children and foster parents participate in evaluating and shaping policy and practice, it is noteworthy that birth parents have not been provided with the same opportunities.

Our French author comments on the conflict between birth families, unrelated foster families and child welfare agencies. This conflict is ascribed to tensions over whether children draw their feelings of identity from the birth or foster family and to the attachment felt towards the children by their foster parents. Birth parents feel that they are seen as 'bad' parents and may, as a consequence, relinquish their parental role. This 'either-or' sort of conflict carries overtones of a bad divorce where the child must choose between parental figures and meanwhile serves as the rope in a tug of war. One solution, in France, has been to reinforce the role and responsibilities of the birth parents by placing the child in kinship care as geographically close to home as possible. Such a solution certainly resolves the conflict since the unrelated foster parent is now out of the picture. On the other hand, a too-enthusiastic reliance on kinship care may deny the child developmental opportunities which only a highly trained carer can provide. An alternative solution is to nurture the ability of people to share. Some divorced parents co-parent admirably, overcoming, for the sake of the child, different views about schedules, house rules, dietary preferences, child-rearing strategies, religious affiliation, and the like. Similarly, some foster parents, and birth parents as well, are able to embrace the idea of the foster family as a complementary rather than a substitute family and to engage in the process of plural or multi or co-parenting. Our French author cites a recent study arguing that the foster family should be regarded as a centre of plural-parenting through focusing on familial links that become manifest during the placement process. Perhaps the birth family might also be regarded as such a centre, focusing on the supports to parenting provided by and through the foster family and child welfare and community agencies.

In Poland, too, researchers have highlighted the strong emotional bonds that often develop between children and their non-related foster carers, and the difficulties experienced by fostered children arising from contacts with birth parents. For example, Przgoda (1998) demonstrated that, whilst strongly attached to their foster families, many foster children feel caught between two families and suffer from conflicting loyalties. In Poland, as we have noted, 80 per cent of foster care placements are in the homes of relatives, usually grandmothers, but there has been criticism about the quality of kinship care and some child-care specialists have sought to prevent children in unrelated foster homes having contact with their birth families despite child welfare regulations that place emphasis on such contact.

South Africa has similar legislation. The Child Care Act states that the birth parents of foster children should receive services aimed at reuniting them with their children. This has proved to be a challenge in practice given that many birth parents experience psycho-social problems that adversely impact their parenting capacities. Social workers' attempts to ensure permanency for children within well functioning families have been undermined in cases where the foster parents constantly fear that children will be returned to birth parents who demand reunification but still lack the necessary parenting capacities. In South Africa, as well, the new model of social welfare has theoretically removed all racial and other discriminatory barriers to social service delivery. However, the stigma of Apartheid clings to the committee of inquiry that produced the new guidelines for standards and procedures in foster care, and the post-Apartheid government has been unable to ensure that child and youth services receive the priority they require. These struggles have been exacerbated by the HIV/AIDS crisis that has overwhelmed all social services agencies.

Recruitment and Retention of Foster Carers

There is no doubt that HIV/AIDS has contributed both to the acute level of need in South Africa for foster families and to an equally acute shortfall of foster parents. However, difficulty in recruiting sufficient numbers of foster carers is a more or less ubiquitous feature of foster care systems around the world. There are various reasons for this. We have noted already the impact on recruitment in Japan and Sweden of the predilection of young women to pursue careers and delay or reject child-rearing. There are additional obvious factors. One may consider, for example, the difficulty and cost involved in mounting a recruitment drive that will reach suitable candidates, or the distrust felt by ethnic minority candidates towards the dominant system that wants to recruit them, or the lack of government interest in foster care, as mentioned by our Swedish author. But essentially, the problem lies in the small number of people who have the two basic characteristics necessary to becoming a foster parent: motivation and capacity. Prospective foster parents must want to take in a child, for whatever reason, and they must have the capacity – financial, emotional, mental, physical and spiritual – to be able to adequately care for the child.

Motivation

Motivation, of course, has many aspects and motives are usually mixed but there are four possible motives which emerge particularly from the chapters in this book:

- The desire to have a child of one's own to raise and love. Applies to prospective parents who would rather adopt than foster. We return to adoption below.
- A sense of duty or obligation. Applies mostly to kinship carers.

- The altruistic desire to help a child or family in need. Applies to the vast majority of unrelated foster carers.
- The desire to improve one's own condition through exploiting the child or system. Applies to the small minority which recruitment systems do their best to repel.

China, because of its singular one-child-only policy, presents an example of people who foster because they want a child of their own. As Robert Glover remarks, the recruitment of foster carers by the Joint Shanghai Foster Care and Training Programme has exceeded expectations. Programme staff found that there was considerable interest in fostering on a long-term basis because many couples had had the one permitted birth child and wished to raise another, often a girl if they already had a son. In Japan, as well, many parents who foster really wish to adopt but there are few children available for adoption and the distinction between adoptive foster parents and non-adoptive foster parents is unclear.

Altruism, the motive which drives the majority of foster parents, may be a personal characteristic but it may also derive from culture and tradition. Kozo Iwasaki remarks that one of the reasons foster care is failing in Japan is that Japan lacks a religious tradition, like Christianity, which advocates social care. Similarly, few families are prepared to consider fostering in India because there is no tradition of caring for unrelated children and such behaviour remains unconventional. In places where a behaviour is not supported by the prevailing social and value systems, difficulties associated with the behaviour may seem more insurmountable than they would if social support were stronger. For example, Goriawalla and Telang refer to pilot foster care projects in Madras and Mumbai, set up in the 1960s, which emphasised matching the child's background with that of the foster family and maintaining the child's links with the birth parents. Difficulties were encountered due to socio-cultural factors, such as religion, ethnicity, eating habits, living conditions, and so on, alongside economic barriers like inadequate housing and the meagre allowance paid for the child's maintenance. Not only were prospective foster parents reluctant to accept a child for all these reasons: birth parents, for their part, preferred to place their children in institutions rather than have them cared for by an unknown family. It may be argued that the difficulties cited, while real enough, were accorded more importance than they might have been had it been traditional in India to care for unrelated children.

Capacity

However, even in countries like France where charity to non-relatives is a valued tradition and the altruistic component is much in evidence, recruitment is still difficult because motivation without capacity is not enough. Capacity to foster, as noted earlier, includes financial, emotional, mental, physical and spiritual capacity. In Japan, foster parents must be healthy in mind, spirit and body, be knowledgeable about child rearing and be financially comfortable. The same conditions apply in most other countries and are usually enforced through licensing standards. In the United States licensing standards include verification that the foster carers' home has adequate space for a child and meets sanitary and safety standards. Verification is also required that the applicants are sufficiently healthy, have adequate income, have no history of child maltreatment, and have the necessary level of parenting ability.

While these conditions seem reasonable enough, it is easy to see why there is a dearth of prospective foster parents who satisfy all of them and are also prepared to take in a child. Michel Corbillon writes that recruitment has proved particularly difficult in large cities such as Paris where housing conditions often result in a lack of space. Lack of space is a problem in most cities. Adequate income may be a problem for many prospective foster parents, particularly given the present-day reality that a single income (traditionally the male partner's income) is no longer sufficient to raise a family and both partners may need to be in the workforce in order to provide the comfortable standard of living — and space — required by the licensing standards. The additional task of caring for a foster child with relatively high needs may be expected to compromise that income since one partner at least must now devote what used to be work time to child-related tasks.

One can envisage a pool of prospective foster parents, highly motivated, physically healthy and morally without flaw who are yet unable to foster because they cannot afford to. The obvious answer is adequate remuneration. But all the authors in this book have commented on the lack of adequate remuneration for unrelated as well as kinship carers and the impact of this on recruitment and retention.

In Sweden, for example, foster carers receive remuneration for the child's board and lodging and also a payment for their own work which is taxable and considered to be pensionable income. A study by Hojer (2001) found that half the foster carers surveyed felt that the payment they received was too low. Further, some carers felt ambivalent about the payment, fearing that people (including case workers) would see them as greedy and their foster children would suspect that they were looked after for money not out of a sense of personal commitment. This 'love versus money' issue is one we will return to below.

In Sweden as in other countries, foster carers engaged by private agencies generally receive higher fees than those engaged by the public sector. Because foster carers in Sweden are treated as receiving a 'paid commission' rather then as 'paid employees' of the social services they are not eligible to receive any unemployment benefits when placements end. Thus, taking on the role of foster carer in Sweden clearly entails a degree of financial insecurity – a state of affairs which has been acknowledged by the government and made the subject of further investigation.

In Japan, as in other countries, reimbursement varies depending on the level of difficulty being experienced by the child and the corresponding level of skill required of the foster parent. The monthly allowance paid to specialised foster parents is almost three times that received by other foster parents. This kind of discrepancy has historically given rise to conflict both between public and private agencies and between foster care agencies and residential centres. Often, 'professional' levels of payment have been introduced in an ad hoc fashion through the development of specialised foster care services for hard-to-place children, and also through the retention of a residential care level of funding for children transferred into home-based care. Moreover, the diversion of funds from residential centres to treatment foster care has exacerbated the ongoing conflict between proponents of residential care and foster care respectively. Nevertheless, despite higher payments to specialised carers, our Japanese author argues that the amount of money generally paid to foster carers in Japan must be increased with respect to both salaries and child maintenance.

In France, carers receive a monthly allowance to cover the child's medical, educational and living costs. The philosophy underlying payment is that people should not be able to make money from fostering but neither should they lose it. At the time the chapter on France was drafted it was anticipated that there would shortly be a Parliamentary Bill to improve the terms and conditions of foster carers in respect of matters such as allowances and paid holidays. Indeed, France appears to have made substantial progress in the professionalisation of foster carers not only with respect to reimbursement but in terms of employment benefits.

In India, by contrast, inadequate financial allocations for foster care have seriously undermined the quality of service. Our Indian authors write 'Whilst caution is required to ensure that economic incentive is not the sole factor motivating prospective foster parents, it is contended that increases with respect to fees and the costs of care are necessary to encourage more families to consider fostering.' Similarly, our author in South Africa argues that a top priority of government must be to develop a sound and adequate system of financial support for foster carers. Financial support to foster parents in South Africa is bluntly described as 'pathetic to say the least'.

However, according to our Swedish contributor, increased pay for foster carers would not be sufficient in itself to resolve recruitment and retention issues. Attention also needs to be paid to the motivation to foster – often to feel that one is doing a good job and making a difference in the life of a child. Recruitment and retention will be facilitated if programmes pay more attention to training, and acknowledge and accept foster carers as equal partners with social workers and other professionals.

This statement from Sweden serves to remind us that, if motivation to foster is insufficient without capacity, so is capacity insufficient without motivation. It will probably be a long time before the process of 'professionalising' foster parents reaches its logical conclusion: that foster parents are genuinely accepted as professionals and not only paid appropriately but accorded the same status and trust as the other professionals in the foster care team. There are links here to the status of women in general and to the societal value ascribed to child-care, which is widely viewed as 'women's work'. The vast majority of foster parents are women (in France, the figure is 99%) and so are the majority of social workers. There is a massive disconnection between the importance of child-rearing and the status afforded it, and it is hardly coincidence that such a huge discrepancy between the importance of a task and the payment provided for performing it occurs, almost solely, in a domain traditionally reserved for women.

Be that as it may, the 'pathetic' financial support devoted to foster care has resulted in a shortage of foster care placements which, in turn, has had a number of consequences. In the UK, the shortfall has meant that, for too many children, foster placements are simply not available and, when a placement can be found, it is not the placement of choice. The crisis faced by local authorities in recruiting and retaining requisite numbers of foster placements has fuelled a rapid growth of independent fostering agencies.

In Sweden, the number of children placed in foster care increased by 20 per cent between 1993 and 2000 and the shortage of placements is acute. Forty one per cent of social workers in a survey undertaken by Parliament Auditors have had the experience of placing children in institutional care because a foster placement could not be found. In order to resolve the problem, social workers are placing more children in the same foster home than was hitherto the case, and are increasingly seeking placements within the child's biological family and social network. Another unfortunate consequence of the shortage of foster homes is the increasing number of children placed far from their birth families because more local placements are not available.

Steps have also been taken in other countries to increase the supply of foster carers and placement choice. Although kinship carers provide the largest share of foster placements in Poland, increased professionalisation and specialisation are seen as means by which to increase the number and diversity of placements, including short-term and respite care options as well as long-term or permanent placements. In Argentina, Fundacion Emmanuel is attempting to raise the profile of foster care through public awareness campaigns, drives to recruit foster families, and training for professionals and volunteers from both government and non-governmental organisations.

Many countries have mandatory procedures for the assessment and licensing of prospective foster carers. The process of recruiting foster carers in Japan, for example, is the responsibility of the local Child Guidance Centre (CGC) and Child Welfare Council. On being approved, the foster parents are registered as foster care candidates for five years and must complete a training session to develop their child-rearing knowledge and skills. Foster carers must be reviewed every five years to maintain their status and in order to receive the support services provided by the CGC.

Our Swedish author describes the PRIDE process, used in many countries, where people interested in becoming foster parents meet in a group with a social worker and experienced foster parent to receive information and discuss the possible impact of fostering on their own lives and families. The hope here is that unsuitable applicants will realise themselves that fostering is not for them and withdraw. Indeed, whatever the assessment method, emphasis is usually placed on helping a family evaluate and decide whether fostering is appropriate for them. In the United States, decision-making may be facilitated through a series of interviews between the child welfare worker and the applicants, home visits, and contact with the wider family. Foster carers are required to complete pre-service training in most states. Although it is hoped that the agency and the applicant will reach the same decision regarding suitability, the agency has the final decision-making responsibility in respect of licensing and applicants have no right to appeal such decisions outside the agency.

Research in the United Kingdom has succeeded in highlighting effective practice in relation to the recruitment, assessment and training of prospective foster carers, and the support and further training of approved foster carers. Foster care agencies in the UK are increasingly adopting a competence-based, strength-focused, approach whereby potential carers are well informed and prepared prior to seeking formal approval as foster carers.

Some degree of training is now widely required of foster carers. Professional training is compulsory in France, and the foster carer is paid during the training period. In Poland, professional foster parents are required to complete appropriate training and to obtain a license to foster. However, in some countries, it is not only the training of foster parents that is at issue but the training of social workers. Our Japanese author argues that one of the reasons for the failure of foster care to prosper in Japan is the lack of training evidenced by social workers who are employed by the Child Guidance Centres to work with foster families. On a similar note, in India, there is considerable variation in the quality of service provided and the level of professionalism shown by staff in the non-governmental organisations responsible for operating foster care programmes. Our Indian authors argue that the authorities in their country have failed to seriously address the training needs of such agencies regarding the knowledge and skills required to run an effective service.

The training of social workers has a major impact on the provision of the support to foster carers that is essential for retention. Lack of support, particularly to kin carers, is common to all the countries represented in this volume. In South Africa, the Child Care Act stipulates that all children in foster care as well as the foster parents and biological parents should receive social work services. However, in practice, agencies overwhelmed by the HIV/AIDS crisis find it very difficult to provide services and, in rural areas particularly, services are often non-existent, over-stretched or too expensive for carers to access. In Poland, one of the major issues remaining to be addressed is the provision of support services for foster carers, organised through the non-governmental sector. In China, support is felt to be so important that Care for Children staff are reluctant to allow people to adopt without the initial support of foster care. The argument here is that unsupported adoptive placements are more liable to breakdown or abuse whereas a period of supported foster care allows both child and family time to adjust. After a period of three to five years, most couples do adopt the foster child placed with them.

Foster Care and Adoption

Adoption by Chinese couples with existing children has been restricted under the one-child-only policy and it is only since the amended Adoption Law went into effect on April 1, 1999 that these restrictions have been eased. Adoptions of Chinese children within China soared from 201 in 1989 to 5,053 in 2002 and this enormous change will certainly affect the face of international adoption since children adopted from China are estimated to represent somewhere between one-quarter to one-third of the worldwide total of out-of-country placements.

In Sweden, childless couples often turn to international sources in order to adopt because adoption without the consent of the birth parents does not exist and children in care are not free for adoption. In some other countries – for example, the United Kingdom and the United States — children in care are free for adoption once guardianship of the child is permanently transferred from the birth parent to the state. The question then becomes whether the foster parents ought to be allowed to adopt the child they have fostered. In the past, the answer has been 'no' in order to reduce the likelihood of 'child shopping' whereby foster parents only continue to foster until they find the child they wish to adopt. More recently, it has been argued that the permanency afforded by adoption is to be desired and that parents who have succeeded in giving a child a home through fostering ought not to be penalised for their success.

In other countries, the distinction between adoption and foster care is less clear. In India, for example, the earlier initiatives under the Children Acts were treated by the implementing authorities, as well as by the respondents (foster parents), as an adoption-in-waiting programme. Similarly, in Japan, many of the parents who foster really wish to adopt but there are few children available for adoption and the distinction between adoptive and non-adoptive foster parents is somewhat blurred.

In South Africa, foster care, which provides some financial compensation, is used as a substitute for adoption, which provides none. Many children, orphaned because of AIDS, need to be adopted rather than being placed in foster care but, since there is no system of subsidised adoptions, foster care is the only alternative. Our South African author argues that the adoption of children in foster care must be addressed in legislation much more vigorously and financial support for parents who adopt children should also be negotiated.

Love versus Money

In countries less besieged by the AIDS crisis, there is no expectation that people who adopt children should be eligible for financial support in the same way that foster parents are. People support their natural children, after all, out of their personal pockets and one of the differences between adoption and long-term (or permanent) foster care is that an adopted child 'belongs' to the parents in a way that a fostered child does not. 'Belonging' implies love and commitment, and love, in turn, tends to be associated with the absence of financial profit. Not-for-profit social services agencies, for example, are perceived as far more worthy than for-profit agencies which blatantly hope to make money out of human misery, whether that misery takes the form of an ill person in the health care system or a child in the foster care system needing a home.

Nevertheless, for-profit agencies do play a role in welfare systems, particularly in North America where they are lauded for three reasons: first, they do not use public money; second, they are in tune with the individualistic philosophy that people ought to be responsible for their own welfare; and, third, they are seen as more efficient and 'professional', not subject to the bumblings of often over-lapping government departments.

In Britain, the New Labour government has sought to bring about fundamental change in welfare by charting a 'third way' between state monopoly welfare and private market services. Local authorities have been encouraged to commission foster care provision from NGOs, including private sector agencies. A major government initiative, *Choice Protects*, has provided additional funding to help expand and strengthen fostering services. This includes measures aimed at retaining the services of foster carers and to help them develop their skills. New placement and health and educational services for foster children have also been commissioned. In addition, *National Minimum Standards* have been established in respect of the assessment, training, approval and supervision of foster carers, and the conduct and organisation of all foster agencies. It may be noted that the financial costs of NGO sector foster placements in Britain are often three times that of local authority placements. However, NGO foster care agencies frequently provide additional therapeutic and educational services for children and higher levels of support for foster carers. Moreover, an increasing number of foster carers receive a fee in recognition of the occupational nature of fostering. The tax burden has also been simplified and standardised for foster carers, and foster carers are entitled to receive state pensions. However, fees and allowances vary greatly both within and between sectors and no minimum standards have been established.

The increasing professionalisation of foster carers has brought the conflict between love and money into sharper focus. Professionals expect to be paid for their skills, and recruitment, already very difficult, may be expected to become even more so if foster carers continue to be inadequately paid. Our American authors comment that the rate of pay for a foster family providing full care to a child 4–11 years old in Rhode Island is USD 13.64 per day – less than it costs to keep a dog in a kennel. One of the justifications for this is that a higher, professional-level, rate of pay will attract people who want to foster for financial rather than altruistic reasons. The assumption underlying the argument is that money and altruism are essentially incompatible: one cannot love a child for whose care one is paid: receiving reimbursement destroys the nobility of the deed.

The same assumption extends to the funding of organisations which have an altruistic purpose. In Argentina, as we have already noted, foster care is conceived as a family right and an expression of social solidarity. Our Argentinian author writes with understandable frustration that 'many public policy bureaucrats seem to believe that because foster care represents an expression of social solidarity within communities it does not have to be paid for.' The underfunding of foster care programmes is thus justified on the basis that noble aspirations will somehow be rendered ignoble if they are contaminated by contact with money.

It is not only bureaucrats who act on this belief. Foster carers themselves believe it and are torn between thinking that they deserve to be paid for the work they do and guilt lest they are perceived to be greedy by case workers and, worse yet, by their own foster children. Foster children, too, believe it and it will doubtless require a sweeping change in public attitudes before children can accept that a person who is paid at a professional rate for looking after them is yet capable of loving them deeply.

Paid parental love faces a particular challenge when the child reaches the age of majority, graduates perforce from the child welfare system, and payment ceases. Children outside the system rarely leave their parental home smoothly and cleanly as soon as they become legally adult. Instead, they may leave and return a number of times, requiring varied levels of continuing support before they finally achieve independent living. Foster children, who usually have even greater difficulty achieving independent living, cannot rely on the system for support past the age of majority and must depend on the former foster parents' love or charity. Some systems do make provision for adult graduates, but there are usually conditions. In Poland, for example, additional financial support is provided for young people who reach the age of majority (until their 25th birthday), who continue to live with their foster family and who remain in full-time education. Young people who reach the age of majority and choose to live independently also receive additional allowances. Roughly four out of five young people reaching the age of majority choose to stay with their foster family rather than live independently. However, children who receive any kind of income or survivor's benefits have their foster care allowance reduced by half the amount of the income or benefit. In other countries as well, attention is now being paid to the plight of former foster children experiencing difficulty in independent living but the support provided tends to be grudging and is a matter of debate.

The money expended on children by their foster parents is also a matter of contention. In Japan, in addition to monthly payments to cover the child's living costs, foster carers also receive payments to cover the entire costs of the child's schooling, including the costs of stationary and other equipment, school lunches, medical expenses, school trips and vocational training. In the United Kingdom, foster carers receive an allowance to cover the costs of such things as clothing, food, sports, cultural and leisure activities, and birthday and other gifts. The same is true, theoretically, in other countries but the fact of the matter is that often these payments are not sufficient to afford the foster child the same opportunities as other children in the same family or in the same school or community who are not 'in care'.

Some would question whether such payments ought to be sufficient. Their argument runs that if children from failed families (i.e., foster children) have more advantages than children from struggling families, it will invite struggling families to give up their struggle, which will ruin society and bankrupt the state. This may seem a trifle extreme but there is some truth to the argument that strife is likely to result when foster children flaunt their new possessions on visits to their birth parents and siblings. Furthermore, if foster children are expected to relinquish their new standard of living when they are reunited with their birth parents, is this not bound to negatively impact reunification, always the desired plan? If one believes that both reunification and contact with birth families will suffer from the provision to foster children of material goods, it is easy to justify the position that foster children should be provided with treats, vacations pocket money, and so forth – but to a lesser extent than the foster parent's natural children – and possibly not to a greater extent than the non-apprehended siblings left at home.

All this brings to mind the concept of 'less eligibility' which formed the bedrock of the deterrent Poor Law in Victorian Britain. According to the principle of less eligibility, public relief benefits should be minimal and less than the wages of the lowest paid worker so as to discourage people from becoming dependent on the government. This principle still enjoys great popularity today and seems to find its echo in the idea that the benefits accorded to foster children should be less than the benefits received by other children in order to ensure that unfit families do not just relinquish their responsibilities and leave the raising of their children to someone else. The results can be seen in the stigma associated with foster care and in the fact that foster children have generally lower levels of educational attainment, poorer health, less self-esteem and worse prospects overall than children outside the child welfare system.

However, the foregoing argument assumes that the foster family enjoys a higher socio-economic status than the birth family. Generally, this is the case because eligibility criteria require a certain standard of economic security from unrelated foster parents. But it is not always the case. In Sweden, for example, a survey by Hojer (2001) found that 61 per cent of carers were categorised as working class, compared with 26 per cent who were middle class and only 13 per cent who were upper class. Perhaps this is because working class people tend to place less emphasis on the career aspirations which often act as a barrier to foster parent recruitment. But, be that as it may, the presence of foster children can serve to enhance the condition of foster families who are no better off than the foster children's own birth families.

An example here comes from the joint Shanghai Foster Care and Training Program in China which was established in 1998 to provide long-term family environments as an alternative to institutional care for abandoned children. The foster carers in one village feared that they would be blamed if their foster children became sick as a result of the poor condition of the village drains. So the authorities offered to improve the drains on condition that they would be used properly. Later on, foster carers in the same village voiced concern that their foster children were receiving greater educational opportunities than their own children. Consequently, the authorities offered to enlarge the school on condition that the foster carers ensured that their own children attended regularly at all times.

Outcomes of Foster Care

Some of the chapters comprising this book contain encouraging comments with respect to the pivotal issue of fostering outcomes. The chapter on China, for example, reports that significant positive changes have been observed in many children following their move to foster families. Research referred to in the chapter on Poland found that family foster care provided better developmental conditions than residential group care (Luczak, 1994). The chapter on France also refers to research reporting better long-term outcomes for young people who were fostered as compared to those who had lived in residential care (Gheorgiu, 2002). Further, the chapter on the United Kingdom cites research showing that close emotional attachments and participation in family life contribute to good outcomes (Schofield et al., 2000; Beek and Schofield, 2004).

However, most outcome studies show that children in family foster care do worse in every realm than comparable children who have no involvement with the system. A particular worry is school performance. Poor school performance, dropping out, truancy, and so forth are prime indicators for a troubled adulthood (Jackson, 2001). Research reported in the chapter on Sweden shows that children and youth placed in family foster care have problems in school and problems establishing themselves in the labour market when they leave care (Vinnerljung, 1996).

Yet, despite the worries about school performance there seems to be little success in achieving co-operation between education and child welfare authorities. In France, the Education Ministry, which is directly involved in education and remedial classes for children with emotional and behavioural difficulties, is hardly involved at all in the administration of family foster placements. On a more encouraging note, the chapter on the United Kingdom relates that, in England, children's education and social work services, together with some health services, are being combined to form new Children's Trusts. These Trusts will employ multi-agency teams based in schools and children's centres with the purpose of providing integrated children's services.

Research highlights the general failure of public care systems in relation to helping children and young people overcome educational difficulties. Despite this, the assumption underlying actual practice too often seems to be that emotional and behavioural problems are the real obstacle to educational progress. This represents an insidious form of 'victim blaming' that serves to obfuscate the failure of child welfare agencies to address the adverse impact that the trauma of being taken into care and other aspects of children's histories such as abuse, neglect, instability and insecurity may have on their educational attainment and skills. Indeed, sadly, abuse, instability and insecurity may be part and parcel of children and young people's experience in family foster care (Colton et al., 2001).

Children enter care systems not so much because of their own problems or disorders but more because of parental dysfunction compounded by a dearth of social supports and acute environmental pressures. Fostered children tend to have a history of insufficient parental nurturing, exposure to intra-familial and extra-familial violence, and separation from attachment figures. One American study usefully provides the following breakdown in respect of the reasons why children were placed in foster care in New York (Tatara, 1993):

- 50.2% – neglect and abuse
- 20.9% – parental conditions such as illness, death, handicap, financial hardship, etc.
- 11.3% – offences such as running away, truancy, or delinquent behaviour
- 12.5% – other reasons, including parent-child relationship problems, a plan for adoption, or deinstitutionalisation
- 1.9% – child's physical, mental, or emotional disability.

Stelmaszuk reports that many children in family foster care in Poland come from birth families affected by alcohol and related problems. A study by Luczak (1994) of a representative sample of foster children from Warsaw found that 46 per cent of their birth parents had substance abuse problems, 34 per cent suffered from alcohol related problems and 37 per cent had committed a crime. Our Swedish contributor notes that the majority of birth parents of children that are placed in family foster care in Sweden had drug and/or alcohol and/or psychological problems. The salient picture that emerges from Swedish research is of birth parents that are economically and socially marginalised: principally single parents (mainly mothers) who are unemployed and who lack vocational training. In the United States, race, poverty and single parenthood are inter-related factors associated with the placement of children in family foster care. Single parenthood and poverty disproportionately affects children of colour. Therefore, as national data and other research clearly show, children of colour are overrepresented in the family foster care system in the United States. It is also apparent from the chapter on Argentina that hunger, poverty, unemployment, ill-health and lack of educational opportunity and vocational training are all factors underlying the placement of children in family foster care in South America.

Family foster carers are thus increasingly expected to cope with children whose difficult circumstances have resulted in them developing emotional and behavioural difficulties. In the United Kingdom family foster care has long since ceased to be reserved for the less challenging child in need of care. In many parts of the United States, family foster care serves delinquent, homeless or runaway youth, as well as providing care for abused and neglected children. In France too, foster care is no longer restricted to any given category of children, but rather is used for all children whose parents are temporarily or permanently unable to look after them owing to psycho-social problems. Although our Indian contributors acknowledge that the numbers placed in family foster care in their country is miniscule compared to the vast numbers of children who might benefit from such placement, family foster care programmes are inclusive in that they are geared both to de-institutionalisation and the prevention of institutionalisation.

Increasing levels of challenging behaviour increase the risk that placements will be disrupted (Colton et al., 2001). Children in family foster care in the United States who manifest emotional or behavioural difficulties, or who have special medical needs, are usually placed in treatment foster care with specially trained carers. More attention has focused in recent years on the special needs of children who have been abused prior to entering family foster care. It also seems likely from the chapter on South Africa that increasing numbers of children and young people who have lost parents through HIV/AIDS will be placed in family foster care. South Africa alone will have an estimated 2.6 million HIV/AIDS orphans by 2010.

Whilst outcome studies show that children in foster care do worse in all respects than comparable children who have no involvement with the system, research has not distinguished the effects of pre-existing factors from family foster care factors. The dearth of longitudinal research compounds the difficulties associated with attempts to assess the impact of family foster care in respect of children's health and development. An extensive discussion of this issue is beyond the scope of this chapter. Here there is only sufficient space to briefly comment on what we do know. One of our contributing authors, Sellick, has, with Thoburn, reviewed the so-called *What Works* research literature from the United Kingdom. Sellick and Thoburn (2002) provide a useful summary of the current state of knowledge with respect to the outcomes of permanent foster care measured largely in terms of placement longevity and the child's well being and satisfaction. The key points include the following:

- Age at placement makes an important contribution to the success or failure of a placement.
- Placements with relatives or friends tend to be more successful than other placements.
- There are few significant differences in outcome between adoption and permanent foster care.
- Placement with siblings is a protective factor.
- Contact with birth parents reduces the likelihood of placement breakdown.
- Although trans-racial placements are no less successful in terms of breakdown rates than same race placements, children placed in the former may experience a strong sense of cultural loss.
- Infants are more likely to be adversely affected by delay in permanent placement than older children who may require more time to adjust to the change in circumstances.

Some Final Thoughts

In many countries, foster care still sits at the crossroads of a complex web of public, private and for-profit agencies, situated within the multiple systems of health, mental health, child welfare, social welfare, education and justice. One may dream of a single, seamless service which may be accessed by a child in need of out-of-home placement at any one of a number of points, and which will then liaise with all the other systems to provide the child with whatever care is necessary, into adulthood and beyond. Such a dream may never be realised but there are moves towards service integration and there is an increasing recognition that a child is a whole person whose interrelated needs cannot be met through separate systems.

However, some trends can be identified. Decentralisation is a thrust common to most industrialised countries, running in parallel to the move towards community-based services. For-profit agencies seem to be playing an increasing role, particularly in North America but their emergence is countered by a distaste for the idea of allowing organisations to make money out of human misery. Continuing tensions between the individualistic and institutional philosophies are often leading to attempts to find a middle path between state monopoly welfare and private market services. As always, we compromise as we struggle to achieve the primary and unchanging aim of foster care: to care for abused, neglected and abandoned children from every race and culture, wherever they may be.

In closing, we would like to say that editing this book has been a fascinating journey. A greater degree of international sharing of problems, experiences and innovations must surely contribute in considerable measure to caring for the children of us all.

References

Beek, M. and Schofield, G. (2004) *Providing a Secure Base in Foster Care.* London: BAAF.

Colton, M., Casas, F., Drakeford, D., Roberts, S., Scholte, E. and Williams, M. (1997) *Stigma and Social Welfare: An International Comparative Study.* Aldershot: Ashgate.

Colton, M. and Williams, M. (Eds.) (1997) *The World of Foster Care.* Aldershot: Ashgate.

Colton, M., Sanders, R. and Williams, (2001) *An Introduction to Working with Children.* Basingstoke: Palgrave.

Davies, T.W. and Morris, A. (1993) A Comparative Quantification of Stigma. *Social Work and Social Sciences Review.* 1: 2, 109–22.

DiNitto, D. (2000) *Social Welfare: Politics and Public Policy.* 5th edn. Needham Heights, MA: Allyn and Bacon.

Gheorghiu, M. et al. (2002) *Rapport final de la recherche longitudinale sur le devenir des personnes sorties de l'ASE de Seine-Saint-Denis entre 1980 et 2000.* Document dactylographié.

Hassett, S. and Austin, M. (1997) Service Integration: Something Old and Something New. *Administration in Social Work.* 21, 9–29.

Hessle, S. (1988) *Familjer i sönderfall.* Göteborg: Norstedts.

Höjer, I. (2001) Fosterfamiljens inre liv. Diss. University of Göteborg.

Jackson, S. (2001) *Nobody Ever Told Us School Mattered: Raising the Educational Attainments of Children in Care.* London: BAAF.

Leatt, P., Pink, G. and Naylor, C. (1996) Integrated Delivery Systems: Time to Experiment in Canada? *Journal of the American Society of CLU and ChFC.* 9, 54–9.

Luczak, E. (1994) Srodowisko wychowawcze rodzin zastepczych *Opieka-Wychowanie-Terapia,* 17, 13–8.

Lundström, T. and Sallnäs, M. (2003) Klass, kön och etnicitet i den sociala barnavården. *Socialvetenskaplig tidskrift,* nummer 2–3.

Martinson, K. (1999) Literature review on service coordination and integration in the welfare and workforce development systems. Washington, DC: Urban Institute. Retrieved on February 16, 2004 from the World Wide Web: www.urban.org/ welfare.

Przygoda, J. (1998) Biografie i start zyciowy usamodzielnianych wychowankow roznych form opieki. in: Kolankiewicz M. (Ed.) *Zagrozone dziecinstwo. Rodzinne i instytucjonalne formy opieki.* Warszawa: Wydawnictwa Szkolne i Pedagogiczne, 193–220.

Schofield, G., Beek, M., Sargent, K. and Thoburn, J. (2000) *Growing up in Foster Care.* London: BAAF.

Segal, E.A. and Brzuzy, S. (1998) *Social Welfare Policy, Programs, And Practice.* Itasca, IL: F.E. Peacock.

Sellick, C. and Thoburn, J. (2002) Family Placement Services. in McNeish, D., Newman, T. and Roberts, H. (2002) *What Works with Children: Effective Services for Children and Families.* Open University: Buckingham.

Short, R. and Talley, R. (1999) Services Integration: An Introduction. *Journal of Educational and Psychological Consultation.* 10: 3, 193–200.

Tatara, T. (1993) *Characteristics of Children in Substitute and Adoptive Care: A Statistical Summary of the VCIS National Child Welfare Database.* Washington, DC: American Public Welfare Association.

Vinnerljung, B. (1996) *Fosterbarn som vuxna.* Diss. Lund, Arkiv.

Waldfogel, J. (1997) The New Wave of Service Integration. *Social Service Review.* 71: 3, 463–84.

Bibliography

Abrahamson, P. (1993) Socialpolitikmodeller i Europa: forskelle og konvergens. in Nordisk Sosialt Arbeid nr. 1.

Abrile de Vollmer, M.I. (1997) *Las Políticas Públicas y la Programación Social para la Protección de los Derechos de los Niños y Adolescentes*. Mendoza.

Ashenden, S. (1999) Rethinking the Welfare State in the Face of Cultural Pluralism. In Chamberlayne, P. et al. (Eds.) *Welfare and Culture in Europe*. Philadelphia: Jessica Kingsley Publishers.

Balbo, L. (1983) The Servicing Work of Women and the Capitalist State. *Political Power and Social Theory*. 3.

Baron, G., Baudel, M. et al. (1993) *Le placement familial, un lieu commun?* In Bass, D. and Pellé, A. (Eds.) Les recherchers du grape. Toulouse.

Bermúdez, I. (2002) *Subió a $702 la canasta básica*. Clarín, Economía, 5.

Bislev, S. and Hansen, H. (1990) The Nordic Welfare State and the Single European Market. in Lyck, L. (ed.) The Nordic Countries in the Internal Market of the EEC. Copenhagen: Handelshojskolens forlag.

Cahiers de la Féderation des Services de Placement Familial (1993) *Placement familial: principes méthodologiques*, Nro. 8.

Cartry, J. (1985) *Les parents symboliques*, Paris: Editions fleurus.

Castro, Á. (2003) *Por día ingresan en la pobreza 1570 chicos en la Argentina*. La Nación. 17.

Child and Adolescent Act, Province of Mendoza – Law 6354 (1997). Mendoza, Argentina.

Cirillo, S. (1994) *Familles en crise et placement familial*. Paris: ESF Éditeur.

Comisión para los Derechos del Niño (2002) *Consideración de los informes presentados por los Estados Parte en virtud del artículo 44 de la Convención. Conclusiones de la Comisión para los Derechos del Niño:* Argentina.

Colton, M., Sanders, S. and Williams, M. (2001) *An Introduction to Working with Children: A Guide for Social Workers*. Basingstoke: Palgrave.

Colton, M. and Williams, M. (1997) *The World of Foster Care: An International Sourcebook on Foster Family Care System*. Aldershot: Ashgate.

Colton, M. and Williams, M. (2002) Editor's Note. in Colton, M., Roberts, R. and Williams, M. (2002) Residential Care: Last Resort or Positive Choice? Lessons from Around Europe. *International Journal of Child and family Welfare*. 5: 3.

David, M. and Appel, G. (1973) *Lóczy ou le maternage insolite*. París: Scarabée.

David, M. (1989) *Le placement familial de la pratique à la théorie*. Paris: Les Éditions ESF.

De la Harpe Bourgault, F. (1989) *L'enfant en famille d'accueil*. Centurion.

Delfos, M. (2001) *Me escuchas? Cómo conversar con niños de cuatro a doce años*. Bernard van Leer Foundation.

Department of Economics, University of La Plata (2002), *Demographic and Poverty Characteristics in Argentina*. http://bisi.siempro.gov.ar/bisi/eds/cuadros/cuadro.jps?cuadro = B8.

Dezeo de Nicora, M.E., Perauer, M. and Menéndez, C. (2003) *Construir junto a los verdaderos Protagonistas del Acogimiento*. Buenos Aires: Fundación Emmanuel.

XXI Encuentro Nacional de Magistrados y Funcionarios de la Justicia de Menores y Familia (2002) *La Justicia y la Familia: Forjando Vínculos*. Tucumán, Argentina.

Esping-Andersen, G. (1990) *Three Worlds of Welfare Capitalism*. Cambridge: Polity Press.

Geroge, S. and van Oudenhoven, N. (2003) *Apostando al Acogimiento Familiar- Un Estudio Comparativo Internacional*. Apeldoorn. Países Bajos: Garant.

Guagnini, L. and Calvo, P. (2004) *Casi el 20% de los hogares vive de planes para pobres*. Clarín. 28–29.

Infancia, Boletín del Instituto Interamericano del niño (1990) – OEA, Nr.230, Tomo 63, Jul.

International Convention on the Rights of the Child, National Law No. 23.849, enforced on September 27th, 1990.

Jackson, S. (2001) *Nobody Ever Told Us School Mattered: Raising the Educational Attainments of Children in Care*. London: BAAF.

Kinoo, P. et al. (1993) *Les interactions en accueil familial*. Wetsch-Benqué, M., Vugteveen, W. and Meliarenne, B. (Eds.) érés. Toulouse.

Lotersztain, G. (1993) *Condenados al olvido*. Clarín. Opinión. 14.

McElwee, C.N. (Ed.) (2002) *Irish Journal of Applied Social Studies*. SocSci Consultancy, Leap Cottage, Kildalton, Piltown, Co. Kilkenny, Ireland.

Minoridad y Familia (1996) Nro.1, Delta Editora, Paraná.

Minoridad y Familia (1998) Nro. 5, Delta Editora, Paraná.

Minuchin, P., Colapinto, J., Minuchin, S. (2000) *Pobreza, institución, familia*. Amorrortu/editores. Buenos Aires.

National Board for Childhood, Adolescence and the Family (2003) Policies and Strategies of Rights in the Childhood, Adolescence and Family Area. *Chronicles of the Regional Meetings*. Buenos Aires.

National Board for Childhood, Adolescence and the Family (2003). *2002/2003 Report*. Buenos Aires.

Nicora, L.M. (1999) Fundación Emmanuel. *Relaciones Internacionales*. 16, 307–308.

Nouvelles Feuilles Familiales (NFF) (1978) Nr. 3.

Oficina Pastoral del Adolescente y el Niños (1996) *I Congreso Andino de Jueces de Niños y Adolescentes – Memorias*. Quito.

Plan para sustituir subsidios laborales. (2004) Clarín. 7

Prieto Castillo, D. (2000) *Programa Regional Piloto Contra la Violencia Intrafamiliar*. Mendoza.

Rentería, M. et al. (1990) *Piden pan … y algo más. Un estudio sobre crecimiento y desarrollo infantil.* UNICEF y CIC (Eds.) Siglo veintiuno de España Editores, sa. Buenos Aires.

Revista de la Asociación Argentina de Magistrados y Funcionarios de la Justicia de Menores, (1996) Año 1-Nr. 3.

Sainsbury, D. (1994) Gendering Welfare States. London: Sage.

Sajón, R. (1995) *Derecho de menores.* Abeledo-Perrot. Buenos Aires.

Sanicola, L. (1996) *Redes sociales y menores en riesgo – Solidaridad y servicios en el acogimiento familiar.* Buenos Aires.

Sanz, P. (1997) *Le Placement familial: ses secrets et ses paradoxes.* L'Harmattan. Paris.

Schearer, S.B. et al. (1998) *Sostenibilidad de la Sociedad Civil. Estrategias para la movilización de recursos.* En Fox, L.M. y Schearer, S.B. (Eds.) Civicus. Colombia.

Secretaría de Desarrollo Social, Presidencia de la Nación (1998) *Derechos de Niños, Niñas y Adolescentes.* Buenos Aires.

Sellick, C. and Thoburn, J. (2002) Family Placement Services. in McNeish, D., Newman, T. and Roberts, H. (2002) *What Works with Children: Effective Services for Children and Families.* Open University: Buckingham.

Sued, G. (2003) *Planes sociales: investigan a los municipios bonaerenses.* La Nación. 1.

Tatara, T. (1993) *Characteristics of Children in Substitute and Adoptive Care: A Statistical Summary of the VCIS National Child Welfare Database.* Washington, DC: American Public Welfare Association.

Tejero, E. and Torrabadella, L. (1999) Family Relationships in Democratic Spain. In Chamberlayne, P. et al. (Eds.) *Welfare and Culture in Europe.* Philadelphia: Jessica Kingsley Publishers.

Triseliotis, J. (1997) Foster Care and Adoption. in Davies, M. (Ed.) (1997) *The Blackwell Companion to Social Work.* Oxford: Blackwell.

Trocmé, N. et al. (2003) *Child Welfare: Connecting Research, Policy and Practice.* En Kufelt, K. y McKenzie, B. (Eds.) Wilfrid Laurier University Press.

Tulkens, F. (1990) Le placement familial: problemes socio-juridiques, Cap. VIII. en Klein Meulders, M. T. *Adoption et forme alternatives d'accueil.* Bruxelles.

Index